D0556000

Lady Chatterley's Legacy in the Movies

Lady Chatterley's Legacy in the Movies

Sex, Brains, and Body Guys

PETER LEHMAN AND SUSAN HUNT

RUTGERS UNIVERSITY PRESS
NEW BRUNSWICK, NEW JERSEY, AND LONDON

Library of Congress Cataloging-in-Publication Data

Lehman, Peter.

Lady Chatterley's legacy in the movies : sex, brains, and body guys / Peter Lehman and Susan Hunt.

    p. cm.

Includes bibliographical references and index.

ISBN 978–0–8135–4802–9 (hardcover : alk. paper)

1. Sex role in motion pictures.   2. Sex in motion pictures.   3. Stereotypes (Social psychology) in motion pictures.   4. Women in motion pictures.   5. Men in motion pictures.   I. Hunt, Susan.   II. Title.

PN1995.9.S47L44   2010

791.43′653538—dc22

                                                                          2009048297

A British Cataloging-in-Publication record for this book is available from the British Library.

Copyright © 2010 by Peter Lehman and Susan Hunt

All rights reserved

No part of this book may be reproduced or utilized in any form or by any means, electronic or mechanical, or by any information storage and retrieval system, without written permission from the publisher. Please contact Rutgers University Press, 100 Joyce Kilmer Avenue, Piscataway, NJ 08854–8099. The only exception to this prohibition is "fair use" as defined by U.S. copyright law.

Visit our Web site: http://rutgerspress.rutgers.edu

Manufactured in the United States of America

For Robert Flynt, friend and photographer
Peter Lehman

For Michael Hart, who inspires my writing,
and for my parents, Charles and Marian Hunt,
who inspired this book
Susan Hunt

Contents

List of Illustrations   ix

Acknowledgments   xi

1. "Everything You Are Is between Your Legs"   1

2. Rebels, Outsiders, Artists, and . . . Brutes?   27

3. "Fuck Me like a Cop, Not a Lawyer"   53

4. "Brain Work Isn't Much of a Spectator Sport"   79

5. Hung like a Horse . . . or an Acorn   105

6. Unmaking Love   136

7. "Why Do You Say That as if It Were a Weakness? It's Not."   161

Notes   185

Bibliography   191

Index   195

Illustrations

1. *Titanic*   2
2. *Titanic*   3
3. *Legends of the Fall*   6
4. *The Piano*   7
5. *Two Moon Junction*   10
6. *The Blue Lagoon*   16
7. *A Night in Heaven*   17
8. *Lawn Dogs*   29
9. *Lawn Dogs*   30
10. *Munich*   43
11. *Twentynine Palms*   50
12. *Asylum*   64
13. *Fur: An Imaginary Portrait of Diane Arbus*   67
14. *The Last Seduction*   71
15. *Any Given Sunday*   73
16. *Any Given Sunday*   76
17. Jews facing execution during the Holocaust   87
18. *Sunshine*   89
19. *Oz*   91
20. *Enemy at the Gates*   94
21. *Sideways*   95
22. *Sideways*   97
23. *The Governess*   100

24.   Speaker at a nudist gathering   121

25.   Nudists at a public rally   122

26.   Nude men at the Toronto Gay Pride Dance, 2002   123

27.   Base layer of photomontage (detail), Robert Flynt, 1990   124

28.   *Kinsey*   125

29.   *9 Songs*   131

30.   *Lie with Me*   134

31.   *Lie with Me*   134

32.   *40 Days and 40 Nights*   139

33.   *1–900*   142

34.   *Sirens*   149

35.   *Sirens*   149

36.   *Angels and Insects*   154

37.   *Man of Flowers*   158

38.   *Man of Flowers*   159

39.   *Forgetting Sarah Marshall*   162

40.   *Lady Chatterley*   176

Acknowledgments

This book has grown out of work we have been doing together for ten years, and there are many more people than we could ever thank who have helped and encouraged us with feedback on conference papers, journal articles, and book chapters over the years. We are especially grateful to Bill Luhr, Bob Eberwein, and Santi Fouz-Hernández. We'd also like to thank the editors who have published the revised and expanded versions of our conference papers. Leslie Mitchner at Rutgers University Press read an early draft of the manuscript, and we benefited immensely from her insightful suggestions. We also want to thank Leah Abriani, Peter Lehman's research assistant at Arizona State University, for her excellent help in the preparation of the manuscript, the compilation of the Works Cited, the index, and her general interest in and enthusiasm for the project.

We owe a special thanks to film and television writer-producer-director Zalman King, who is, in our view, the creator of the body-guy film genre, the subject of this book. Zalman has been kind and generous with us, granting interviews and inviting us into his home as guests on several occasions. Most important, he has listened to our analyses and critiques and responded with great candor, always participating in a spirited, positive exchange of ideas. We hope our book supplies a historical and cultural framework in which to appreciate, understand, and even constructively critique his films and other films of the genre he presciently founded.

From Peter Lehman: I would like to thank Melanie Magisos for once again cheerfully putting up with the many hours that my devotion to writing requires and to watching and talking about countless movies and TV shows with me. Without her support I couldn't do it. I also want to thank Robert Flynt, to whom I have dedicated my work on this book, for his friendship and for his work. I have spent so much time looking at images of the male body and the male nude only to come away with the feeling that I've seen it all before and to lament the limitations of the assumptions about masculinity and male sexuality that cling to those images. But Bob's work is fresh, challenging, complex, ambiguous, and, rarest of all things in this field, mature. He is the most important photographer of his generation and one of the most important in the history of his medium working in the male nude. And he is a great lunch companion, with a wonderful appetite for both good food and good conversation.

From Susan Hunt: I would like to thank Michael Hart for his many generous "read-throughs," excellent editing suggestions, and stimulating insights about movies that sometimes made him squirm. His eternal optimism has helped me throughout the process. Thanks also to friends from the various communities in my life for their support and understanding, especially Jay Atkinson and Russ and Dorothy Balisok. Gene Hart and Toodie Beutler deserve a special mention for listening to me say "one more chapter" for months. I'm grateful to my department chairs Barbara Baird, Alex Kritselis, and Frank Dawson for the "flex" time to develop this book. And, of course, my students at Santa Monica and Pasadena City Colleges have always been a source of inspiration—a special appreciation goes out to Ikko Suzuki and Yuta Okamura.

Although this book includes no reprints, we have drawn on some previously published essays and would like to acknowledge the following: "Exposing the Body Guy: The Return of the Repressed in *Twentynine Palms*," in *Mysterious Skin: Male Bodies in Contemporary Cinema*, edited by Santiago Fouz-Hernández (London: I. B. Tauris, 2009), 207–19; "The Naked and the Dead: The Jewish Male Body and Masculinity in *Sunshine* and *Enemy at the Gates*," in *The Persistence of Whiteness: Race and Contemporary Hollywood Cinema*, edited by Daniel Bernardi (New York: Routledge, 2008), 157–64; "'Something and Someone Else': The Mind, the Body, and Sexuality in *Titanic*," in *Titanic: Anatomy of a Blockbuster*, edited by Gaylyn Studlar and Kevin S. Sandler (New Brunswick: Rutgers University Press, 1999), 89–107; "Passion and Passion for Learning in *The Governess*," *Jump Cut* 44 (2001): www.ejumpcut.org/home.html.

Lady Chatterley's
Legacy in the Movies

CHAPTER 1

"Everything You Are Is between Your Legs"

Titanic (1997) is still "king of the world" at the box office, grossing more money worldwide than any other film in history. For his epic tale, writer-producer-director James Cameron masterfully intertwines a broad array of genres: romance, action, adventure, and historical drama. The film belongs to yet another category, which has flourished virtually unnoticed for the past twenty years: the "body-guy" genre, as we call it. In the genre's classic form, a beautiful, intelligent, but discontented woman is engaged or married to a cultured, intellectual, upper-class male. The woman's discontent is quelled when a working-class man, often tied closely to the land, awakens her sexuality and energizes her life. The body guy's masculinity and sexuality are so compelling that he rescues the woman from the stultifying world of the successful "mind guy," who is boring, controlling, and, significantly, a poor lover who fails to recognize, let alone fulfill, her sexual needs.

   Titanic contains many of the genre's key conventions. From the ship's lower tier, Jack (Leonardo DiCaprio), a penniless itinerant worker, sights the beautiful, well-dressed Rose (Kate Winslet), above him on a deck reserved for the far-from-penniless. He knows in an instant that her beauty is tinged with melancholy. With equal immediacy he knows that he has the right stuff to fix whatever is haunting her. The two meet when Jack prevents Rose from committing suicide. Soon, he is whisking her away from the upper-deck dining room and her cultured but arrogant fiancé, Cal (Billy Zane), to show her a good time at a "real party" in steerage. Cal quietly sips his cognac over conversation about politics and business while inarticulate men in steerage happily fall down drunk. The fun continues for Jack and Rose when they have first-time sex in the back of a car in the ship's frigid cargo hold. Even though they have just fled from Cal's assistant, who pursued them with a gun, Jack's sexual performance is perfect. In a graphic image, we see Rose's hand slap against the rear window and trace a pattern in the steamy condensation, the PG-13 signal

Figure 1. *Titanic*

of intense orgasm from vigorous penetration sex. To confirm our imagination, the next shot shows Jack and Rose in afterglow, their bodies glistening with sweat. At this point, there's no going back for Rose. She risks her own death to be with Jack, who, as she says, "saved her in every way a person could be saved."

Rose's attraction to Jack is repeatedly tied to frenetic bodily energy. She's giddy when emulating Jack's Celtic step dancing, and the two of them spin gleefully in circles on the dance floor (figure 1). This playfulness is starkly contrasted with her corseted world of propriety. She learns how to spit over the upper-deck rail (to her priggish mother's chagrin) and nearly swoons thinking she and Jack will someday drink cheap beer and ride a roller coaster till they throw up. Rose is revitalized by an uncommon common man. Cal only shows physical vitality when he violently slaps Rose and chases her in order to kill her. In fact, the film's cutting pattern dramatically associates Cal with isolation and stillness. He is shown alone, surveying his stateroom's private promenade immediately after a scene in which Jack negotiates a bustling corridor to enter a third-class stateroom he shares with three other men. Rose and Jack's frivolity at the steerage party is intercut with rigid and restrained images of Cal and the other upper-class men conversing in a drawing room, subtly denigrating the mind's potential as a locus of erotic energy (figure 2).

Typical of body guys in the pattern, Jack is a manual laborer, but he is somewhat unusual in that he's also an aspiring artist. He is, however, far from intellectual. Jack lived in Paris at the height of the modernist movement, a time when artistic style and political action coalesced, but he seems untouched by the innovative milieu, sketching instead in a highly conventional, realist style against which the philosophical artists rebelled. Perhaps most key to his body-guy status, Jack sketches female nudes and body parts, and his models are prostitutes. His art is that of the sexed body and the working-class streets. In one of

Figure 2. *Titanic*

the film's integral scenes, he sketches Rose nude in what becomes a type of foreplay. His art, his sexuality, and body-guy persona are fused.

Jack's masculinity is dramatically privileged over Cal's, so emotion reigns over intellect. In establishing the mind/body opposition in this manner, Cameron plugs firmly into an anti-intellectual ideology so familiar to American culture. He reinforces the popular myth that the mind is a boring place—a site that could never be stimulating, erotic, or even fun. Those qualities are attached instead to the party in steerage. When Jack urges Rose to dance, she says, "I don't know the steps," to which he replies, "Neither do I. Go with it. *Don't think*." When Rose tells Jack that she will go with him when the ship docks, he says, "This is crazy," to which Rose responds, "I know. It doesn't make sense. That's why I trust it."

The world of the mind represented by Cal and other "real-life" men on the *Titanic* such as Benjamin Guggenheim and John Jacob Astor is dismissed as the "snake pit" by the loveable nouveau-riche but social pariah, Molly Brown (Kathy Bates). Obviously, the first-class world of cigars, cognac, and conversation could be presented as one of pleasurable vitality rather than deadly boredom, and just as obviously, Rose could find erotic fulfillment with a man from that world. And, indeed, the film potentially contains such a man in the character of Thomas Andrews (Victor Garber), the designer of the *Titanic*.

Cameron seemingly contradicts his project of privileging working-class Jack by creating Andrews as a kindred spirit to Rose. Andrews is the only upper-class man at the captain's table who is amused by Rose's impertinent Freudian-laced comments about *Titanic*'s size. Though she publicly impugns the *Titanic*, Rose's private remarks to Andrews are glowing: "The ship is a wonder, Mr. Andrews, truly." In many ways, Andrews is the upper-class, educated equivalent of Jack in that they are, in a sense, both artists. They are even linked visually as both interact with Rose on the elegant stairway to the upper-deck dining salon.

Perhaps the most compelling similarity between Andrews and Jack is that they both "see something" in Rose. Although Andrews may seem to be a type of father figure, he appears barely middle-aged, and his place within the narrative structure makes it clear that Cameron could just as easily have made him a potential lover for Rose—one who attractively represents the world of the mind. Although Jack and Andrews are linked, the relationship between Rose and Andrews functions ultimately to emphasize the impotence of the educated, upper-class man as compared to working-class potency. Jack is able to motivate Rose and effect her survival in a way that Andrews cannot. As the ship is sinking, Andrews's parting words to Rose are, "I'm sorry that I didn't build you a stronger ship." Not surprisingly, the most iconic image from the film celebrates the liberating bodily experience Jack provides as he and Rose stand on the ship's prow, sensuously feeling the rush of the wind; the "king of the world" moment.

Although *Titanic*, an extremely big-budget production, is the most well known film within the body-guy narrative pattern, it is part of a vast array of international, multigeneric films ranging from low-budget "indies" to blockbusters directed by both women and men. To name just a few: 1988's *Two Moon Junction* jump-starts the genre, followed by *Henry & June* (1990), *At Play in the Fields of the Lord* (1991), *The Piano* (1993), *Legends of the Fall* (1994), *I.Q.* (1994), *The Bridges of Madison County* (1995), *Antonia's Line* (1995), *Box of Moonlight* (1996), *Lawn Dogs* (1997), *Titanic* (1997), *The Horse Whisperer* (1998), *The End of the Affair* (1999), *Fight Club* (1999), *Enemy at the Gates* (2001), *Sweet Home Alabama* (2002), *The Notebook* (2004), *Asylum* (2005), *Fur: An Imaginary Portrait of Diane Arbus* (2006), *Lady Chatterley* (2007 in the U.S.), and *Australia* (2008). At least one significant body-guy film has been released per year for the last twenty-plus years. This pervasive pattern suggests a deep, broad appeal.[1]

Novels and plays have placed women like Rose in *Titanic* between men of opposing categories such as working class and upper class for centuries. We trace this particular incarnation of the genre to the publication of D. H. Lawrence's *Lady Chatterley's Lover* in 1928, a novel that pits an intellectual, paraplegic, impotent upper-class landowner against his virile gamekeeper for his wife's affections, with the latter winning out in all ways. In 1928, when agrarian societies dwindled in the face of the industrial revolution, glorifying and sentimentalizing the men of the earth had an obvious appeal. But what does it mean to revive this scenario in the 1990s? Why offer the body guys' model of sexuality to intelligent women in the films and simultaneously to women in the audience? Why denigrate intellectual males in the current information age, where education and specialized training is crucial? Why promote a "cowboy" masculinity in modern America? Or in Europe? Or Australia?

Who is this contemporary body guy? Which actors portray him? What physiques typify him? And what is his unique appeal? Arguably the most popular movie star of his generation, Brad Pitt stars in at least four key films of the genre: *A River Runs Through It* (1992), *Kalifornia* (1993), *Legends of the Fall* (1994), and *Fight Club* (1999). Pitt burst onto the film industry's radar with 1991's *Thelma & Louise*, in which his small role as J.D. solidified his sex appeal and the genre's classic characteristics: cowboy hat and boots, tight blue jeans, trim but chiseled body, and a studly sexual performance that causes Thelma to squeal, "I finally understand what all the fuss is about. It's a whole 'nuther ball game." In a sense, in 1991 Pitt provided the look and persona to create a cultural shorthand for the body guy's role in film narrative. One look and we all know this character and what he's capable of doing, particularly in the bedroom.

This contemporary body guy packs the same kind of punch that Lawrence's gamekeeper provided in 1928. Connie Chatterley swoons at the initial sight of the shirtless Mellors:

> He was naked to the hips, his velveteen breeches slipping down over his slender loins. And his white slim back was curved over a big bowl of soapy water. . . . Connie backed away round the corner of the house, and hurried away to the wood. In spite of herself, she had had a shock . . . in some curious way it was a visionary experience: it had hit her in the middle of the body. . . . Perfect, white, solitary nudity. . . . Not the stuff of beauty, not even the body of beauty, but a lambency, the warm, white flame of a single life, revealing itself in contours that one might touch: *a body*. (68, emphasis added)

A whole 'nuther ball game.

In the body-guy movie genre proper, *Legends of the Fall* is the exemplar for both the man of the earth's body type and his sex style in R-rated representation. The character Tristan, played by Brad Pitt, makes first-time love to the beautiful woman, his hairless chest highlighting his sculpted pecs and abs. His absent body hair only enhances the glorious blond tresses flowing from his head as his lover runs her fingers through them in a moment of all-consuming passion. He kisses her gently; dissolve to him pinning the woman's hands above her head as he undulates atop her; dissolve to a slow pan up their bodies as he caresses her thigh and continues sprinkling her with kisses; dissolve to him taking the woman from behind, a look of ecstasy on her beautiful face as she grips the headboard (figure 3); dissolve to the woman lying on top of him wearing the same ecstatic expression; cut to daybreak and a rooster crowing. There you

Figure 3. *Legends of the Fall*

have the salient features of the body guy's sexual performance: chiseled, buff body on display; penile penetration in various positions with an emphasis on how long he can last, both in the sense of endurance during a lovemaking episode and in the sense of his recuperative power: doing it all night.

Dead Presidents from 1995 foregrounds another facet of this privileged sex style: deep, forceful penile thrusting—what we call "pound, pound, pound" or "pound-cubed sex" for short. Anthony and Juanita decide to have intercourse for the first time before he goes to war in Vietnam. Initially they fumble. He can't unhook her bra. He tries to insert his penis, but she cries out, "Ouch, that's not it. Up, up, up, up. That's too high . . . wait . . . down." Once he finds the right place, she winces with the pain of her torn hymen. But then, in a moment, he gets his stride and she is as instantly delighted. He thrusts atop her so vigorously that the headboard bangs against the wall. The vibrations from their vigorous sex literally shake a bed in an adjacent room, and Juanita's sister must cover her head with a pillow to muffle the lovers' moaning. After a brief interlude, the sweat-soaked couple go at it again. Cut to an exterior view of the house with a low angle of their bedroom window and the rhythmic sounds of the thwacking headboard and Juanita's zealous screams. Dissolve to the same shot of the house as dawn breaks. It's the urban version of *Legends*, but no rooster crows this time. This style of sex is now virtually synonymous in the movies with good sex, and even teenage boys losing their virginity are expected to perform it well if we are to regard them as real men and good lovers.

Some of the R-rated movies, however, are even more explicit than either *Legends of the Fall* or *Dead Presidents* in that they bring a feature to the genre

Figure 4. *The Piano*

unimaginable and virtually impossible prior to 1968: frontal male nudity featuring a good-sized penis in a manner that once again recalls Lawrence's *Lady Chatterley's Lover*. The novel created an international scandal in the early twentieth century, with its graphic sexual explicitness. The novel is so vivid in its descriptions of sex, including the penis, that Lawrence actually titled an earlier version after the main characters' pet names for their genitals, *John Thomas and Lady Jane*.[2]

In 1991 and 1993, major American movie stars Tom Berenger and Harvey Keitel appeared frontally nude in well-regarded independent films, Hector Babenco's *At Play in the Fields of the Lord* and Jane Campion's *The Piano* respectively. Here were two well-known actors baring all in what would become a key genre convention. Whereas *Titanic* was a wildly successful Hollywood blockbuster, *The Piano* (Australia/New Zealand/France, 1993) was a critically acclaimed art film. In this film, a woman is married to a prosperous landowner but passionately succumbs to the sexual advances of an illiterate neighbor who has "gone native." Amid the critical accolades, little attention was paid to the shot in which Harvey Keitel's penis is prominently displayed for a fairly prolonged period of time to the woman in the film and the film spectator (figure 4). After Berenger and Keitel, a string of nude body guys appear: Mark Gerber in *Sirens* (1994), Douglas Henshall in *Angels and Insects* (1995), Ewan McGregor in *The Pillow Book* (1996) and *Young Adam* (2003), Sam Rockwell in *Box of Moonlight* (1996) and *Lawn Dogs* (1997), Jonathan Rhys Meyers in *The Governess* (1998), and Jean-Louis Coullo'ch in *Lady Chatterley* (2006), to name a few.[3] As the genre developed, it inextricably linked the body guy's typically good-sized penis to the frenetic, pound-cubed lovemaking style described above. This foregrounded penis is what pound cubed is all about, and the displayed penises are all of good size with rare exceptions that prove the rule.[4]

Which returns us to Lawrence's *Lady Chatterley's Lover*. In his novel, Lawrence describes the intensity of Connie's orgasm in a manner that emphasizes the all-powerful penis:

> Then as he began to move, in the sudden helpless orgasm, there awoke in her new strange thrills rippling inside her. Rippling, rippling, rippling, like a flapping overlapping of soft flames, soft as feathers, running to points of brilliance, exquisite, exquisite and melting her all molten inside. It was like bells rippling up and up to a culmination. She lay unconscious of the wild little cries she uttered at the last. But it was over too soon, too soon. . . . She could do nothing. She could no longer harden and grip for her own satisfaction upon him. She could only wait, wait and moan in spirit as she felt him withdrawing, withdrawing and contracting, coming to the terrible moment when he would slip out of her and be gone. Whilst all her womb was open and soft, and softly clamouring, like a sea anemone under the tide, clamouring for him to come in again and make a fulfillment for her. She clung to him unconscious in passion, and he never quite slipped from her, and she felt the soft bud of him within her stirring, and strange rhythms flushing up into her with a strange rhythmic growing motion, swelling and swelling till it filled her all cleaving consciousness, and then began again the unspeakable motion that was not really motion, but pure deepening whirlpools of sensation swirling deeper and deeper through all her tissue and consciousness, till she was one perfect concentric fluid of feeling, and she lay there crying in unconscious inarticulate cries. (141–42)

Zalman King's *Two Moon Junction* (1988), which launched the modern film incarnations of *Lady Chatterley's Lover*, retains precisely this emphasis on the extraordinary penile-centered orgasm that only a gifted man of the earth can give to a woman. King stated in a 2008 interview that he was unaware of the trend he helped set in motion (King). Although he was working in a marginal film genre that he believes many critics mistakenly label soft-core porn, his depiction of the body guy and the narrative conventions he employed would essentially become the models for the future of the genre. In *Two Moon Junction* the narrative tension is built around what the hero "has" that the cultured mind guy does not have. Although the hero has a number of attractive qualities, it is his sexuality that lures the beautiful woman away from the upper-class man, who lacks in a variety of ways but particularly in the sexual arena. As is frequently the case, the mind/body polarity is the structuring opposition of the film, but the body guy is so central to the plot dynamic (which is why we name the genre after him) that the mind guy essentially becomes a secondary figure.

King describes the body guy's compelling quality as a "physicality" and his ability to perform penetration sex as a "gift":

> Ultimately that's his gift. Young men know whether they have a gift or not in that area. It happens very young in life where they know that this is a particular gift that they've been given and basically, the ability to fulfill—seriously fulfill—a woman. Sometimes that's the only gift that a man has, like let's say the carnival guy, maybe that's his only gift—in *Two Moon Junction*, that might be his *only* gift. It is not easy to seriously fulfill a woman. I think basically, that there normally is a culmination the woman has to experience, or the man and the woman need to get together, in these films that we are talking about, yeah it happens. And it usually then haunts the women. That encounter haunts them. And I believe *that* sex is addictive, especially for women.

King goes on to associate this gifted sexual performance with penis size, noting that body guys usually have "really big" penises, even regretting that he didn't make that fact explicit in *Two Moon Junction*: "When women make love a lot, that's very important to them, the size of a man, when they're really promiscuous to the max. And basically, that's how it is in reality. In *Two Moon Junction* I should show that; I should actually show that, but I don't" (King).

Two Moon Junction's opening scenes establish the extreme wealth and social status of the film's protagonist, April Delongpre (Sherilyn Fenn), as she descends a lavish staircase in an equally lavish gown, queen of her college sorority's spring graduation ball. Her wealthy, Harvard-bound fiancé, Chad, awaits her on the ballroom floor, and as a mind guy he's immediately linked to a world of pretension and regimentation, a genre staple: "I like things to work and I like them nice and neat," says Chad. Just as quickly, April craves life outside the rigid code of southern propriety: "What I want, Chad, is to run away to a tropical island somewhere and live in a grass hut [eating] coconuts, mangoes and papayas."

April's discontent is primarily sexual in nature, demonstrated in the film's second sequence when, while showering at their country club, she removes a previously loosened tile from the wall to spy on men in the adjacent shower room. In a point-of-view shot, April gazes at the naked men, their buttocks and penises fully visible to the film spectator, then swoons with desire. This scene is intercut with shirtless muscled men assembling attractions for a carnival that has rolled into town. April later crosses paths with the man of the earth, Perry (Richard Tyson), and in the next few scenes key conventions of the future genre are laid out. At first sighting, the long-haired Perry is sweaty and shirtless with a "cut" body straight out of Calvin Klein (figure 5). He takes one look at

Figure 5. *Two Moon Junction*

April and immediately reads her needs. She notices him in return, his posture signaling self-confidence, even cockiness. Indeed, he flirts with the clearly upper-class April with ease and no self-consciousness. He is so sure of himself and his knowledge of April's wants and needs that he essentially breaks into her home when he knows she's alone and begins taking a shower, saying to April, "I knew you wouldn't mind." Sure enough, an initially enraged April is soon having sex with the hypnotic Perry.

Perry's association with the carnival allows the elaboration of most of the body-guy hero's other characteristics. The carnival presupposes a nomadic lifestyle, linked to people considered "Other" (the owner is a dwarf, and the first carnival sequence begins with "native" bungee jumpers leaping from a platform). Perry has a beloved dog and shows an affinity for animals and nature in general, doing manual labor with ease. Although Perry opts for a transient life over the values of materialist American culture ("I ain't got nothing except a bike, a truck, and a post office box in Clearwater, Florida"), he is different from and superior to the others in the carnival. When he pulls his hair back, puts on glasses and buttons up his white dress shirt, he can easily pass for an educated, higher-class person (as does Jack in a tuxedo in *Titanic*), and, indeed, his knowledge of things such as pongee silk suggests a suppressed worldliness.

Perry belongs neither to the world of the carnival nor the world of high society, but this is indicative of his "specialness," his *je ne sais quoi*, which is a key trait across the genre. Perry is appalled by the greedy and unscrupulous attitudes of the carnival owner and his lackeys, but he is superior, as well, to the upper-class men who, in Chad's bachelor party scene, are shown to be part of a male world that is insensitive to and controlling of women—not a place that April or any woman should be.

Indeed, this notion of the body guy saving the woman from a world that is stultifying at best and dangerous at worst is another staple of the genre. For April, the entry into her fiancé's world of social convention marks the death of her individuality. She confides her qualms about marriage to her grandmother: "I haven't had enough time for me," a concept her aristocratic grandmother finds insignificant in relation to the power alliance between families that will result from April's marriage. April's grandmother, father (a U.S. senator), and fiancé (linked to The Law) come to stand for control and loss of self, but Perry will be the one to save her from this personal and spiritual ruin. This issue of freeing the woman is what puts Perry in trouble with the law, another feature of the genre. Perry is literally outside the law when he breaks into April's home, but the temptation he offers April is the real transgression, inciting characters on the side of the mind guy, such as April's controlling grandmother and the town sheriff, to eliminate his influence.

In essence, Perry's manhood, with its liberating effect on women, is out of control. In a scene near the end of the film April goes to Perry on the night before her wedding. She initiates sex with him by first removing her dress and standing before him completely naked. Her lovemaking with Perry is intercut with images of Chad at his bachelor party. As April frees herself of clothing, a performer dressed like a police officer handcuffs Chad while his grandfather, an actual sheriff, looks on with patriarchal approval. One of the faux law officers then rips off her uniform to reveal a lacy bra, garter belt, and stockings, signs of conventional femininity in the service of male fantasy. Chad is handcuffed and subjected to a world of conventional sexuality that views women in derogatory ways while April actively seeks her own sexual liberation.

In 1988, as now, women in many facets of American society had more opportunities to define, locate, and act on their passions in life than ever before in American history. Yet simultaneously, society attempts to channel, control, and limit those opportunities by promoting a particular kind of sexual experience as the ultimate value. In *Two Moon Junction*, April has an array of opportunities which she succinctly states when she tells her grandmother that what she needs is "having time for me." Instead, however, Perry looks into April's soul, and out of all the possibilities "the world" offers for personal fulfillment, the satisfaction of her libido, as he refers to it, takes precedence; and she immediately succumbs to it.

And Perry has the look, confidence, and sexual prowess to excite and satisfy April's libido instantly. That's the body guys' gift in these films. And the importance of this gift is articulated when an elderly male carnie says of Perry, "You got it all, kid." April repeatedly says of Perry, "Everything you are is between your legs." She says this with disdain but keeps coming back for more. Perry may "have it all," but the main thing he has, according to the film, is, indeed, between his legs. Perry's magnetism and masterful lovemaking abilities are central to the genre, and Zalman King even points to the erotic appeal that this model of lovemaking will hold for future filmmakers in this genre when he has Perry videotape his first lovemaking session with April. Later, we see her become sexually excited while watching the tape; thus, the film's address to female spectators makes explicit that this kind of lover and sex style is what they should desire and seek for their fulfillment: this is the way it should *look*, as well as the way it should feel.

April decides to go through with her marriage to Chad, but the film's final scene has Perry return to his motel room to find her showering—a direct rhyme with the scene in which he sneaks into April's home to shower before seducing her. The mind guy just doesn't have what it takes to attract and keep the desirable, experienced woman. The idea that the body guy has something that the mind guy lacks may not be totally new, but within the current climate of sexual explicitness, the films we examine create new dichotomies and new variants of established ones: penis/brain, sexuality/intellectualism, preferred masculinity/inadequate masculinity. Although these films are made worldwide, and those made in America enjoy a global audience, this disparagement of the mind resonates in a uniquely intense manner within American culture, which has long embraced anti-intellectualism. The 2004 hit country song by Trace Adkins, "(This Ain't) No Thinkin' Thing," concisely articulates American anti-intellectualism as it revels in the pleasures and truths of the body and emotions over the brain and mind. The title says it all, even flaunting bad grammar. Love is the thing that we should not think about: "It's a chemical, physical, emotional devotion" with "nothing that we need to analyze." Forget psychology, economics, sociology, or history. On the 2004 music video of the song, Adkins clearly displays body-guy tropes. Referencing the western film genre, he wears a cowboy hat and duster as he gyrates and thrusts his pelvis to throngs of screaming women and men who reach out to touch him, evocative of "Ladies' Night" at a strip club.

Body guys can be found in novels, movies, songs, music videos, and on the concert circuit. Their ubiquity is a symptom of America's obsession with the body, the creation of a virtual body culture. The body culture defines identity and power as residing in the body as opposed to the mind. This belief places undue emphasis on surface appearances and visible display of bodily coordination and performance. The political commentator George Will concisely summarizes the current moment by saying that we as Americans have gone from "I have a body" to "I *am* a body."

The rise of the new American body culture begins in the late 1970s and early 1980s with Arnold Schwarzenegger and Jane Fonda, but of course there are predecessors to Schwarzenegger's pumping up and Fonda's aerobic workouts. Jack LaLanne opened his first gym in 1936, and was a television celebrity from the 1950s to the 1980s. This book, however, focuses on the increasing excesses of 1980s and 1990s body culture perhaps epitomized by the trajectory of the running-jogging phenomenon that essentially began in 1977 with Jim Fixx's *The Complete Book of Running*. Casual jogging soon gave way to the rising popularity of the marathon, a 26.2-mile run. In 1976, 25,000 people completed a marathon in the United States, and that number has increased every successive year to 412,000 in 2007. Triathlons arose in the early 1980s, complete with the grueling "Ironman" category (26.2 miles running, 2.4 miles swimming, 112 miles biking). The early 1980s also launched "Ultra Runs," 100-mile treks through challenging terrain such as Pike's Peak or Death Valley. By the late 1980s, we had Extreme Sports (a.k.a. action or adventure sports), activities with a high level of inherent danger, such as backcountry snowboarding, ice-climbing, and high-wave surfing, as if marathons and other conventional sports—already a national obsession—were just way too dull. Big, bigger, biggest.

Masculine display escalated during this same time period with a new emphasis on the penis and male sexuality. Penises, obviously, had been the subject of endless fascination throughout history and across cultures. Early in the twentieth century Freud placed great importance on the penis in psychoanalytic development; by the middle of the century the famous Kinsey Report spotlighted it within the context of anatomy and sexual behavior; and late in the century William H. Masters and Virginia E. Johnson gave it prominence in the realms of medicine and sexology. But something new was happening in popular culture and the media.

In the turnabout-is-fair-play guise of empowering women by making men sex objects, *Playgirl* magazine was first published in 1973 and featured full-frontal male nudity, and in the early 1980s Chippendale male dancers stripped to their thongs for howling female club-goers. Along with liposuction and breast implants, the early 1980s also introduced phalloplasty, surgical techniques for lengthening and thickening the penis. Continuing the late 1960s trend of public nudity associated with Woodstock and the sexual revolution, in the 1970s naked male streakers ran through public events in order to disrupt them, bringing attention to the ridiculous reverence previously granted the penis by not showing or talking about it. In the 1980s radio shock jock Howard Stern extended streaking's taboo-smashing legacy by frequently talking about his self-described small penis on the air. Penises even began to appear in mainstream Hollywood movies with Richard Gere fully nude in *American Gigolo* (1980).

After he appeared naked again in *Breathless* (1983), *Newsweek* featured a scant-ily clad Gere on its cover and dubbed him one of Hollywood's new "male idols."

In the same vein, Calvin Klein Underwear for Men launched a fashion line in 1982 with male models "heralding a new era in imagery of men in advertising—the sexualized male as a hairless muscular object of desire" (gayfortoday .blogspot.com). If the 1980s broke new ground with "outing" the previously hidden and unexamined penis, the 1990s intensified the spectacle. In 1992 a giant billboard in New York City's Times Square featured rapper Marky Mark (the now famous film star Mark Wahlberg) buff and provocatively clad in Calvin Klein briefs that revealed the outline of his large penis. This image entrenched the prototype for a less-pumped-up but finely toned male physique that would set the standard for many leading men in 1990s cinema, a standard that foregrounds the good-sized penis. At the same time, the big penis got further attention when the National Endowment for the Arts came under attack for funding *The Perfect Moment*, a traveling exhibition of Robert Mapplethorpe's photographs that included his pictures of well-endowed African American men.

Mainstream media's polite silence concerning "penis talk" was shattered in 1993 with the John Wayne Bobbitt saga. Bobbitt's enraged wife, Lorena, severed his penis while he slept and threw it into a field from her car while leaving the scene. A police officer retrieved the member after a long search, and it was sur-gically reattached in a nine-and-a-half-hour operation. Bobbitt went on to act in porn films, but had his penis surgically enlarged after it was mocked as too small—a procedure that he videotaped and used in one of his films! Not sur-prisingly, in the following year penis-size jokes go prime time with the now-famous "shrinkage" episode of *Seinfeld*. As George removes his swimsuit, his date sees him and laughs. He fears that she has mistaken his small penis that was shrunken from cold water as his normal size. Such penis-size jokes also ran rampant in movies of the 1980s and early 1990s. Toward the end of the decade, former vice president Bob Dole brought attention to yet another kind of penis. With his Viagra television commercials, Dole made it okay to talk openly about erectile dysfunction. The 1990s also saw the rise of Web sites that featured the penises of celebrities in one category and "amateurs" in another with pictures they or their partners submitted on user-generated content sites.

Gigantic, shrunken, or useless; famous or amateurish; the penis emerges from hiding in the 1990s, setting the stage for the twenty-first century, when Calvin Klein meets Robert Mapplethorpe in the form of Oscar-nominated actor Djimon Hounsou, who graced billboards and magazines in his "CK" briefs. A *twenty-seven-story* Hounsou billboard erected in Hong Kong was reputedly the largest in Asia, and slyly referring to Hounsou's very formidable bulge, his girlfriend remarked, "He's the biggest one in the world, honey" (Slonim and Tapper). Also in 2008, mainstream film critics gave prominence to the star Jason Segel's penis in their reviews of *Forgetting Sarah Marshall*. In 2007 on the CBS hit comedy *Two and a Half Men*, Charlie teases his brother, Alan, about wearing his Jockey underwear in the shower in high school because other boys called him "shrinky dink." Alan replies, "I'm a grow-er, not a show-er," meaning his flaccid penis shows little shaft before erection, but expands significantly when erect. By June 2009, the large penis had its own TV show with the premiere and consequent renewal of the HBO series appropriately entitled *Hung*.

The ultimate absurdity of where all this body-penis mania has been heading can be seen in a 2008 media happening. On YouPorn, a free adult Web site, a thirteen-minute video entitled "Hot Alpine Sex" features an attractive, athletic-looking man and woman running out of gas in their SUV in alpine backcountry. They decide that in order to get help they must rappel down the mountain from what seems to be a seven- or eight-thousand-foot elevation. They rig up and begin their descent, but don't get more than fifty feet when they're overcome with sexual desire. As they dangle from the mountain ledge on ropes, clearly thousands of feet above the ground, the couple engage in classic vigorous porn maneuvers in various positions until the man ejaculates onto the woman's face. Extreme sports, a large penis, and porn-style sex—itself a kind of extreme sport—combined. (But alas, the couple fall two minutes short of their Warholian fifteen minutes of fame.)

This brief historical overview progresses much like a Hollywood narrative, building in a nearly hysterical intensity toward the atomic climax that we've yet to reach. Pumped up bodies. Pumped up breasts and lips (on excessively trimmed down bodies). Pumped up penises. Extreme sports. Ultimate fighting. What is going on here? In short, that's the question this book attempts to answer, as it were, by going to the movies.

"Everything you are is between your legs," says April to Perry in *Two Moon Junction*. If the body guy's sex style is the apex of his appeal, his good-sized penis is the linchpin of his penetration-based sexual performance, emphasized by the inordinate amount of male frontal nudity in the genre. For our purposes, the title of Robert Mapplethorpe's photo exhibition from the early 1990s, *The Perfect Moment* is, well . . . perfect. The critical brouhaha surrounding the black nudes in the show foregrounded the inordinate cultural importance placed on the penis in defining male sexuality at precisely the same moment that the body guy began to appear nude in films.

Before the 1970s, the penis was seldom if ever seen in mainstream American cinema. Perhaps partly in response to the "outing" of the penis in the late 1960s

Figure 6. *The Blue Lagoon*

and 1970s with Woodstock, streaking, and other exposures related to the free love and counterculture movements, frontal male nudity began seeping into Hollywood cinema. Beginning in the 1980s, Christopher Atkins is a key actor who repeatedly appears frontally nude. He even modeled fully nude for magazine photographs at the time, some of which currently circulate on the Internet. In *The Blue Lagoon* (1980), Atkins and Brooke Shields play adolescents shipwrecked on a nearly deserted island. Atkins's penis is displayed multiple times, including when he swims in the ocean, and his nudity evokes Woodstock in that it is not presented to impress the film spectator. Both Atkins and Shields display the tropes of flower children—muddied bodies, living off the earth, and going *au naturelle*. Atkins's overall body, however, portends the soon-to-appear "Calvin Klein" physique: he's buff, scantily clad, and adopts an array of sports poses that maximize and show off his muscle tone. His penis may not be intended to impress, but his body is (figure 6).

Just three years later, in 1983, Atkins's penis appears again in *A Night in Heaven*, a film that centers on a mind/body opposition or, perhaps more accurately phrased, a penis/brain opposition. The representation of Atkins's penis, however, takes a turn from flower child innocence toward impressive spectacle. Atkins plays Rick Monroe, a charismatic college student who fails his public speaking class taught by Professor Faye Hanlon (Leslie Anne Warren). Faye admonishes him by saying, "You say what you say well, but you have nothing to say. You have a natural gift and you are constantly abusing it. If you don't take yourself seriously, why should we?" Faye is married to a recently laid-off NASA engineer, Whitney, who is too distracted and depressed to respond to

Figure 7. *A Night in Heaven*

her sexual desire. The opening credit sequence establishes Whit's nerd status when we see him riding a wacky-looking self-designed recumbent bicycle.

Faye reluctantly parties one evening with her sister at a strip club featuring male performers, a la the Chippendale "Ladies' Night" phenomenon. To her initial horror, her student Rick is one of the dancers with the stage name "Ricky the Rocket," a double entendre referring both to her husband's NASA connection and Ricky's penis. When he spots her, Rick seductively approaches Faye, and while he essentially performs a lap dance for her, the club manager directs her hand to the prominent bulge in his crotch (figure 7). He then kisses her and she's hooked—the hook, though, begins with the promise of his penis. Rick pursues a seduction, and Faye is receptive. In a close shot during their first liaison, Rick guides her hand to his crotch, a direct rhyme with the earlier scene at the club. When Atkins removes his pants, we see his partially erect penis. He may have had nothing to say as a student, but he clearly has something to show and give as a lover.

Earlier, the penis was granted a near magical power when a male dancer at the club simulates sex with a female patron by wildly thrusting his pelvis, and she is so overcome that she slumps to the floor. We see the dancer from behind as the woman reaches up and pulls down his thong, literally fainting at the sight of his penis, which the audience does not see. Even though Rick's penis is only briefly glimpsed in the hotel lovemaking scene, its impressiveness is confirmed for the film spectator as the penis literally moves from a visual spectacle inducing fainting to a tactile, penetrating penis inducing blissful orgasm. Earlier, Faye noted that Ricky had a "natural gift" for public speaking, but now, within the terms of the genre, the teacher has been taught about her pupil's "true" natural gift.

Unlike the future body guys, however, Rick is no savior, and he is ultimately not exalted. He does not really awaken Faye's sexuality but rather eases her temporary loneliness. Instead of generously wanting to give something to the woman, Rick wants to get something—a grade change. Also, the mind guy Whitney ultimately puts Rick in his place, not by proving his sexual potency to Faye with his penis but with a phallic gun. When he learns of the affair, Whit, clad in military fatigues, takes Rick at gunpoint to a boat and makes him strip. Rick weeps and begs for his life as Whit abandons him naked in the middle of a lake in a flimsy skiff into which he shot a hole. Our last image of the frontally nude Rick has him teetering in the boat screaming, "Hey, what about my clothes?" his penis looking smaller and much less impressive than earlier. Whit then returns home to the repentant Faye with the promise of a renewed marriage. Faye's experience with the doltish body guy is ultimately unsatisfying instead of liberating, and she has a greater appreciation for her mind-guy husband who is not depicted as negatively as he will be a few years later.

A Night in Heaven was released during the heyday of the "hard body" phenomenon. Schwarzenegger and Stallone were thriving, as was a buffed-up Bruce Willis in the early *Die Hard* films. Body building became a bona fide national craze in America. In her book *Hard Bodies*, Susan Jeffords argues that the excessively muscled men of the 1980s offered an image that many facets of American culture seized on as a means of imagining manhood, and this includes then President Ronald Reagan. Although Christopher Atkins is buff and not pumped up in *A Night in Heaven*, both leading male characters, the not-so-bright Ricky and the "egghead" Whit, are conventionally masculine in the Reagan mode: Ricky with his captivating manhood vis-à-vis his penis and lovemaking style, Whit with his captivating gun and militaristic readiness for violence. Thus, the film ends up affirming two different forms of body-guy masculinity.

A Night in Heaven foreshadowed the shift that would occur when the hard-body phenomenon began to wane in the 1990s, as the pumped-up heroes aged and were legally deprived of anabolic steroids. Historically, the hard-body figures offered an image of manhood directly after, or in response to, America's loss of the Vietnam War and the massive influx of college-educated professional women into the American workforce in previously male-dominated fields. The long-standing clichés associated with female inferiority—women's emotionality, physical weakness, irrationality, moodiness, indecisiveness, and lack of leadership skills—were eroded by the large number of women who succeeded in their fields. *A Night in Heaven* makes clear that a professional woman—an academic who publicly belittles her male student by insulting his intelligence—must be brought to her knees. It's not a body builder and his muscles who does it but a body guy and his penis.

A Night in Heaven predates by five years the moment we identify as the formal start of the body-guy genre. The bodybuilder was ultimately ineffective in restoring a milieu of masculine superiority and awe, and the intervening years elevate the importance of the penis. The 1980s magnified the spectacle of the steroid-infused physique at the expense of the hidden testicles and scrotum, which were known to shrink as a side effect of steroid use. In the 1990s, the previously hidden penis is inflated to compensate for the deflated overblown physiques. The penis packaged in a buff rather than pumped-up body is granted the magical quality of Ricky the Rocket, but in the emerging genre it is never diminished by a more powerful phallic symbol such as a gun: it fully embodies that power itself. Appropriately, the hard-body actors of the 1980s starred in action-adventure films; they used swords, guns, and their fists in combat to complement their enormous bodies. In the 1990s, the body guys' main mode of action is not fighting but lovemaking. The emphasis moves from weapons to the penis and an ability to perform with it.

The grunting, strutting, fighting, and pounding to demand the superiority of an awesome masculinity occurred at a time in history when the categories of femininity and masculinity were openly discussed as cultural constructs, not biological absolutes. All this frenzied activity just when the conflation of the penis with the phallus was under fire, critiqued with eloquent language such as Richard Dyer's "the penis isn't a patch on the phallus. The penis can never live up to the mystique implied by the phallus" (*Only Entertainment* 136). Within academia in the United States, women's studies programs established in the 1970s and 1980s expanded their curriculum to encompass the growing area of men's studies, which flourished by the 1990s. Some women's studies programs were even renamed "gender studies."

The notion of "multiple masculinities" challenged the belief that one fixed and secure masculinity exists in polar opposition to a fixed femininity. Early work in masculinity studies was extensive.[5] Academia opened a door to realistically confront and discuss the social and personal ills perpetrated in the name of masculinity or "being a man" such as gang and domestic violence, hate crimes, and homophobia. Scholars and others opened a space to examine the damage from pressures to conform to cultural norms of masculinity and the male body. Adopting a confessional mode, Stephen S. Hall poignantly articulates the personal pain of oppressive masculinity in the beginning of his book *Size Matters*, in which he details the trials of growing up much shorter than other boys his age. Similarly, in *The Adonis Complex*, men with small penises relate the trauma they've experienced. Hollywood, like much of American society however, missed the opportunity this historical emergence of masculinity studies provided. Movies gave us body guys, and instead of engaging in a meaningful national dialogue about the horrors perpetrated in the name of being a man, we reveled in awe at this new embodiment of masculine power.

Cinema rejected multiple, sometimes radical masculinities in favor of an overly insistent intensification of one fixed, highly limited, powerful, phallic masculinity. That masculinity involved the denigration of intellectual males. The genre affirms the importance of the penis for the woman's pleasure by insulting the sexual and penile inadequacies of the intellectual men to whom the women are initially attached. In John Duigan's *Sirens* (1994), a learned minister scores points in a battle of wits with his nemesis. Energized by the repartee, he later has sex with his attractive, sophisticated wife, bobbing up and down atop her while she stares vacantly at the ceiling. As her husband sleeps in a post-sex stupor, the woman sneaks out to the bungalow of a well-endowed handyman who has fascinated her since she saw him frontally nude on several occasions. The handyman lives up to her expectations, eliciting moans of ecstasy with his first touch, in marked contrast to her husband.

In Fred Schepisi's *I.Q.* (1994), a haughty college professor and his beautiful, brainy fiancée pull into a service station with car troubles. The auto mechanic takes one look at the woman and spark plugs fly. Instantly, he knows that she is unhappy and sees the nature of her discontent. After surveying the car engine, he says to the professor:

> MECHANIC: That's your problem right there. You got no spark.
> PROFESSOR: What?
> WOMAN: You have no spark.
> PROFESSOR: . . . is it the generator, the coil, what? What is wrong with the car?
> MECHANIC: Well, my guess is your stroke is too short and you're getting premature ignition. [*To the woman*] Does it ever feel that way?
> WOMAN: Like what?
> MECHANIC: Like the stroke is too short and you're getting premature ignition?
> WOMAN: [pause] Well . . . I'm sure I don't know what you mean.

The mechanic takes one look and knows the Ivy League professor is a bad lover, and his incompetence centers on his implied short penis, poor thrusting technique, and premature ejaculation. We are asked to accept the mechanic's assessment of the professor's sexual inabilities and endowment in that through casting and acting performance we see him as an unattractive, overweight, pompous individual *in the first thirty seconds that he's on the screen.*

The assault on intellectuals in these movies is particularly nasty in that it often involves the humiliation of men who clearly enjoy using their minds and language in the world of ideas. In *Antonia's Line*, directed by Marleen Gorris (Netherlands 1995; Academy Award winner for Best Foreign Film), Therese, a mathematics professor and one of the film's brainy, attractive female protagonists, sits in bed, bored with her doting sexual partner. A voice-over says, "She experimented with a few intellectuals, but found them wanting." In the next scene Therese is in a bar listening to a bespectacled, overweight man talk animatedly about capitalism and its impact on human relationships. She looks uninterested but signals the man to follow her out of the bar. The next scene shows the same man stumbling naked from the door to Therese's apartment building as she throws his clothing out of a window. Covering his genitals, he repeats the line, "What did I do? What did I do?" A female narrator's voice-over spans both the bar and apartment scenes: "Their [the intellectuals'] self-indulgent blather insulted Therese's intelligence. *Nor was she compensated physically*. And Therese, who was used to the best, refused to put up with this." Again, the intellectual is a poor lover with an inadequate penis, and he's too naive to know that his brain is not supposed to be his main locus of appeal.

The mind/body opposition in narrative began in earnest in 1988. The 1980s, however, had just witnessed cogent challenges to the way intelligence was assessed and defined in the United States. Influential American researchers advocated for broadening the boundaries of how we define intelligence and who is considered intelligent. In Stephen Jay Gould's *The Mismeasure of Man*, first published in 1981, the Harvard professor challenges biological determinism with regard to intelligence. He exposes the fallacies in theories that claim to prove "unitary, innate, genetically fixed, rankable, unchangeable intelligence" (21, 22, 28), and he lambasts the misapplication of the Stanford-Binet I.Q. test as a tool for measuring and ranking intelligence. Gould contends that the fallacious arguments of biodeterminists are used for sociopolitical purposes to "rank people in a single series of worthiness, invariably to find that oppressed and disadvantaged groups—races, classes, or sexes—are innately inferior and deserve their status" (21). Shortly thereafter in 1983, Howard Gardner, also of Harvard, published *Frames of Mind: The Theory of Multiple Intelligences* in which he outlines "a new theory of human intellectual competences," challenging, like Gould, the notion that individuals are "born with a certain amount of intelligence" that can be measured and ranked in definitive ways. Gardner argued that humans have at least six intelligences (linguistic, logical-mathematical, musical, spatial, bodily-kinesthetic, and intra- and interpersonal) but that the American school system teaches to only the linguistic and logical-mathematical learners. With his eloquent aphorism, "It's not how smart you are, but *how* you're smart," Gardner challenges educators and educational systems to include the previously excluded learners in their curricula and pedagogical methods.

Both Gardner and Gould would become public intellectuals, with Gardner's theory adopted by teacher-training programs in major American colleges and promoted by school districts on a national level, including the massive Los Angeles Unified School District and the New York City Department of Education. Gould made numerous appearances on television talk shows such as *Larry King*, *The Today Show*, and *Crossfire* and frequently wrote popular science essays for magazines such as *Natural History*, the *New Yorker*, and the *New York Review of Books*. In other words, in their heydays (the 1980s and, then again, in the late 1990s, when both expanded, revised, and republished their research), Gardner and Gould achieved widespread, public attention for challenging stereotypes about intelligence with regard to race, class, and gender. Gould's and Gardner's theories make it clear to a degree that mostly anyone who chooses to develop his or her mind and see the brain as a site of empowerment can do so. They contend that attitudes and practices in American society are fundamentally to blame for the perpetuation of elitist and exclusionary beliefs about intelligence. As Gould so eloquently states, "But we must never forget the human meaning of lives diminished by these false arguments—and we must . . . never flag in our resolve to expose the fallacies of science misused for alien social purposes" (50).

American culture could have taken the cue to promote the idea that "big brains" are far more important than big penises to individual empowerment and social harmony. A good mind can essentially be developed by everyone, but for all practical purposes, the size of a man's penis is genetically predetermined, then apparent at birth, and physiologically fixed throughout the rest of his life; he can do nothing about it. In contrast, the mind and what one does with it is not fixed. Imagine the liberating potential of these theories for individuals who had been labeled ignorant by parents, teachers, administrators, education systems, and the very society in which they live. Gould and Gardner provided moments in American history when developing one's mind could have been honored, defined as a pleasurable and vital thing to do for people of all classes, races, and sexes. Instead of seizing a cultural moment to affirm and promote ideas that could result in the real empowerment of American citizens, facets of American culture "go postal," insisting that the body is the primary if not sole locus of power.

There is a fascinating connection, as well, between Gould's and Gardner's work on intelligence and our analysis of the penis and its dominant sexual role. Although Gould only noted in passing the similarity between measuring I.Q. and penis size, the details are revealing. Penis size-measurement establishes the average erect penis as six inches with a five- to seven-inch normal range, which is exactly analogous to how I.Q. testing establishes 100 as the average and

90–110 as the normal range. In reality, penises have a wide range of different shapes and sizes. Similarly, with reference to Gardner, men are not born with a certain amount of masculinity and sexuality measurable in their penises; there are a multiplicity of penises but the history of representation is one of a limited range that establishes a norm.

The norm is based on the assumption that the penis reveals something significant about masculinity and male sexuality: good sex requires a large penis for sustained deep penetration. Good-sized penises are also intended to impress and awe women, and their significance lies therein. Short penises, however, are excluded from representation. They can be described as short with little or no shaft, round, soft, tactile, less dramatically visible, and not resembling something meant to penetrate—descriptors traditionally more feminine than masculine. We are suggesting that multiple penises and male sexualities exist, just like multiple intelligences. The normative flaccid penis has the traditional masculine properties of being long and straight and dramatically visible; demonstrating the potential to penetrate a woman. By excluding the short, rounded penis from representation, culture solidifies the notion of a natural impressive masculinity and male sexuality and prevents contemplating alternative possibilities. The shape and size of a man's penis does not determine his masculinity or sexuality (anatomy is *not* destiny). If, however, the variety of penises repressed from representation is made visible, this may lead to an awareness of a similar variety of masculinities and sexualities: some may be penetration-centered; some may not. One type of penis representing an all-encompassing ideal masculinity and sexuality is oppressive, limited, and overdetermined, as is defining intelligence by one single category out of many.

This attempt to fix "proper" penis size occurs after a historical period in which there was a relative acceptance of a range of body types. In the late 1960s to mid-1970s, getting naked was, for many, a political gesture in itself, regardless of body type or penis size—a collective "mooning" of patriarchy and sexually repressed dominant culture and a celebration of sexuality and diversity. Of course, this was not a golden era without judgments and comparisons, and there were counter efforts to standardize, normalize, and idolize bodies, including penises. But again, a perfect moment was missed. A cultural happening could have been seized to promote inclusiveness and challenge dominant definitions of masculinity based on a normative penis. Instead, we turned to the body guy.

In a sense, all those body guys to whom we turned in the movies, and whom we analyze throughout this book, are all Lady Chatterley's lovers, and all the women to whom these men appeal and to whom these films are addressed are Lady Chatterley. We therefore conclude this chapter with some detailed reflections on Lawrence's unbelievably influential novel. It has entered the worldwide popular consciousness even for those who have never read a word of it, which is ironic from the perspective of literary critics who have never held it in high esteem and have, in fact, frequently been embarrassed by it in relation to much of Lawrence's other work. The novelist Lawrence Durrell includes himself among those who believe it is not Lawrence's best work but nevertheless concludes, "Nobody concerned with the novel in our century can afford not to read it" (xii), to which we add no one concerned with film in the late twentieth and early twenty-first century can afford not to read it.[6]

The first few chapters of *Lady Chatterley's Lover* deal centrally with Lady Constance Chatterley as a new kind of woman in post–World War I England, and her sexuality is central to that newness. She and her friends become sexually active around age fifteen with students at school. The environment is one of freedom and intellectual exchange: "It was the talk that mattered supremely; the impassioned interchange of talk. Love was only a minor accompaniment" (3). The relationship of conversation and intellectual activity to sex is formative to Connie: "The arguments, the discussions were the great thing: the love-making and connection were only a sort of primitive reversion and a bit of an anti-climax" (3).

Connie believes that "this sex business" (3) is and has always been really the doing of male artists and thinkers and that women are interested in something "higher" (3): "Neither [Connie or her sister] was ever in love with a young man unless he and she were verbally very near: that is unless they were profoundly interested, TALKING to one another" (4). Within this context, instead of being the main event, sex becomes a kind of afterthought or anticlimax: "And if after the roused intimacy of these vivid and soul enlightened discussions the sex thing became more or less inevitable, then let it be. *It marked the end of a chapter*" (4, emphasis added).

Lawrence's notion of the "new woman" involves early sexual experience with a variety of men but within a context in which the sex is a "minor accompaniment" and the inevitable "end of a chapter." With that background Connie marries Clifford Chatterley: "He had been [a] virgin when he married: and the sex part did not mean much to him. They were so close, he and she, apart from that. And Connie exulted a little in this intimacy, which was beyond sex, and beyond a man's 'satisfaction.' Clifford anyhow was not just keen on his 'satisfaction,' as so many men seemed to be" (9).

All this in chapter 1. The pattern continues with the first affair she has after marrying Clifford. Michaelis, a young writer, is "the trembling excited sort of lover, whose crisis soon came and was finished. . . . He roused in the woman a wild sort of compassion and yearning, and a wild craving physical desire.

The physical desire he did not satisfy in her" (28). Lawrence even writes of Michaelis's "little orgasm being over" (29), connecting how quickly he comes with the intensity, or more precisely, the *size* of his orgasm.

Within the first three chapters of the book, Lawrence defines Connie's ideas on sex as naive and pathetically limited because of her childlike belief that intellectual conversation with her lovers is more important than the sexual climax to which it leads. Lawrence also excoriates Connie's initial contentment with a man who has no sexual experience and little interest in it, and who does not care much about his "satisfaction." Lawrence further humiliates his character for finding a way to actively bring about a powerful orgasm with a trembling, overexcited lover who himself has only a "little orgasm." All this sets the stage for the entrance of Mellors, the gamekeeper with the "true" powerful phallic sexuality that Connie has never imagined, let alone experienced. The student boyfriends, Clifford, and Michaelis are almost literally straw men waiting to be blown away by the real thing. From this perspective, *Lady Chatterley's Lover* is a novel about the sexual education of its heroine.

From our perspective, however, the remaining chapters are about the miseducation of its heroine. And the miseducation doesn't stop there. Our analysis of Lady Chatterley's many lovers within the movies of our time suggests that Lawrence may have had it backward, overvaluing one kind of sexuality while failing to see the very real sexual and erotic possibilities in the straw men. The students, the paralyzed husband who cares little about sex, and the overexcited writer who comes very quickly are all intensely excited about the world of ideas. These men may hold the potential for an exhilarating sexuality as opposed to the phallic gamekeeper. What if the gamekeeper conned Connie?

We close by returning to the overexcited lover and Lawrence's words that unwittingly betray the gaps in his own beliefs. Lawrence describes Connie's lovemaking with Michaelis: "But then she soon learned to hold him, to keep him there inside her when his crisis was over. And there he was generous and curiously potent; he stayed firm inside her, given to her while she was active . . . wildly, passionately active, coming to her own crisis" (28). *But then soon she learned!* She learned. No body guy showed her what she needed and then gave it to her; on the contrary, *she learned* how to address creatively her desire with a lover who Lawrence describes only in the most utterly humiliating way as a childlike failure with his premature "little orgasm." But even here, Connie learns an alternative way to get her satisfaction, though Lawrence can't grant any real significance to such a scenario where the woman is totally active in bringing about her orgasm while the man (nothing but a failed lover for Lawrence) is totally passive. But even the language about his passivity betrays something more: *he was curiously potent.* Curiously? Yes, because for Lawrence anything other than the active powerful phallus as a sign of true masculine potency must of necessity be curious. For us it is this total belief in the power of the phallus as the basis of awakening and fulfilling female desire that is truly curious. And for us it is even more curious that it is alive and thriving in the beginning of the new millennium. And Lawrence's total belief in the active powerful phallus explains the most curious thing of all: that it never seems to cross his mind to grant any sexuality to Clifford after he is paralyzed.

The paralysis is more than, or, perhaps more accurately, also less than, symbolic—it is a clichéd, trite stereotype. What good is a man who cannot actively use his penis? Given the way Lawrence has described the intimacy between Connie and Clifford, it is curious, indeed, that he can't even imagine that Clifford could use his hands or his tongue to give her pleasure. But we can, and we will imagine alternatives in the coming chapters, including in films about paraplegic men. But we will imagine much more: a world in which it does not take catastrophic paralysis to move away from a total, misplaced, and ultimately limiting belief in the central power of the penis to pound, pound, pound until a woman knows what true pleasure is. And a world in which the excitement of intellectual conversation and trembling writers who come quickly are not signs of naiveté or masculine failure but are, instead, alternative erotic opportunities leading to scenarios where men and women "learn" to give each other intense pleasure in "curious" ways.

CHAPTER 2

Rebels, Outsiders, Artists, and . . . Brutes?

In *Moonlight and Valentino* (1995), Rebecca, a widowed college instructor, is having "too delicious" sex with the guy who's painting her house. At one point she asks him if he's "really an artist—an oil painter who just paints houses as a sideline." He replies, "No, I'm a house painter. I paint signs as a sideline." No, the classic body guys in cinema are not intellectuals in disguise, bringing in a few dollars on the side to enable their loftier goals and passions. They're working class through and through, but they have something that upper-class intellectuals do not have. And all these films appear at a historical moment when the issue of socioeconomic class difference and inequality has been nearly erased from American national consciousness and public discussion. Labor Day is a holiday that marks the end of summer and offers yet another occasion for department store sales, not its original intent of a national tribute to honor the contributions workers have made to the strength, prosperity, and well being of our country.

Despite this cultural erasure of socioeconomic class difference, our cinematic mythmakers and preservers gleaned that in the 1990s the time was—and remains—right to foreground the issue of class in movies. Why? What's at stake that a quieted issue must be brought back from exile to assist in the work of culture? This question is particularly weighty given that the celebration of the working-class male in representation is a false privilege. These narratives often grant undereducated, close-to-the-earth men a power that is inconsistent with the lived experience of working- or lower-class people in America. The hysterical extremes with which the body guy is feted also point to this bogus advantage: clearly not every working-class man of the earth is sensitive and wise and a fabulous lover, just as we know that not every person of intelligence and/or economic means is a miserable egomaniac incompetent in bed, as these narratives would have us believe.

These movies glorifying working-class men appear at the same moment cultural analysts such as William Greider and Barbara Ehrenreich begin to publish books about class inequality in America: Greider's *Who Will Tell the People: The Betrayal of American Democracy* in 1992, and Ehrenreich's *Fear of Falling: The Inner Life of the Middle Class* and *The Worst Years of Our Lives: Irreverent Notes from a Decade of Greed* in 1990 and 1991 respectively. Both journalists finger American capitalism as the root of both cultural and personal malaise in the United States. Near the beginning of the new millennium Greider writes: "Despite the class differences, I have heard people from nearly every income level express an oddly similar sense of confinement, as if their lives were trapped by the 'good times' rather than liberated. *Short of renouncing modern life and going off to live in the woods,* they do not see any sure way to break free of what binds them. Think of the paradox as enormous and without precedent in history: a fabulously wealthy nation in which *plentiful abundance may also impoverish our lives*" (*The Soul of Capitalism,* 14; emphases added). A long tradition of rags-to-riches tales in American cinema touts the capitalist system as the liberating force that allows down-and-out movie heroes with pluck, integrity, and ingenuity to get ahead. The American-produced *Box of Moonlight* (1996), directed by Tom DiCillo, and the British-produced *Lawn Dogs* (1997), directed by Australian John Duigan, however, offer a critique of American capitalism that echoes Greider and Ehrenreich. Both films pose the working-class body guy as the solution to social ills attributed to the capitalist ethos.

In *Box of Moonlight,* the mind guy Al Fountain (John Turturro) is an electrical engineer and supervisor of a construction crew building a small factory. Al is also the troubled character in the film, a man impoverished in the land of plenty: alienated from his wife and son and described by his crew as a "damn machine on automatic pilot . . . who probably masturbates to the company's construction manual." Corporate mentality and corporate America's indifference to the environment are key causes of Al's malaise, but the Kid (Sam Rockwell) restores Al's sense of childlike wonder and appreciation of nature and thus saves him. In his signature Davy Crockett outfit, the Kid recalls Greider's man who renounces modern life, residing in a mobile home open to the outdoors in the back, with living room spilling into the nearby woods. Kid proclaims he's "off the grid," earning money by selling stolen lawn ornaments and refusing to pay taxes. *Lawn Dogs* presents an even more scathing view of capitalist-consumerist America through the trailer-in-the-woods character Trent (once again played by Sam Rockwell), who exposes various hypocrisies of the social-climbing, mansion-dwelling residents of Camelot Gardens, a gated and guarded community where he mows lawns.

THE REBELLIOUS BODY

The rebellious nature of Kid and Trent is typical across the genre, but unlike other films, Sam Rockwell's body is integrated into the political themes of both *Box of Moonlight* and *Lawn Dogs*. Like some of the other heroes in the genre Rockwell is shown frontally nude in both films, but his penis functions as a sign of defiance against dominant culture, not of his sexual ability. In *Lawn Dogs*, Trent strips with the specific intention of disrupting and disturbing. After a sweaty day of mowing lawns, he stops his truck in the middle of a bridge to tie up traffic from both sides. The upper-class residents of Camelot Gardens get out of their cars and watch as he undresses and performs a perfect jackknife dive into the river below. They continue watching as he walks calmly back to his truck, his penis fully exposed to the film spectators as well (figure 8). In *Box of Moonlight*, Kid undresses to jump into a quarry while trying to get Al to loosen up. His comfort while naked in a quasi-public place is evocative of the counterculture skinny dippers and streakers from the Woodstock era. Conventional American culture is too hung up about sex, the body, and the penis, and Kid attacks those taboos. He doesn't care who sees him and doesn't worry about offending someone, and since no women are present and the scene has no homosexual overtones, his penis is not linked to sexual bravura. Indeed, he displays it not to impress a woman or to awaken her sexual desire but to awaken in Al the dormant sensuality of his own body. At the beginning of the film, we also briefly see Al nude as he emerges from a motel shower, but unlike the Kid, his nudity and penis are linked to a troubled masculinity. He's talking to himself in an imaginary dialogue with the body-guy construction

Figure 8. *Lawn Dogs*

Figure 9. *Lawn Dogs*

workers he supervises, revealing that he desires to belong but is excluded from
their group. Al's sense of his own failed masculinity is not directly tied to sexuality but rather an estrangement from his body and identity as a man, and this
is what the Kid seeks to remedy.

The characters in both films display a comfort with their body and sexuality, but their nudity also has a power to shake things up, perhaps even for the
film audience. Trent exposes himself in *Lawn Dogs* to show contempt for his
upper-class employers. In other films of the genre, the display of the penis is
directly linked to the stellar sexual performance of the male characters, a sexuality that lures women from their upper-class mates. Once these women have
sex with the body guy, there is no going back. Not so in *Lawn Dogs*. Trent has
an ongoing sexual affair with a beautiful single woman from Camelot Gardens,
but "Trailer Man," as she calls him, is just a fling for her. Trent is soundly
rebuffed when he asks to meet the woman's parents and wants to be seen in
public with her. The film emphasizes the relative powerlessness of Trent's penis
and sexuality in the face of class difference. The upper-class woman does not
want to be seen with "Trailer Man" (figure 9).

In *Lawn Dogs*, the penis's radical potential lies elsewhere than in its ability
to impress or seduce upper-class, educated women. Indeed, Duigan films
Rockwell's nudity in a manner that denies a view of his penis as an impressive
spectacle. Classic films of the genre attempt to impress us with the good-sized
penis and/or pound-cubed sex. We are asked to oooh and aah over the sexual
spectacle rather than think, displacing serious social critique. In Zalman King's
full-length feature pilot for the Showtime cable series *Red Shoe Diaries* (1992)

the body guy tells a woman to look at his crotch because he can balance a block from a pyramid on the front of his pants. Later, when the woman, who's engaged to a successful architect, goes to the same man's low-rent apartment, she says, "I don't know what I'm doing here." The man replies, "I told you I can move stone blocks with my cock. Your curiosity was piqued; now here you are." The woman later commits suicide for her inability to resist the man's brazen appeal. The alleged powerful penile-centered masculinity of the body guy that attracts, mesmerizes, and controls women erases the issue that, in reality, class difference is more likely to alienate than transcend relations between people.

Unlike *Red Shoe Diaries*, *Lawn Dogs* suggests that penises, even when they are good-sized, do not have the power to confer anything on working men in their lives. In accordance with common usage we use the term "good-sized" penis throughout the book to describe men in the average range who conform to the ideal cultural norm. It is true that some men have a larger penile display than others, and we acknowledge that. Culture and representation, however, frequently attempt to fix a connection between such penile plenitude and a superior, masterful masculinity and sexuality. No such connection exists, and the belief in the possibility of such a masculine plenitude is the product of cultural fantasy. In that sense, there is nothing "good" about the good-sized penis. The display of a good-sized penis and athletic sexual performance are not the solution to, in William Greider's words, breaking free from a sense of confinement. A belief in the power of the big penis only contributes to the sense of being "trapped by the 'good times' rather than liberated." The patterns of penile display across the genre falsely empower the body guy's sexuality. An erotic utopia of beautiful, wealthy women is not likely to await them; the penises that seem to be everything, including those that meet the cherished norms of representation as they dangle impressively before us, are closer to nothing. In Greider's terms again, they could be seen as the "plentiful abundance" that also "impoverish[es] our lives."

OUTSIDERS AND INDIVIDUALS

As with the Kid and Trent, body guys across the genre either literally live outside of town or are transient in some other way, a trait that enables their rebellious nature. In most instances, the outsider status involves being an outlaw, perhaps epitomized by Tristan in *Legends of the Fall*, who deliberately breaks the law of the land with his bootlegging business and religious and civic laws of monogamy and relationship fidelity (as does nearly every other body guy in the genre). Indeed, it's this outsider status that marks these men as special, somehow more than just any working-class townie in the films. The Kid of *Box of Moonlight* is different from and better than the crude, violent car mechanic who beats him up. Trent is different from his well-meaning but entrapped trailer-dwelling parents. The special quality of these characters is paraded in a number of other films in the genre. *Sirens* (1994) differentiates the handyman Devlin, who lives in a tent in the woods, from the beer-guzzling boorish men who live in town. In Pascale Ferran's *Lady Chatterley*, as in Lawrence's novel, when the gamekeeper, Parkin, tells his lover, Connie, that he is leaving the country estate to work in her husband's coal mines, she begs him not to because "it's not in his nature." Jack in *Titanic* bonds with his working-class buddies, but his sensitive artistic nature also sets him apart from them. All of these films, typical of the genre, confer a scarcity on the body guy. They tell women that because he is not like other men, he is not easy to find. But once he's found, it will all be worthwhile.

As we have seen in *Box of Moonlight* and *Lawn Dogs*, however, outsider figures can potentially disturb and offer a critique of existing political and power systems by actively refusing to participate in those dominant cultural systems. They are individualists marching to the proverbial beat of different drummers. Their distance from the enveloping and standardizing quality of community gives them their insight and specialness. Across the genre, however, the body guy's link to nature and frequent reference to cowboys invokes the well-known American cliché of the rugged individualist. Ruggedness masculinizes individualism in these films. Tristan in *Legends of the Fall* is one of this kind, but he's a gun-totin,' horse-ridin,' grizzly-wrestlin,' hard-fuckin' type. The man of the earth's individualism yokes him to masculinity, and his athletic penis-centered lovemaking epitomizes this masculinity, thus closing down other ways of seeing individuality. The rebellious outsider has the potential to be an incisive social observer and critic, but that potential is normally decentered, eclipsed, and displaced.

Robert Redford's 1992 film *A River Runs Through It* illuminates the body guy's individualism as a potential threat to dominant culture. In this instance, two brothers are divided along the lines of mind and body. The younger brother and body guy, Paul (Brad Pitt), adopts what might be called a working-class lifestyle by choice, even though he was raised in a middle-class home. The older brother and mind-guy narrator, Norman (Craig Sheffer), feels a kinship to their Presbyterian-minister father in that they both admire the poetic potential of language, and, indeed, Norman goes on to become an English professor at the University of Chicago. Paul openly rebels against the righteous world of his father and even changes the spelling of his last name from Maclean to MacLean so, to his father's chagrin, he'll be "mistaken for a lowland Scot."

Despite their differences, the brothers and their father are united by a compelling bond: their love of fly fishing. Even here, Paul rebels against his father, but his rebellion is two-pronged. One side of Paul's rebellious behavior is stereotypically masculine: he drinks, gambles, and carouses with "wild" women to excess. His compulsive gambling takes him into an ugly world of boorish body guys, the rugged side of his individualism that is not linked to nature. His rebellion as a fisherman, however, takes him on a different path. Norman describes Paul's fishing technique: "I then saw something remarkable. For the first time Paul broke free from our father's instruction and into a rhythm all his own." Later, after observing Paul's triumphant struggle with a huge fish he says, "At that moment I knew surely and clearly that I was witnessing perfection. . . . My brother stood before us, not on the bank of the Big Blackfoot River but suspended above the earth, free from all its laws like a work of art." Paul's connection to nature here is not reduced to the category of rugged individualist as is the Brad Pitt character of *Legends of the Fall*, who sails the high seas, breaks horses, and wrestles with grizzly bears. This prong of Paul's rebellion links nature and his individualism to art, not masculinity, and it is appealing even to the father he has rejected. The good son, Norman, is boring while Paul captivates his parents with his storytelling about his job as a newspaper reporter, a position he uses to expose corrupt businessmen. The lure of traditional but boorish masculinity leads to Paul's demise, laying waste also to Paul as artist. His artist side is a threat that must be eliminated. This makes explicit the usual manner in which the body guys are outsiders and individualists, but masculinity controls the subversive potential of individualism. In other words, the notion that art can be "free from all laws" poses an alternative to the masculinizing aspect of individuality; it enables us to see the body guy as a creative, not rugged, individualist.

Body Guys as Artists

In light of the above, a subset of the genre features the body guy as an artist of some kind: novelists/writers in *Henry & June* (1990), *The End of the Affair* (1999), *Young Adam* (2003), and *Ask the Dust* (2006); painters/sketchers in *Titanic* (1997) and *A Perfect Murder* (1998); a photographer in *The Bridges of Madison County* (1995); an actor in *Sideways* (2003); and sculptors and designers in *Inventing the Abbotts* (1997), *Sweet Home Alabama* (2002), *The Notebook* (2004), and *Asylum* (2005). Most of the artist body guys are urban instead of rural, but they are still outsiders and individualists through the trope of artist-as-bohemian. They live alone, poor and struggling on the margins, and act on a strong internal drive rather than one dictated by society. Although the stereotypical starving artists are commonly viewed as losers in economic terms, they can also be viewed as defining their self-satisfaction around something other than consumerism and bourgeois morality.

The mind guys and body guys of Philip Kaufman's *Henry & June* conform to most conventions of the genre. In an early scene, the protagonist, famed author Anaïs Nin (Maria de Medeiros), refuses to go to a dinner party with her well-to-do businessman husband, Hugo (Richard E. Grant), because it will bore her. She says to Hugo, "All that crowd talks about is bad loans or trusts or estate planning," and he rather pathetically replies, "Estate planning can be very creative," to which she answers, "I need to know people who are alive, Hugo." In the following scene, Anaïs meets author Henry Miller (Fred Ward), and the two exchange glances that signal their immediate interest in one another. Henry is, in effect, an urban cowboy, an American expatriate in Paris who prefers the company of a curious mix of artists, prostitutes, magicians, pickpockets, and clowns among whom he lives in a crumbling lower-class neighborhood. A hard drinker and smoker, Henry is part blue-collar stud as well, marked as lower class with his coarse Brooklyn accent, lack of table manners, and ineptitude at eating the fine foods Anaïs serves. Neil Jordan's *The End of the Affair* echoes the representations of the mind and body guys in *Henry & June*. In London during World War II, writer Maurice Bendrix (Ralph Fiennes) attends a party at the home of upper-class diplomat Henry Miles (Stephen Rea) to research the life of a civil servant for a book he's writing. At the party he meets Henry's wife, Sarah (Julianne Moore), and the attraction between them is immediate. Like Henry Miller, Maurice is an outsider, marked as lower class by the shabbiness of his abode that's located on the other side of the tracks.

The artist as body guy presents a contradiction, however, in that artists are often associated with the world of the mind and culture, addressing or appealing to intellectuals with their artistic creations. So, why are they so frequently portrayed as body guys? The urban settings offers one explanation, but then why not present a carpenter, construction worker, or some other figure doing blue-collar work in the city? An artist's individualism is for the most part anti-materialistic, counter to the interests of consumer capitalism. Artists may also rely on intuition and the unconscious for their work, using them to discover and define themselves outside of social definitions and control. In short, artists may present a radical threat to dominant culture and the body culture in particular by valuing interior life over what we see on the surface; conventional behavior, appearance, and material possessions may count for little or nothing.

In the genre, however, the artist's greatest talent, or perhaps we should say "possession," is his stellar lovemaking style, a gift identical to his rural man-of-the-earth counterpart, thus controlling any real threat to dominant culture posed by individualistic outsiders. The genre values artists not for their social critique but for their hypermasculine sexual performance—their visible displays of manliness. In *Henry & June*, it is said of Henry Miller that he writes about fucking for the man in the street. We learn in the film's opening scene that, unbeknownst to her husband, Hugo, Anaïs is indeed interested in fucking as we see her transfixed by pornographic images. Hugo is so clueless about Anaïs's sexual desires that he is repeatedly shown sleeping while she lies next to him, writing about sex in her diary. But Henry knows what Anaïs needs. Before their first sexual encounter, he says to her, "I saw your true nature when you were dancing out there." He is so confident in his ability to satisfy her that he has sex with her in quasi-public spaces, the first time backstage in a cabaret with Hugo in the next room and later under a bridge. In *The End of the Affair*, Maurice's hypermasculinity comes from sexual performance, and once again, Sarah's husband, Henry, is marked as clueless, oblivious to Sarah's discontent, even though they have a sexless marriage. When Henry arrives home as Sarah is climaxing with Maurice, Maurice covers her mouth and asks, "What if he heard?" to which she replies, "He wouldn't recognize the sound."

The artists as lovers are similar to other body guys in that they are able to perform under extraordinary circumstances. Immediately after their first outing, Maurice makes love to Sarah in *The End of the Affair*. He grabs her from behind as they climb a staircase. His impetuosity flames her desire on the spot, and, after a kiss, she leads him to a room in their apartment. She briefly strokes his genitals as she unbuttons his pants, then he flings her on a couch and makes love to her. He is instantly erect, and she is immediately ready to receive him, requiring no further foreplay or stimulation. She is still fully dressed and he simply pulls his pants down and enters her without a moment of fumbling or hesitation. The sustained thrusting begins immediately. In a later lovemaking scene, we see Maurice perform remarkably in the midst of a bombing raid with sirens blaring and bombs detonating dangerously close to the house. Yet, he calmly sustains a variety of sexual positions: Sarah rides him from above, then they go to a sitting position, then to her lying on her back while he kneels, then back to a sitting position when she reaches orgasm.

The first lovemaking scene between Anaïs and Henry in *Henry & June* eerily resembles that in *The End of the Affair*. This time the husband, Hugo, is present with them in a cabaret. When Hugo decides to join the band for a set, Henry goes into a hallway, where he encounters Anaïs. After barely beginning to kiss her, he sweeps her up in his arms and carries her backstage behind a translucent curtain. While the music plays and we see silhouettes of dancers, he puts her down on a table, effortlessly enters her even though she is resisting, and begins thrusting. They each have all their clothes on. Although they have had no foreplay and she is initially reluctant, she soon pants and moans with pleasure, wrapping her arm around his neck. The scene ends as she repeatedly says his name with intense desire. In a later scene, he makes love to her under a bridge. As she nervously looks around, he confidently tells her, "I'm going to fuck you, teach you things. I'm going to make you come with me."

Both films are adapted from well-known literary works, and in each case the adaptations underscore the manner in which the 1990s films grant a false privilege to body-guy artists as stellar lovers with nearly magical penises and extraordinary performance abilities. *Henry & June* is adapted from the unexpurgated diary of Anaïs Nin, published also as *Henry & June* in 1986, although some material appeared first in volume 1 of *The Diary of Anaïs Nin*. *The End of the Affair* is adapted from Graham Greene's novel of the same name, first published in 1951. Maurice is depicted as a good lover in Greene's novel, but the film omits a surprising excerpt from Sarah's diary about Maurice that appears in the novel: "His love is like a medieval chastity belt: only when he is there, with me, in me, does he feel safe. If only I could make him feel secure, then we could love peacefully, happily, not savagely, inordinately, and the desert would recede out of sight. For a lifetime perhaps" (91). The reader has been led to believe by the male narrator that the love affair has been one of mutual pleasure until this unexpected revelation. The precise language Greene uses to reveal Sarah's dissatisfactions and longings is remarkable: she interprets Maurice's emphasis on penetrating her during their lovemaking not as a sign of his skill as a lover but rather as a sign of a psychological insecurity that is only alleviated when he is in her. She desires lovemaking that is peaceful rather than that which is inordinate and savage. Far from being an erotic haven, her sex life with Maurice is a desert from which she seeks escape. The description of the sex she finds unfulfilling is strikingly like that attributed to the body guy in the 1990s paradigm and repeatedly presented as the kind of sex (and implicitly as the only kind of sex) women need and want for their pleasure. Yet Greene attributes such a sexual performance to the needs of the man who performs, not to the pleasures or desires of the woman with whom he makes love. Furthermore, insecurity drives this inordinate, savage, penetration-centered sexual performance. Far from being admirably skillful lovers, the men in the many films we have identified might more perceptively be represented as Greene represents Maurice—as performers of highly physical sex to prove something about their masculinity to themselves. In Greene's terms, the sexual performance of the men in the dominant movie paradigm imprison women in "a medieval chastity belt" rather than liberate them.

Something similar emerges in Anaïs Nin's diary of her actual love affair with Henry Miller, and although Philip Kaufman acknowledges it, he does so in a manner that once again contrasts sharply with his literary source. In the film, an exchange takes place between Anaïs and Henry after they make love. Henry lies back in the bed in satisfied postcoital bliss when Anaïs remarks, "We fit so well together. With Hugo it's so difficult sometimes. We have to use Vaseline.

His penis is so big. But you and I fit so well." As she speaks, he makes repeated satisfied grunting sounds until she says, "His penis is so big," at which point Henry gives a distressed grunt and his facial expression shows concern. Henry's response turns the entire episode into a penis-size joke that, at the time of the film's release, provoked loud audience laughter. Compare this with the passage in Nin's diary: "The first time Henry made love to me, I realized a terrible fact—that Hugo was sexually too large for me, so that my pleasure has not been unmixed, always somewhat painful. Has that been the secret of my dissatisfaction? I tremble as I write it. I didn't want to dwell on it, on its effect on my life, on my hunger. My hunger is not abnormal. With Henry I am content" (76). The film scene actually makes the episode more about Henry's momentary distress at learning that he is noticeably smaller than Hugo than about Anaïs's pleasure. And the manner in which she states it contrasts sharply with the book. In the film the problem with Hugo's large penis is simply that "it's difficult sometimes." Yet, in her diary, Nin characterizes the large penis as a "terrible fact," saying it always leads to pain and dissatisfaction. The realization is so important to her that she "trembles" as she writes it.

And this points to the most significant change Kaufman makes in adapting the scene: Nin, as she makes explicitly clear, is writing in her diary, not talking to Henry. Henry's response is totally absent; this passage is about Nin's discovery that her pleasure is linked to the smaller penis. Far from being a joke or even containing one, Nin's entry deals with what will become a central fact of her sex life. Throughout the film, Kaufman has maintained the device of using Nin's voice-over as she writes in her diary. Indeed, several such scenes take place immediately after she makes love with Hugo and we see him sleeping while Nin writes, her words heard in voice-over. Thus, Kaufman breaks a formal pattern in the film in this scene when he transforms a reflective diary entry into an actual, real-time exchange between Anaïs and Henry; rather than speaking to herself, she speaks to him. Kaufman's strategy of minimizing the importance of the small penis to Anaïs affects yet another lovemaking scene in the film. Within the paradigm it is virtually unimaginable that the desiring woman would want a small or smaller penis because the body guy is so strongly linked to conventional notions of masculinity and male sexual performance.

The body-guy-as-artist movies subordinate the artists' work and accomplishments to their stellar sexual performance, often significantly altering or embellishing concomitant scenes in the novels from which they are adapted. Also, the masculinity that becomes the centerpiece of their appeal effaces the radical social, political, and cultural dimensions of their artistic creations and in the process erases the radical individualism that allows the artists to care more about their work than social convention. Is it a coincidence that one of the most culturally aware characters of the genre, the Kid from *Box of Moonlight*, is also an artist, of sorts, with his outdoor space decorated with lights and tchotchkes in a Rauschenberg-type installation? It seems dominant American culture, of which the film industry is a major part, cannot bear to expose the potential political potency of either working-class males or artists.

PLAYFUL REBELS

Another universal characteristic of both the men of the earth and body-guy artists is playfulness, and this trait may also work to contain the radical potential of the outsider individual. In *Box of Moonlight*, Kid teaches the robotlike Al to get in touch with his inner child. The men leap from boulders, pelt each other with tomatoes, shoot out windows of abandoned buildings, and break the law in a number of other teenage prankish ways. Through these games Kid helps Al see what he must do to improve his life. *Lawn Dogs* literally introduces a child in a central role, foregrounding childhood and play. Trent bonds with a client's daughter, Devon, a precocious ten-year-old who also disdains her parents' superficial conspicuous consumptive ways. Trent and Devon have burping contests, steal chickens, and moon fishermen. Playfulness and fun in the genre is specifically couched in an upper-class/lower-class opposition and is consistently linked to the body and frenetic activity. Jack and Rose in *Titanic* abandon the upper-deck bores, who sit around drinking cognac and conversing, to dance wildly in steerage. In *I.Q.* (1994), Albert Einstein is almost unimaginably shown having the time of his life while racing around on a motorcycle with a garage mechanic. We see horseback riding tricks and racing in *Legends of the Fall*, clowning on a bicycle in *Henry & June*, screaming on an amusement park ride in *The End of the Affair*, and on and on.

The issue of play raises two troubling aspects in the portrayal of the body guy. This playfulness risks celebrating immaturity (as evidenced by the name "The Kid"), valorizing a stunted figure rather than a fully developed adult. Second, the genre suppresses the possibility of locating playfulness in intellectual activity. The "aha" of intellectual insight is never seen as exciting. All thrills are on the side of the "waa-hoo" of bodily activity. Writing in his 1964 Pulitzer Prize–winning book *Anti-intellectualism in American Life*, Richard Hofstadter says of playfulness: "certainly the intellectual relishes *the play of the mind* for its own sake, and finds in it one of the major values in life. What one thinks of here is the element of sheer delight in intellectual activity," and "in the United States the play of the mind is perhaps the only form of play that is not looked upon with the most tender indulgence" (30, 33, emphasis added). The "play of the mind" is absent in the body-guy genre just as it is in American culture.

The frenetic activity of play in the films is in a league with the hyperathleticism of the body-guy sex style. Once again, it's the body, not the mind, which engages in exciting movement. In words remarkable for their relevance today, Hofstadter conceives of a kind of "mental movement" that is suppressed in culture: "But intellect is always *on the move* against something: some oppression, fraud, illusion, dogma, or interest is constantly falling under the scrutiny of the intellectual class and becoming the object of exposure, indignation, or ridicule" (45, emphasis added). Hofstadter connects mental movement to involvement with political causes and social action, acts that could be exhilarating, but exhilaration isn't defined in such terms by dominant American culture. Although body-guy play often involves breaking the law—stealing tomatoes and chickens—such rebellion against mainstream society is not a productive form of social critique.

The suppression of the playful mind supports an ideology of anti-intellectualism, and *Box of Moonlight* reinforces this through the depiction of Kid's intelligence. One evening, Kid tries to cheer the morose Al with his enthusiasm for the beautiful moon that is shining on a nearby open box. He suddenly jumps up and closes the box, proclaiming to have captured the moonlight, and warns Al not to open it for fear the light will escape. When a rejuvenated Al eventually departs for his own home, Kid gives him a gift of the box of moonlight. Al later opens it and discovers his lost rental car keys inside. The Kid was not as naive as he seemed, possessing instead an incisive insight into Al's psyche and the aspects of consumerist America that shaped and reinforced Al's dysfunctional behaviors. The Kid's type of knowledge, however, is linked to intuition rather than rigorous critical thinking. The Kid says to Al, "And this is what's happening all over America. This country's being taken over by smart people with no common sense, and that's why I'm out here, man—just *me, my instincts, and nature.* That's all you need. See that moon up there? Look at that moon! Shit, in the city you wouldn't even be able to see that." The Kid's rant taps into long-standing discourses in America regarding intelligence. As Hofstadter notes: "there is a persistent preference for the '*wisdom' of intuition*, which is deemed to be natural or God-given over *rationality*, which is cultivated and artificial" (48, emphasis added). The prescient author even hypothesized a connection between nature, frenetic activity, and capitalism, writing of the constant action endemic to the businesslike character of American life: "*business activism* has provided an overwhelming *counterpoise to reflection* in this country" (49–50, emphases added). He goes on to say that the need to make quick business decisions and to promptly seize opportunities is not compatible with deliberative, precise thought.

In their ostensible attempts to critique American capitalism, these films imagine rebellious heroes whose traits would leave their real-life counterparts most susceptible to the manipulations of capitalism and consumerism: frenetic, impulsive bodily activity over calm sustained reflection; common sense and intuition over rational critical thought. It's one thing to view the world with childlike wonder and enthusiasm; it's another to remain childish into adulthood. Indeed, in his 2007 book *Consumed: How Markets Corrupt Children, Infantilize Adults, and Swallow Citizens Whole*, Benjamin Barber addresses the childlike attitude with which the Kid and Trent embrace life. He argues that we have a worldwide phenomenon of a citizenry consisting of perennial adolescents (*kidults, rejuveniles, twixters, adultescents*), "an ethos of induced childishness: an infantilization that is closely tied to the demands of consumer capitalism in a global market economy," an ethos that will "undo not only democracy but capitalism itself" (3, 5). Does dominant culture fear that the body guy will discover the playfulness of the mind? Defining this intellectual playfulness may have profound implications for the cultural move toward class equality.

BRUTES

The childlike innocence linked to body guys through their playfulness may also mask a larger truth of the actual lived experience of working-class or underclass males: violence as a way of life. Interestingly, a film entitled *Fight Club* (David Fincher, 1999) lays bare the underlying cultural project of most body-guy films and points to a generic subcategory that curiously contradicts the mission of the more conventional films of the genre. Like *Box of Moonlight* and *Lawn Dogs*, *Fight Club* begins as a critique of American consumerist culture. The protagonist, an unnamed narrator (Edward Norton), works for an insurance company and is depicted as the ultimate consumer: a high-rise condo owner who's addicted to designer clothing and the IKEA catalogue. His consumerist ways leave him unsatisfied, and he develops acute insomnia. To medicate his pain, he attends support groups for people who suffer from various addictions and illnesses. He bonds best with a group of men who have testicular cancer, tying his own malaise to masculinity: these guys can't get an erection, procreate, or have a strong sexual drive. In fact, his best friend in the group is Robert Paulsen (Meat Loaf), who has developed humongous "bitch tits" as a result of hormone treatments. Paulsen, a man of massive height and girth, is now marked as female, and he behaves as a stereotypical woman, weeping onto the narrator's shoulder as they hug.

When the narrator is able to cry in return, he begins to sleep, a catharsis that is disrupted when a literal female starts attending the testicular group—a female whose speech and behavior is masculine and who dresses in Madonna-like abominations of feminine attire. Secure categories of masculinity and femininity are breached, and the narrator is incensed. His own cathartic foray into femininity would be secret and secure if a literal woman were not present. The narrator's desire to rid his life of "the tourist" Marla Singer (Helena Bonham Carter) leads to the emergence of Tyler Durden (Brad Pitt), whose status as the schizophrenic "better half" of the narrator's ego is not revealed to us or him until near the end of the film. "Tyler" shows the narrator what he must do to regain his masculinity, which includes literally blowing up his condo and all his IKEA possessions (shopping is a woman thing) to squat in a crumbling abandoned house. He must also win over and control the sexually experienced "butch" Marla through a phenomenal pound-cubed sexual performance; and he must leave the weepy masculine-impaired support group to start a fight club—a group "for men only," comprising macho types who confirm their manhood by beating the crap out of each other.

As the club develops, the film's dialogue seems as if it's taken straight out of William Greider or Barbara Ehrenreich. Tyler says things such as "we're consumers, by-products of a lifestyle obsession. Murder, crime, poverty . . . these things don't concern me. What concerns me are celebrity magazines, television with 500 channels, some guy's name on my underwear. Rogaine, Viagra . . . fuck Martha Stewart." Later Tyler says, "Advertising has us chasing cars and clothes, working jobs we hate so we can buy shit that we don't need. . . . Our great war is the spiritual war. Our great depression is our lives." Tyler couches this national malaise in socioeconomic class terms: "Man, I see in fight club the strongest and smartest men who've ever lived. I see all this potential and I see it squandered. Goddamn, an entire generation pumping gas and waiting tables. The slaves of white collars." Media is even self-reflexively cited as a contributor to the wasted lives of consumerist America: "We've all been raised on television to believe that one day we'll all be millionaires and movie gods and rock stars; but we won't. We're slowly learning that fact and we're very, very pissed off." Tyler develops a plan of action to deal with this consumerist malaise: "Project Mayhem," a national corps of fight club guys who are domestic terrorists. They blow up corporate sculptures and destroy Starbucks shops, with the ultimate goal of bombing all major credit card companies.

This fantastical and impractical terrorist plan is the end point of the capitalist consumer subplot; therefore, the film seems to be less about critiquing materialism than about restoring traditional masculinity, the demise of which is the cause of the narrator's original melancholy and the resurrection of which is the purpose of fight club. The narrator tames the feisty woman in the end and retains the awe of fight club guys by refusing help after he shoots himself in the face (to destroy his Tyler persona). A key question therefore arises: what are the signs of this proper masculinity, and who best displays them? Well, Tyler is

Brad Pitt, the consummate body-guy actor—all buff and strong-jawed and leather-clad, who, with reference to being raised by single mothers, utters things like: "We're a generation of men raised by women. I'm wondering if another woman is really the answer we need." And like other body guys, Tyler performs athletic sex but even more excessively. We don't actually see Tyler and Marla in the act, but by 1999, this hyperkinetic sex style was so well established that we know what it looks like even when it's offscreen, making it even more awesome when we repeatedly hear Marla screaming as a bed bangs against a wall while plaster falls from the ceiling into the room below and lights flicker on and off. Although we don't see Pitt's genitals, we see what Marla likes in the form of a huge rubber penis and scrotum sculpture she keeps on a bureau in her apartment. When Tyler jiggles it, Marla assures him, "Oh, don't worry, it's not a threat to you."

Fight Club suggests that consumerism most damages disenfranchised people and that the failure of consumerism and media to make good on their promise of prosperity and personal well-being will result in mounting anger. The film also links the working class with this festering anger, yet the imagery romanticizes the resulting testosterone-fueled violence of the fight club with its slow-motion emphasis on the rippled abs and full biceps of the fighters. By the time the narrator sees the error of his ways and destroys his violent hypermasculine side by killing off Tyler in the end, the damage is done.

What is America's love affair with violence? *Fight Club* proposes that the violent fighting is about restoring masculinity. If the penis has come to stand for what a man has that a woman does not have, thus distinguishing masculinity from femininity and maintaining sexual difference with a male advantage, then violence is the action men perform that trumpets and valorizes such sexual difference to male advantage. Having and doing. Perhaps this helps explain vigorous thrusting as the dominant movie sex style. If you mute the sound and just look at the visuals of that kind of sexual performance, it looks a lot like a violent assault. Two movies with a critique of violence at their core, *American Psycho* (2000) and *Munich* (2005), depict the frenetic performance of the male protagonists as, well, psychotic. *American Psycho*'s "hero," Patrick Bateman (Christian Bale), has materialist values similar to those of the narrator in *Fight Club*. Bateman's obsession with success, status, and style, however, is linked to insanity. His schizophrenic other half rapes, murders, and dismembers his primarily female victims. At one point he has pounding intercourse with a woman in various positions as he admires himself in a mirror, flexing his muscles and smoothing his hair while videotaping the whole thing. In *Munich*, the protagonist, Avner (Eric Bana), has sex with his wife after a long separation. Avner has been on a mission to assassinate the terrorists responsible for the murder of

Figure 10. *Munich*

Israeli athletes during the 1972 Olympics, a violent retaliation that he eventually questions. We see images of him during intercourse intercut with shots of the Israeli athletes being killed in a horrific manner, implying that Avner is thinking of this violent act. The expression on his face is a combination of rage and fear as his thrusting becomes increasingly frenzied (figure 10).

It is within this context of violence linked to women and sex that Bruno Dumont's 2003 film *Twentynine Palms* offers a pungent critique of the American body-guy genre. *Twentynine Palms* was directed in America by Bruno Dumont, a French filmmaker, in the tradition of such films as the Italian director Michelangelo Antonioni's *Zabriskie Point* (1970), the German director Wim Wenders's *Paris, Texas* (1984), and the Australian director John Duigan's *Lawn Dogs*, suggesting that often outsiders offer insightful views of America. Perhaps not coincidentally, three of the above films are titled after the names of places in the United States. In *Twentynine Palms*, David, an American photographer, scouts locations in the California desert with his French girlfriend Katia. David's status as a body guy is immediately established: his scouting links him to the land; he has a buff body and rugged good looks, wears jeans, and drives a Hummer. His style of lovemaking resembles other body guys as he has rough sex with Katia in a motel swimming pool, eliciting moans of pleasure from her even as her body is arched awkwardly over the concrete pool edge.

As a photographer, David is an artist as well, but *Twentynine Palms* deviates from the classic paradigm in that there is no rival mind guy. Dumont's use of this variation, however, undercuts the usual body-guy savior / mind-guy destroyer pattern. Typically, the woman in between is enlightened and impassioned by the hero. In *Twentynine Palms*, however, instead of liberating the beautiful woman, David ends up brutally killing her and then committing suicide. The usual hero is the destroyer, not the savior. *Twentynine Palms* subverts the mythic quality of the normal sexual performance style, as well, by linking it to insecurity, aggression, and ultimately violence, signaling the return of a repressed representation: the body guy as brute, a character type that can be traced to the Victorian era before mass industrialization and urbanization relegated the man of the earth to a figure of nostalgia, à la *Lady Chatterley's Lover*. This beastlike character is described by Wilkie Collins in his 1886 novel *The Evil Genius* in a chapter aptly titled "The Brute":

> The man . . . was one of the human beings who are grown to perfection on English soil. He had the fat face, the pink complexion, the hard blue eyes, the scanty yellow hair, the smile with no meaning in it, the tremendous neck and shoulders, the mighty fists and feet, which are seen in complete combination in England only. Men of this breed possess a nervous system without being aware of it; suffer affliction without feeling it; exercise courage without a sense of danger; marry without love; eat and drink without limit; and sink (big as they are), when disease attacks them, without an effort to live. (63)

This is hardly a description of the blue-eyed, yellow-haired Brad Pitt of *Legends of the Fall* or even *Fight Club*. Note how Collins ties this figure to having grown from the soil, and how the muscular buff features admired in present time here suggest a violent coarseness: "the tremendous neck and shoulders, the mighty fists and feet." Instead of the sexy handsome faces of contemporary body guys, Collins describes his brute's face as having "no meaning in it." Indeed, he goes so far as to suggest that such a man lacks all self-awareness, let alone possess a special sensitivity and insight to the erotic or innermost feelings of women. Also in 1886, Robert Louis Stevenson presents an even more brutish character in Mr. Hyde, the infamous body-guy alter ego of the brilliant Dr. Jekyll. Like David of *Twentynine Palms*, Hyde murders his victims with a horrific intensity. The discourse at the time of Collins and Stevenson was not tied to a denigration of the intellect as it is constructed today; on the contrary, it elevated the world of the mind, but it did so based on strong repression of the sexually explicit.

For D. H. Lawrence to elevate and extol the man of the earth as a sensitive and stellar lover, as in *Lady Chatterley's Lover* (some thirty years after Collins and Stevenson), the body guy as brute had to be repressed. But as with all things repressed, he occasionally erupts to become the focus of representation, the return of the repressed. So it is with the recent films of the genre. Though not as prolific as the purely "noble" body-guy hero, films featuring brutes appear during the same time period in question: *Dead Calm* (1989), *Cape Fear* (1991), *The Indian Runner* (1991), *The River Wild* (1994), *Sling Blade* (1996), *The Gift* (2000), *Killing Me Softly* (2002), *High Crimes* (2002), *Asylum* (2005), and

Derailed (2005), to name a few. In all of these films, the body guy is depicted as curiously charismatic but is revealed to be, at best, potentially violent and at worst a psychopathic serial killer. Most of the brute films make clear that these male characters specifically threaten women. In Sam Raimi's *The Gift*, the body guy is similar to others in the genre in that he is working class, linked to the land, drives a truck, and speaks with poor grammar, suggesting that he doesn't particularly value education. Donnie Barksdale, played by Keanu Reeves against type, is no saint, however. He's racist, beats his wife, and threatens his wife's friend and her children with violence, an "insecure redneck," as he's called. He's also having an affair with the wealthiest woman in the region, who says of Donnie that he's "the only man in town who knows how to fuck." When the rich woman's fiancé learns of the affair, she says to him, "Maybe I wanted to be with a *man* for a change." Donnie is associated with exceptional sex, but instead of it being "the gift" to which the title refers, here his "fucking" is linked to disturbance and dysfunction.

The Gift and films like it, however, do not signify a complete return of the repressed brute from the nineteenth century since they continue to endow him with a sexual gift or magnetism that is lacking in ordinary men. On the one hand, they don't simply romanticize the gifted working-class man since they make him frightening rather than appealing, but on the other hand, they reaffirm that he is "the only man in town who knows how to fuck." Thus, the brute subgenre acknowledges the "something" that the body guy has, even when it is in the terrifying form of the Robert De Niro character in *Cape Fear* (1991), who mesmerizes a teenage girl with sexual innuendo. Throughout most of the film he is a horrifying figure, yet this one scene establishes his sexual magnetism. Dwight Yoakam's entire career as an actor is particularly interesting within this context. Yoakam achieved fame as a charismatic, sexy country singer prior to becoming a film actor. He performed in videos and concerts in skin-tight, ripped blue jeans and a white cowboy hat with the brim alluringly pulled over his forehead as he swiveled his hips in highly stylized gestures and assumed erotic poses. Yoakam is an outstanding singer-songwriter, and those concerts and videos were serious music wrapped within the cowboy mystique—in short, cowboy sexual cool plus great music. In such films as *Red Rock West* (1992), *Sling Blade* (1996), *The Newton Boys* (1998), *Panic Room* (2002), and *The Three Burials of Melquiades Estrada* (2005), his acting career seemed almost the opposite: he chose roles that invoked his country music cowboy status but as a brute—scary, dangerous, violent, criminal. He didn't dress as a sexy cowboy figure, and in place of the ever-present cool hat he often revealed thinning hair and a receding hairline. Yoakam seems to revel in playing supporting roles with characters that are physically, psychologically, and ethically unattractive—the white-trash loser underside of the country music industry image of both its performers and fans. In these films he is never endowed with the body guy's sexual magic. We do not see him as a lover, and we do not see him successfully making love. These roles are probably made possible by the fact that it is the other side of the coin and that viewers have the image of the sexy country music star in their mind as they watch these unglamorous performances. He is the sexy guy on the stage and the brute on the screen.

In a similar variation, Brad Pitt plays against type in *Kalifornia* (1993); he's a brute in the form of a maniacal serial murderer. The movie cleverly centers on a mind-guy writer, Brian (David Duchovny), who happens to be researching serial killers. Brian travels by car from Kentucky to California with his talented photographer girlfriend, Carrie (Michelle Forbes), stopping at sites of key murders along the way to "get in the skin" and "look through the eyes" of the killers, a tour that he thinks will improve his writing. The couple is low on cash, so they take on riders: Earley Grace (Pitt), a trailer-dwelling parolee, and his girlfriend, Adele (Juliette Lewis). The issue of socioeconomic class is raised immediately and linked to violence. Earley and Adele are marked as poor and ignorant through their stereotypical southern-hick manner of speech and filthy living conditions. When the couple sight Earley and Adele waiting for them, the sophisticated Carrie tells Brian to drive on because they "look like Okies."

We learn after the fact that Earley wants to leave the state because he killed his landlord. Such violence is oddly validated, however. Earley "saves Brian's ass" by fighting with belligerent biker types in a bar, and the two begin to bond. When Earley reveals he is carrying a gun, he teaches the giddy Brian to shoot, much to Carrie's horror. When Carrie demands that Brian get rid of him, Earley takes both of them hostage and soon kills several other people, including Adele. In the climactic scene, a massive fight takes place between Brian and Earley, and although Carrie disables Earley, Brian fires the fatal shots. The intellectual male defeats the brute but becomes a brute himself in order to do so, thus validating violent behavior in the guise of saving a woman.

The manner in which we see Brian having sex near the beginning of the film lays the groundwork for his transformation into a body guy. In a twist on the genre, mind-guy Brian and Carrie are shown having vigorous sex as he literally bangs Carrie against the motel wall while Earley listens from the other side. Carrie is never for a moment attracted to Earley, however, even when she clandestinely watches him doing pound cubed with Adele. At first she is intrigued and takes photos of them but is then repulsed after Earley sees her watching. While staring at Carrie, he even increases his thrusting in a display of masculine bravura, but Adele cries out in pain instead of pleasure. The usually life-altering sexual experience associated with body guys is deromanticized, producing pain for Adele, disgust instead of desire for Carrie, and perhaps even equal disgust for the film spectator.

Carrie is not just any woman. She is a contemporary woman who controls the camera and creates sexualized imagery. She initiates sex with Brian ("Take your shirt off. Come here"), berates him for not "getting off his ass" professionally, and is right about Earley. Before meeting him, Carrie asks Brian about Earley, and he replies, "He was real polite. He kept calling me sir. I like that; maybe you should try it once in a while." Brian is ostensibly kidding, but it's clear that initially he's not in control of himself, let alone Carrie. In the film's denouement, we see that Brian is now more in control, progressing with his book (in an ocean-front cottage, no less) in which Earley and Adele will play a big part. Brian learns something valuable about himself by associating with and becoming a body guy: he got into Earley's skin and looked through his eyes. He is empowered by and progresses toward the film's definition of ideal masculinity through what he has learned from the body guy, which could summarize *Fight Club*'s theme.

With Brian's emulation of Earley, *Kalifornia* validates the body guy's mystique, however contradictorily. *Twentynine Palms*, by contrast, goes several steps further in that the body guy's violent behavior is totally unredeemed, while his sex style links to that behavior. David's appearance at first sight is like that of other males in the genre, and at first glance so is his style of lovemaking, as he roughly penetrates Katia to her ostensible delight in the motel swimming pool. Later in bed, their energetic sex leaves David screaming with animalistic yelps. In another sexual encounter they have stripped while hiking among rocks in the desert, and David takes Katia from behind, the sound of their body impact greatly amplified. David's penis is prominent in several shots in the sequence, as per the genre. The penis in other body-guy films connects to the hero's stellar sex style. In *Twentynine Palms*, however, the narrative development centers on David and Katia's increasingly problematic sexuality, and the trouble stems from his masculinity. In the sex-among-the-rocks scene, Katia begins giggling, and says that she is too dry. The next encounter has them back in the pool where David pushes Katia's head underwater for oral sex, but this time she becomes enraged when she must gasp for air. By this point David displays a clear pattern of aggressive, violent sex, an insistence bordering on hostility. Moments in their earlier lovemaking now take on added significance. The first time David has intercourse with her in the hotel swimming pool, he repeatedly asks, "Can you feel that," fearfully implying that he is somehow inadequate. On the rocks, he shows no sensitivity to her need for adequate foreplay, leading to the failed lovemaking with her giggling and complaining of being dry. Finally, back in the pool she becomes outraged that he would dare to hold her underwater.

Far from fulfilling a fantasy of the body guy as gifted lover, the aggressive and violent David is self-centered to the point of near-total disregard for his lover's feelings or sexual responsiveness, causing her physical discomfort and even fear instead of a blissful orgasm. Far from awakening any sexuality within her, he forces his highly physical thrusting style upon her. In one sense, then, David is a critique of the body guy and his pounding style of penile-centered thrusting so central to the genre's depiction of good sex. Here vigorous intercourse crosses over into something ugly and frightening.

In the town of Twentynine Palms, someone hurls a crude insult at Katia and David from a passing truck. They ignore what seems to be an unpleasant fleeting moment but later notice a truck following close behind them. The truck is filmed in an ominous manner with a dark, impenetrable windshield hiding its occupants. Then the unthinkable happens. David and Katia are forced off the road by the truck, and the men inside pull them from their vehicle. Stripped of her clothing, Katia is forced to watch as David is beaten with a club and anally raped with the same aggressive thrusting techniques and animalistic howling we had earlier observed between David and Katia. Now David, the normally romanticized figure, is brutally victimized by other body guys whose sexual techniques and style recall his own. But they are as far removed from a romanticized ideal as possible. The men of the earth in the dominant movie tradition are completely sanitized, lacking any sweat, smell, or crudeness—they just possess wonderful "natural" bodies, physically coordinated, perfectly equipped sexually, and an intuitive gift for masterful sexual performance that awakens true desire in women whose previous mind-guy lovers have been clueless about such deep sexual responsiveness.

The rape scene in *Twentynine Palms* is as if Wilkie Collins's "Brute" and Stevenson's Hyde suddenly erupted into a contemporary narrative paradigm. The body guy becomes the recipient of his own pounding sex style, and, it is safe to say, he does not like it. Furthermore the men that perpetrate this upon him are in general appearance and behavior what can only be termed brutes. Crude, insensitive, uncaring, violent—they are the mirror opposite of body guys like Robert Redford in *The Horse Whisperer*. They even make Katia watch, heightening David's humiliation. It is hard to imagine how Dumont could present a more shocking eruption of the return of the repressed, but he does, and in the very next sequence. After David's brutal rape, it seems that we have seen it all, and, in classic narrative terms, the climax has occurred, leaving only the denouement. But in fact the climax occurs when David, apparently traumatized by his rape, suddenly dashes naked from the bathroom of their motel room and repeatedly stabs Katia with a large knife while screaming in the same animalistic way we heard at his earlier sexual climax with Katia, and at his rapist's climax. This surprising turn of events involving Katia's murder exceeds the graphic rape we have just seen, and now the critique of the body guy as romanticized, ideal, great lover has been taken to the final level—he becomes a psychotic killer. The dénouement is equally significant in rounding out the critique. We see David's dead naked body lying in the desert, stripped of a potent sexuality on the land once linked to sex and romance. Even the position of the body is telling; he lies on his stomach, his penis not visible as it had been earlier but rather fused with the land, which, in this genre, normally gives it a special potency. But here it is more like the genre's magical penis is on a journey of "ashes to ashes, dust to dust"—dead and impotent like the seemingly vibrant body-guy myth that Dumont has brilliantly deconstructed as being at the heart of American culture.

In ending the film with an assault, rape, murder, and apparent suicide, Dumont invokes that thorny issue at the core of American national identity: violence. In charting the characters' trajectory, Dumont links violence with yet two other American obsessions: masculinity and penis size. In addition to their deteriorating sexual relationship, Dumont impels Katia's and David's personal relationship on a downward spiral toward violence, and masculinity lies at the core of this decline. With each rift in their relationship, Katia's behavior is so emotionally extreme that she seems mentally unstable: she sobs uncontrollably because David will not talk with her about what is on his mind, then has a tantrum when he glances at an attractive woman in a restaurant. She laughs hysterically at David's anger when she scratches his Hummer, then hysterically accuses him of having no heart when he doesn't immediately help a dog that he injured with their over-sized vehicle. In each case, Katia's emotional outbursts are related to stereotypical masculine behaviors: stoicism, sexual appetite, insensitivity, and an obsession with his car. Their personal deterioration culminates in a scene in which Katia emerges after locking herself in the motel bathroom and announces that she's "splitting." Her anger has no immediate motivation. David goes after her, pins her to the ground and slaps her while repeatedly saying, "I hate you." He then drags her toward the motel. They spar while David taunts her, but they ultimately reconcile and return to their room. The climactic sequence follows in which David masochistically tells Katia to again drive the Hummer that she had earlier scratched because of her poor driving skills, and they end up on an impassable road where they are attacked. Katia is the dethroning thorn in the side of both David's Hummer and his masculinity. This trajectory perhaps explains why David kills Katia instead of the men who raped him.

Dumont completes the trifecta of American obsessions by linking David's penis size to masculinity and violence, integrating it with his character in a

Figure 11. *Twentynine Palms*

disturbing manner. David's penis is noticeably smaller than the good-sized norm in representation. A series of posts on Celebrity Nudity Database (cndb.com) is very revealing in this regard. Users can search the website under film titles or actor's names for comments about nude scenes posted by others. Three of the four posts under David Wissak's name (the actor who plays David) refer to his penis size, body, and sexual desirability, in itself demonstrating how noticeable this aspect of the film is to some viewers. One reviewer gets right to the point in a brief post: "he shows off a short, plump weenie; very nice. It has almost no shaft, just a head. Brave guy. Kudos." His description is unusually graphic in noting that the penis is "short" and "has almost no shaft, just a head." But he likes it and the courage it takes for an actor with a penis like that to do a nude scene. Another reviewer is equally graphic, "we see david's [*sic*] little dickhead among his long, dense black pubic hair. pretty and tiny, it's no wonder Katia wants to put her hand on it to protect it from the sun. when she takes her hand away it's lying back slightly, no bigger than a nut, pretty much just a head" (figure 11). Again, the need to describe his smallness in such an explicit and even vivid manner jumps out here: "little dickhead," "tiny," "no bigger than a nut, pretty much just a head." Obviously the two reviewers agree on what they are seeing, and it strikes them enough to go into unusual detail. But a third reviewer forgoes the specifics in favor of a general reaction, voicing disbelief with the first commentator: "This is a very ordinary guy, face and body. I am stunned that another reviewer gave him such a positive review. We do see a lot of him, back & front. But it is unlikely that any of what you see will make you hot."

A close analysis of the film in relation to these comments raises two different issues. It is true that the actor who plays David has a penis that shows little shaft before erection.[1] But the detailed comments just quoted reveal a form of hysteria not borne out by the film: it is not true that his penis has "no shaft" or is "tiny" and "no bigger than a nut." This hysteria shows the profound impact that the careful regulation of the representation of the penis has had on some within our culture. Two of these commentators seem to simply long for a normative, "impressive" spectacle surrounding the penis.

For us the problem lies elsewhere. Initially David's penis may seem a refreshing departure from the usual "big dick" clichés, but it may, in fact, invoke another cliché by the manner in which David's character is developed through both dialogue and visual imagery. As noted earlier, we hear him frantically and repeatedly ask Katia, "Do you feel [that]?" while he's forcefully thrusting during sex in the pool. In other words, his aggressive sexual behavior may be linked to being so small that he fears she doesn't feel him when he is inside her. His attack on Katia at the end of the film with a classic phallic-looking knife, which he plunges into her fifteen times, reinforces his perceived need for a larger penis. This draws attention to the knife-as-phallus, recalling Hitchcock's *Psycho*. After the stabbing, David sits nude on Katia's dead body in a composition that rhymes with their earlier lovemaking.

David's apparent penile inadequacy also relates to an earlier scene in which he and Katia are dining near a marine whose head is closely shaven in the typical manner. The following conversation ensues:

DAVID: "You wouldn't want me to shave my head like them?"
KATIA: "If you do, I'll leave you."
DAVID: "You don't like marines?"
KATIA: "I do. They're really handsome."

David is angered by Katia's contradictory statement. In the scene prior to her murder, we see Katia comforting David, who appears battered but with a full head of hair. Katia then leaves to buy food and is murdered on her return. When David charges from the bathroom to stab her, we see that his head is now mostly shaven, recalling their previous conversation about the phallic marine. The bald fashion look for men transforms the entire male body into a phallus, the bald head resembling the head of a penis. While David only approximates the fashion look, clearly he has attempted to transform his entire body into a penis, referencing the marine. Thus, both the violence of his sexual performance style and his homicidal violence may intersect with a cultural discourse that men with small penises aggressively overcompensate (by doing such things as driving Hummers), another cliché that ties the usually unrepresented penis—one that shows little or no shaft before erection—to an undesired and even dangerous smallness. Far from a refreshing departure.

Normally, the lower-class body guys are endowed with a hypermasculinity exhibited through their strong bodies, athletic sexual prowess, and good-sized penises. This alone diverts attention away from such inherent socioeconomic issues as class inequality. Who's going to feel sorry for a working-class guy with a magical penis who can make love all night long to beautiful, desirable women in such a manner that they can no longer be satisfied with their successful mates? The genre thus promotes traditional masculinity. To employ a spatial metaphor, it is as if there is no room for both the display of the body guy's impressive penis and sexual performance and for serious social critique—the former takes up all the room. Ironically, even the eruption of the brute into the genre does not return it to socioeconomic issues since the brute body guys are seldom, if ever, depicted as unilaterally "bad" without at least the saving grace of sexual appeal and skill. They may beat the shit out of you, but no one can fuck as well as they can. This usually displaces a serious representation of the sociocultural factors that produce violent brutishness in the first place. Examinations of such conditions as poverty, unquestioned traditional beliefs, and lack of education that cause brutish masculinity are elided. *Twentynine Palms*, the film that features the most brutish behavior of a classic body guy— a woman's brutal murder by her lover—is the only film that remotely suggests a cause of the body guy's behavior, a behavior that is linked to his small penis. In so doing, it inadvertently reveals and affirms the other side of the coin—that the unexplained, romanticized, indeed idolized masculinity of the body-guy hero derives from his good-sized penis.

CHAPTER 3

"Fuck Me like a Cop, Not a Lawyer"

The body guys do not offer their gold-medal sex style to just any women in the films of the genre. These women are not only beautiful but intelligent. The Harvard-educated Samuel (Henry Thomas) says of his fiancée Susannah (Julia Ormond) in *Legends of the Fall* (1994), "She's got me spinning. She's got these *ideas and theories*, and she's . . . she's sorta passionate." Samuel confesses to his earthy brother, Tristan (Brad Pitt), that he's afraid he won't meet Susannah's sexual expectations. When Tristan asks if they're going to "fuck before marriage," Samuel haughtily replies, "I'm planning to be with her," to which Tristan playfully snaps, "I recommend fucking." Samuel dies in World War I before "being with" Susannah, but we see that she later enjoys "fucking" Tristan, represented in the conventional all-night, multiple positions montage. In *Enemy at the Gates* (2001), when the man of the earth, a sharp-shooting shepherd (Jude Law), first sees the woman of his dreams, Tanya (Rachel Weisz), she is reading a book. The people of Stalingrad are eating boiled rats during the prolonged siege of their city in World War II, but Tanya has a library of books neatly organized on shelves in a basement where she lives with filthy, ragged families. The mind guy (Joseph Fiennes), a political officer in the Soviet army, also desires Tanya. In his bid to win her affection, he compliments her intelligence and appeals to their common heritage as learned Jews and good students of Marx. Instead of the intellectual, however, Tanya chooses the barely literate shepherd and begins their relationship by seducing him as he lies in a chilly cavern among filthy snoring soldiers who may awaken at any moment from the sound of cannon fire in the distance. Yet the shepherd performs so admirably that he must stifle her orgasmic screams. The film emphasizes Tanya's braininess, but ultimately implies that smart women know in an instant that the best men and lovers are body guys. One line from *American Gangster* (2007) says it all: as a brainy woman rides the film's protagonist, a police officer working on a law degree, she screams, "Richie, fuck me like a cop, not a lawyer." In mainstream cinema, men associated more "purely" with the mind than the body just can't do it right.

What does it mean to address contemporary intelligent, college-educated, professional career women with these narratives? Why construct their sexual desire on a masculinity defined by lack of formal education, outward attractiveness, bodily strength and coordination, and athletic sexual performance with a good-sized penis?

The genre engenders the core body/mind dichotomy as a penis/brain opposition and is a reaction to a significant change in women's self-identity that began in the 1960s and continued into the 1970s and 1980s. Second-wave feminism valued women for their brains instead of their bodies. Affirmative action laws facilitated this vision by opening formerly all-male elite universities and academic programs to women, enabling them to flood male-dominated fields and careers. Indeed, it is now common knowledge that throughout the 1970s and 1980s, women's influx into the workforce steadily increased, especially in professional careers. This major historical event in America dispelled long-standing gender stereotypes: women are too emotional, illogical, moody, indecisive, weak, or just plain too nice to perform "men's work." Clearly not so. Even the last bastion of masculine privilege was infiltrated. In the early 1990s—precisely when the body guy emerged in films—forty thousand American military women served in key combat-support positions in the Gulf War. Women were—and are—doing virtually everything a man can do, in the military and elsewhere.

THE BODY GUY'S GIFT

Never before in American history did women have so many opportunities to define what fulfills them in life—in theory anyway. It is at this moment that a model of pleasure and satisfaction for women is devised and circulated, centered on a highly physical sexuality, a well-toned male body, and the one thing males can say they have that women don't: a penis. Ironically, from this perspective, the proliferation of body-guy films includes a key woman director linked to feminist sensibilities. *Two Moon Junction* may have jump-started the genre in 1988, but the 1993 film *The Piano* "legitimized" it. An independently produced art film written and directed by Jane Campion, *The Piano* brought with it a particular cachet for female audiences in that Campion is one of that rare breed of female directors consistently making feature films; one of only three women to have ever been nominated for a best director Oscar and the only one to win the Palme d'Or at Cannes (both for *The Piano*). In addition to those honors, *The Piano* won American Oscars for Campion's original screenplay,

Best Actress (Holly Hunter), and Best Supporting Actress (Anna Paquin). Campion also consistently makes films with explicit feminist themes. Female protagonists struggle with their socially prescribed roles in various settings: New Zealand, Australia, the United Kingdom, and the United States. Yet, Campion constructs *The Piano* around a mind/body opposition with the protagonist as a charismatic, sensitive, and sexy man close to the earth.

In the 1850s, a Scottish woman, Ada (Hunter), and her daughter, Flora (Paquin), are shipped to New Zealand for an arranged marriage with a landowner, Alistair Stewart (Sam Neill). Since age six, for unexplained reasons, Ada has been psychosomatically mute and communicates by sign language through her daughter or by writing on a pad. Her greatest passion in life is her piano, which she takes with her to New Zealand, but it's abandoned on the beach because of excessive weight. Feeling sympathy for her, Alistair's neighbor, George Baines (Harvey Keitel), accompanies Ada to the beach so that she can play her beloved instrument. As he listens and sees the depth of Ada's passion, George is emotionally moved and swaps a parcel of land with Alistair for the piano, transporting it to his home in hopes of seeing Ada more often. Thus the opposition is established between mind guy, Alistair, and body guy, George, with Ada in between. Though both men are British immigrants to New Zealand, Alistair is a sexually repressed, cultured imperialist who disrespects the indigenous Maori people and is more interested in land ownership and development than the region's native beauty. His house is ringed by the dead trees he's burned to clear the land, an act that creates paralyzing bogs of mud as a result of the torrential rains of the region. George is illiterate but sensual. He lives in the verdant, uncut jungle and mingles with the Maoris, speaking their language and sporting their facial tattoos and jewelry. Most important, he identifies with Ada and reads her "soul" (per the genre). While the piano is still on the beach, Alistair sees Ada practicing on "keys" that she lightly carved into his kitchen table. Instead of acknowledging her intense passion, he reads her behavior as a sign of insanity. George, however, sees her needs in an instant and takes steps to satisfy her longings.

George arranges for Ada to visit his home under the guise of taking piano lessons from her. Instead, he listens to her play, but is increasingly infatuated to a point where he offers Ada a deal: She can buy back the piano one black key per visit if she allows him to do erotic things while she plays. He begins by looking under her skirt while lying beneath the piano, progresses to tenderly touching her arms as she plays, and gradually does more intimate acts that culminate with conventional intercourse. Alistair learns of the affair and, piqued, boards up his doors and windows to entrap Ada, then later cuts off one of her fingers and sends it to George as a warning. George enables Ada's passion; Alistair cripples it.

The severing of her finger is part of a larger motif of chopping linked to Alistair. We repeatedly see him felling trees, symbolically raping the land as he does so. In a play staged at the local church, the character Bluebeard prepares to axe one of his wives in silhouette behind a screen. The native Maoris attending the play think a murder is actually about to occur and disrupt the proceedings to save the woman. George's saving of Ada from her "murderous" husband is a recapitulation. With his axe, Alistair rapes and damages the land, the Maoris, and Ada.

When George finally succeeds in seducing Ada, he appears fully nude in front of her, a sustained shot in which the film audience also sees Harvey Keitel's penis from her point of view (see figure 4). He asks her at this point to lie naked with him, which Ada, who has been resistant, agrees to do. He reveals himself to Ada by dramatically flinging a curtain aside, and the sight of his body and impressive display of his penis overwhelm her. In a moment of guilt soon afterward, George sends the piano to Alistair's home, ending the affair to protect Ada's reputation. Ada goes to him willingly, however, and they have conventional intercourse, which ends their sexual "explorations." It is after this act that Alistair maims Ada, and as she recovers from her injury, he thinks he hears her speak to him: "I have to go. Let me go. Let Baines [George] take me away. Let him try and save me." And he lets her go. George saves Ada from a stultifying life with a sexually repressed man. George has awakened her sexuality so fully that when Alistair, with whom she had not had sex, imprisons Ada in their home, she erotically explores his body in an explicit scene recalling George's explorations of her. Alistair, however, is unresponsive, his masculinity threatened by her controlling manner.

George also saves Ada from a life of displaced sexual energy. She is supposed to be teaching George to play the piano; instead, he teaches her to redirect her passion from the piano to a human body (the abstract to the physical), a body that foregrounds the penis. As they have penile-centered intercourse for the first time, music from the now-absent piano is heard over the imagery of their lovemaking, but the sight of her impassioned physical engagement with the piano as she plays is replaced by the movement of their intertwined bodies. The replacement of the piano with George's body is repeated when the Maoris row George, Ada, and Flora to meet a ship that will take them back to Scotland. Ada impulsively decides to throw the piano overboard because it is "spoiled." She sees the piano as damaged after the loss of her finger, her phallic hands spoiled as well. She is incomplete. As they release the piano, or coffin (as the Maoris refer to it), Ada's foot is caught in a rope attached to it and she is pulled under the water. At first it appears that she is resigned to die with the piano, but she frees herself as if cutting an umbilical cord, and George literally pulls her from the water into his arms.

Back in Scotland, the first time we actually hear Ada's voice in a voice-over (previously her daughter narrated), we learn that she is slowly starting to speak again. We see her practice phonating with a shawl over her head. In the next-to-last shot of the film, George removes the shawl and kisses her. Ada has learned to transfer her displaced desire from the piano onto its "proper" object for her completion: the male body and the liberating penis. Even though George has fashioned a metal prosthesis to replace her missing finger, her per-formance is marred by the tapping of metal against the keys. The restoration of her phallic hands is not enough for her identity completion, but George and his penis are, and she enters the realm of language. George saves and restores her, but at a very high cost, since in so doing she falls under his power and subordi-nates her passion for her piano to her savior. The film's trajectory moves her away from her creative outlet toward the body guy and the good sex that he represents, stifling Ada's passion by an either/or trap: the piano or George. The last image of the film says it all in a way: Ada dreams of her piano at the bottom of the sea and pictures her body still tethered to it, her black dress floating upward to envelop her body. Her attachment to the piano renders her a lifeless corpse. George believed he was giving Ada the gift of her piano, but it turns out that he is the gift.

OLDER WOMEN / YOUNGER MEN

The "gifted" body guy becomes the gift in a subset of the genre featuring older women coupling with younger men. Historically, this pairing has not been accepted equally with the commonplace older man / younger woman couple. But in the new millennium, "Forty is the new twenty, fifty the new thirty, and sixty the new forty." Women are encouraged to spend time and money on their bodies through rigorous exercise, plastic surgery, and other beauty strategies to maintain their youthful appearance because they can then be eligible for the real prize: the virile younger man. This is the prize that body-guy movies emphasize for women—more than a rewarding career, more than commit-ment to political and social causes, more than developing the intellect. This scenario plays to the American and growing international obsession with body culture and youth that has been forcefully linked to women throughout his-tory. It even invokes the Freudian notion that women are defined by lack—a "something missing." In the traditional way of regarding beauty, it is the locus of power for women, but ideal beauty is tied to youth. Aging beauty is an oxy-moron: beauty fades with age and female empowerment fades with it. Classic Hollywood films such as *Sunset Boulevard* treat this as a tragedy about which nothing can be done. Contemporary Hollywood and commercial cinema, however, wasted no time targeting an assumed vulnerable female audience with their message of desire and fulfillment, presuming that mature women will be concerned with the loss of attention from men that accompanies the aging process. This subset of films plays to these alleged fears and specifically addresses the generation of baby-boomer women (and those slightly younger) who were directly impacted by second-wave feminism. The central female characters in these films are played by boomer-aged actresses.

A Night in Heaven (1983) and *White Palace* (1990) are precursors to the late 1990s cluster of *Afterglow* (1997), *How Stella Got Her Groove Back* (1998), and *The Love Letter* (1999). The pattern then takes off in the new millennium with *Lovely and Amazing* and *Crush* (2001); *The Good Girl* (2002); *The Mother* (2003); *P.S.* and *Book of Love* from 2004; *Prime*, *The Squid and the Whale*, and *Heading South* from 2005; *Notes on a Scandal* (2006); and *The Reader* (2008), to name just a few.

How Stella Got Her Groove Back, adapted from the best-selling 1996 novel by Terry McMillan, illustrates the various nuances of the body-guy worldview and how it functions in these films. Stella (Angela Bassett) is a forty-year-old divorced single mom who is a well-paid and highly successful stock broker. Although Stella has a good relationship with her son, owns a gorgeous home, and seemingly loves her work, something is missing in her life, as the film's title implies. If she has to get her groove back, it's been lost; the word *groove* specifically invokes slang from the 1960s, when boomer women were coming of age. Stella's girlfriend and sister tell her she needs a man, and her young son implores her to have fun while he's away visiting his dad. Everyone can see the lack in Stella's life, so she and her girlfriend Delilah (Whoopi Goldberg) decide to vacation in Jamaica, where Stella meets twenty-year-old Winston (Taye Diggs). Winston could model for Calvin Klein, and, of course, he's a great lover. Although his penis is not shown or discussed, the film blatantly draws attention to male endowment, emphasizing the fact that women notice and care about it (this is explicit in the novel). Before their trip to Jamaica, Delilah is shown dressing mannequins in a department store window that will display—of all things—Calvin Klein underwear. She surveys a black mannequin, stuffs a scarf she is carrying into its crotch, and then glances at a male onlooker for approval. She then says to her assistant, "Can you get some more penis material, baby, 'cuz these boys are just . . . it's painful." A few scenes later Stella is bonkers over Winston and his hot body; clearly he does not need more "penis material."

Of course, in order to attract Winston, Stella has to spend time looking good herself. The film opens with shots of her running in a park, clad in a jogging bra and tight capri pants. We later see her in a variety of two-piece swimsuits and sexy lingerie, and her biceps, thighs, and abs rival Winston's. Another early scene shows her getting treatments in a day spa and focuses on her perfectly manicured pink fingernails and hair extensions. The importance of Stella's classic beauty in this scenario is reinforced when the overweight and conventionally unattractive Delilah thinks she has scored hot dates for herself and Stella, two Super Bowl–winning ex-football players. In actuality, the men are out-of-shape "has-beens" with inflated egos, shown by the embarrassingly juvenile ways in which they dress and flirt. At a "pajama disco," one of the flirts strips down to his thong underwear in an attempt to impress Stella, revealing flabby breasts and thighs and a sagging stomach. Women—aging or not—who don't spend time, energy, and money conforming to cultural notions of attractiveness (thus serving the interests of consumerist America and a surface-oriented, see-and-know ethos) will be stuck with men who are "losers" and will not be privy to "special" men like Winston. Delilah only has access to body guys through her role as a designer. In her department-store windows she creates ideal norms that others consume but that are unavailable to her. Ironically, through her profession she perpetuates the body culture's norms of beauty that eliminate her from successfully competing for the real body guys. The losers' bodies reinforce the horrors of aging, even for men. As Super Bowl athletes, these men once had ideal, phallic bodies, but not even their illustrious past can now redeem them.

The film's conclusion reveals the cultural significance of the older woman / younger man subgenre by ultimately overlaying it with a career/relationship opposition. Winston returns to San Francisco with Stella, at which time she's offered a job promotion with an exorbitant salary increase. Stella turns down the offer, however, knowing it will be all work and no Winston. The film's ending implies that the successful career woman poses a threat, but control can be regained by getting that powerful woman focused on what she "really" needs for her completion: a young man with a great body who knows how to use it.

The French and Canadian coproduction *Heading South* (2005) has women once again seeking pleasure in the Caribbean, this time in pre-AIDS Haiti. Whereas both Stella and Winston are black, the women of *Heading South* are white: Ellen (Charlotte Rampling) who says she's fifty-five years old, and the fortysomethings, divorcee Brenda (Karen Young) and Sue (Louise Portal). These women go to the same resort year after year to sexually cavort with local young black "escorts" who work on the premises. A rivalry develops between Ellen and Brenda for the same young man, Legba (Mènothy Cesar), who is around eighteen years old. Like Winston, Legba has a "Calvin Klein" body, and we see him frequently displayed in skimpy swim trunks through the point of view of the desiring woman. *Heading South* goes one step further than *Stella* in that the desiring women are both a careerist (like Stella) and an apparent homemaker. Women in both arenas are missing something, whether they be a suburban housewife from Savannah, like Brenda, or a professor of French literature at Wellesley, like Ellen, who says, "There's nothing in Boston for a woman over forty. . . . I've checked out every bar. . . . If you're over forty and not as dumb as a fashion model, the only guys who are interested are natural-born losers or husbands whose wives are cheating on them."

Essentially, the film offers the solution to the women's ennui by invoking a crude cultural cliché: "What she needs is a good fuck," and a youthful, buff body with a big penis can seal the deal. At one point Legba strips for Brenda and we see him frontally nude, literally showing what was only implied in *Stella*. He is illuminated by moonlight, but we see enough to conclude he is good-sized. Furthermore, the Caribbean setting invokes the cliché of the "big black penis," a stereotype Terry McMillan explicitly raises in the novel *How Stella Got Her Groove Back* when a friend excitedly tells Stella about "all those young Jamaican boys with big flapping dicks" (46).[1] Similarly, in *Heading South* Brenda discusses a prior encounter with Legba in direct address to the film spectator: "His body fascinated me . . . long, lithe, muscular, his skin glistened. . . . I moved my hand down his body . . . slid two fingers into his bathing suit and touched his cock. Almost immediately it started getting hard . . . growing in the palm of my hand until it popped out. . . . I literally threw myself on him. It was so violent I couldn't help but scream, and scream. . . . It was my first orgasm. I was forty-five." Her moment of sexual liberation and initiation into pleasure comes from a cock that grows so big so fast and creates such an impressive spectacle that it makes her lose all self-control.

Though released in 2005, *Heading South* is set in the late 1970s, the historical moment in the Americas in which women (many earning good salaries) began to take initiative in defining their own sexual pleasure. This practice included picking up men in places like singles bars. (The movie *Looking for Mr. Goodbar* was released in 1977.) Female orgasm became part of public discourse. The 2005 film addresses aging "boomer" women, who were in their twenties and thirties in the late 1970s, and asks the "boomer" spectator to recall a time of alleged sexual liberation, then defines that liberation around the buff bodies and big penises of young men.

But the address of the older woman / younger man genre is not restricted to baby-boomer women. In *Stella* we frequently also see young women checking out Winston with approving looks. The British film *The Mother* (2003) features a woman about a decade older than the boomer women of other films; a woman from the generation expected to be homemakers, tending to the needs of husband and children. Indeed, in talking with her adult daughter, the woman confesses resentment toward the sacrificial role that was expected of her. The mother's sense of having missed something was so great that when the opportunity presents itself, she engages in an affair with a married younger man with whom her own daughter is having an affair. Once again, the man who "delivers" conforms to type as played by Daniel Craig (the most recent James Bond). He's a carpenter who works with his hands and whose good-sized erect penis we see in the mother's drawings.

The older woman / younger man scenario implies that sexually experienced, often worldly, women are choosing the "right" males for their pleasure. And those right males happen to be young men who stereotypically have muscular, lean, hairless bodies, can get their firm, big penises up quickly and more often, and can last longer and perform more vigorously than aging men. These films coincide with an existing media-fueled cultural phenomenon so pervasive it's been given a name: older women on the prowl for younger men are known as "cougars." Much buzz surrounds high-profile middle-aged celebrities such as Demi Moore and Madonna, who have husbands and partners twenty to thirty years their junior. The fact that older women now openly search for younger men highlights the primary appeal of the body guy's sexual performance. Even body guys with big penises who perform well will eventually lose their ability to get as hard as they once did, perform vigorously, and recuperate quickly for repeated sexual episodes as they age. The older woman / younger man phenomenon has resonated so potently within American culture that it now has its own TV series: *Cougar Town* (2009) is about a forty-year-old woman (Courtney Cox) who joins the dating scene in search of twenty-year-old men to restore her self-esteem, which, like her beauty, is diminishing with time.

The precursor to the body-guy genre, *A Night in Heaven* from 1983, featured an older woman / younger man scenario, but the older woman was, in a sense, punished for her indiscretion, feeling remorse and guilt for her actions. And although the movie was blatant about the fact that it is a professional woman— a professor—who is wowed by the young man's penis, her career is not her problem. By the 1990s, it's the professional woman's career that is in some way exhausting her, and snagging a younger body guy is the energizing solution. If career isn't the problem, then aging is. In any case, these female protagonists just can't seem to find satisfaction in life without having sex with a younger man, as if nothing that they've gained from their education, work, or life experience in general matters as much. In an article in the *Baltimore Sun* from 2002, the reporter quotes Susan Winter, the coauthor of *Older Women / Young Men: New Options for Love and Romance*: "The suffragists had to fight for our right to vote; women of the '80s had to fight to break the glass ceiling and become CEOs. You may never want to vote; you may never want to be a CEO and you may never want to date a younger man. But you should have the right to do it without criticism, without discrimination, without social censure." With some apparent sarcasm, the author of the article observes, "Ahh, this is what bra burners of the '70s must have envisioned as a necessary victory in the battle for equity." Have we seriously come to the point in history at which the right to have sex with younger men is equivalent to the right to vote and breaking the glass ceiling?

CAREER VERSUS MOTHERHOOD

Films rated PG or PG-13 cannot normally show the penis or even depict the body guy's graphic sex style, but in many films he serves a similar function: he shows the career woman that she's missing something—in this case, motherhood. Perhaps the epitome of this subset is Robert Redford's *The Horse Whisperer* (1998). As the title states, Tom Booker (Redford) has a way of calming difficult horses by somehow communicating with them. It's a gift he has. Tom works on the family horse and cattle ranch in Montana, the trope of the cowboy immediately establishing his masculinity and sex appeal. Annie MacLean (Kristin Scott Thomas), the editor-in-chief of a highbrow fashion magazine in New York City, contacts Booker after a tragic riding accident in which her daughter, Grace (Scarlett Johansson), lost a leg. Grace's horse, Pilgrim, was also critically injured both physically and psychologically, so Annie packs him up along with a reluctant, angry Grace and heads to Montana for Tom's help, while her mind-guy husband, a successful attorney, remains in New York. Tom quickly sees that horse, daughter, and mother require major healing and proceeds to fix all of them. Annie was estranged from Grace even before the accident, and her workaholic ways are identified as the culprits. Early scenes in the film emphasize Annie's competence in a high-pressure career, her importance to the magazine, and her ostensible love of her work; but she is eventually fired because she opts to take time for her daughter, time she ultimately does not regret. The family is further privileged when Annie and Tom fall madly in love, but she returns to New York to her husband for the sake of her daughter and the family. The central importance of family over career or an "outside" world is doubled in the film. Tom's brother and ranch partner is married to a woman whose big dream is to travel to Morocco, a trip she admits, however, is unlikely to happen in that her husband just wants to visit Branson, Missouri, where he "has family." Even though the woman has an unrequited longing for an outside—something different from the life she leads—her three sons seem happy and well-adjusted, and her family seems content and functional overall, the opposite of Annie's relationship with her daughter and husband.

Body Guys / Family

Although Tom Booker has the potential to break up the family, he ultimately restores it while punishing the career woman, but not so in other films of the genre. The body guy may model the epitome of normative masculinity, but he threatens sacred institutions such as monogamous marriage and the family. *Asylum* (2005) and *Fur: An Imaginary Portrait of Diane Arbus* (2006) are particularly illuminating in this context. Both take place in the 1950s, a time in the United States when media was consciously used to disseminate images and messages designed to convince post–World War II women—many empowered by "Rosie the Riveter" wartime employment—that homemaking and mothering are preferable to work outside the home. These films indirectly suggest that the 1950s brand of propaganda is again in effect in the late twentieth and early twenty-first centuries in the United States and elsewhere, and the body guy is a key part of it.

In *Asylum*, a UK/Ireland coproduction, Dr. Max Raphael (Hugh Bonneville), his wife Stella (Natasha Richardson), and their ten-year-old son, Charlie, move to an asylum for the criminally insane outside of London, where Max has accepted an administrative position. *Asylum* specifically uses the 1950s to highlight repressed feminine sexuality and constrictive gender roles. The ambitious, arrogant Max speaks to Stella with lines such as, "Why didn't you speak to any of the other wives [at a reception]? . . . You *will* involve yourself with the life of the hospital. It's expected." And "[institutional] policy . . . is none of your bloody business. Is it really so difficult to behave?" Stella replies, "Like the other wives, like the other little ladies," and Max angrily retorts, "Frankly, yes." Clearly, the beautiful Stella, with her omnipresent cigarette, glass of whiskey, and low-cut stylish clothing, is not like the other stereotypical overweight matrons, in their Sunday go-to-church dresses, who fill their time with tea, scones, and sewing projects. The setting of the prison is both literal and metaphorical. As the hospital director says at a reception for the Raphaels, "We wish you many contented years here among the confined and confused. I refer, of course, to the present company, not to the patients."

Stella soon meets Edgar Stark (Marton Csokas), a patient who's been assigned the job of repairing a conservatory on the Raphael grounds. His body-guy status is established immediately in that he's a carpenter with rugged good looks. Not only is Edgar a manual laborer, but in his outside life he's an artist— a sculptor who's been institutionalized for murdering his wife in a particularly horrific manner for a marital infidelity. Stella's interest in Edgar begins at a staff-patient party when Edgar asks Stella to dance with him during a slow number and their bodies are close together. At one point Stella quietly gasps,

Figure 12. *Asylum*

steps back, and looks at Edgar's groin, apparently noting that he has an erection (figure 12). She continues to dance with him anyway. Soon after the party, Stella initiates an affair with Edgar, going to him in the daytime in a sexy dress while he works in the dilapidated conservatory. Their sex is quick and literally dirty as they engage amid dust, broken glass, and shards of wood, but Stella is clearly moved, revealing that sexual passion is a key lack in her life. Although Edgar's penis is only fleetingly glimpsed at one point, his sketches of male nudes with large penises are prominently displayed in the film, and this, combined with the impact of his erection while dancing with Stella, implies that his penis is large and part of his appeal as a good lover. Their risky daytime trysts continue for a number of weeks until Edgar escapes from the asylum, after which Stella leaves her husband and son to live clandestinely with him in London, driven to him even when his violently jealous tendencies reemerge.

Stella's only regret while living with Edgar is leaving her son, Charlie. When a private detective finds her in London and returns her to her family, she is overjoyed to see her son. Despite her happiness, on a mother-son school outing, Stella is inexplicably paralyzed when Charlie slips under the water in a lake. Her prompt action could have saved him, but the delay causes him to drown. Her deep longing for Edgar distracts her to the point of near psychosis. Stella continues to long for Edgar and eventually commits suicide when she cannot have him. Perhaps more than any other film in the genre, *Asylum* lays bare the social threat played out across the body of the artistic man of the earth: there are passions in life greater than motherhood.

Although Edgar's appeal is linked to his body and penis, he displays another attractive quality that is part of a larger genre pattern. Stella responds with disdain when told that her predecessor sewed tapestries of settings around the asylum to fill her time. This scene is followed by ones in which Stella works outdoors, planting flowers in a garden that Edgar later helps her tend. Before their affair, Edgar gives Stella a bouquet of cut flowers and thanks her for dancing with him. When she hesitantly says that she can't take them, he replies, "You can take what they mean," and leaves them on her lounge. It means that he has noticed what it is that gives her some pleasure in life and is validating it, rather than demanding she sacrifice her personal desire in order to conform to and perform cultural expectations, as does her husband. She grows things, not sews things.

This idea of sensitivity to each particular woman's "nature" is played out in several other films and has a direct relation to art. In *Phenomenon* (1996), a garage mechanic secretly buys large numbers of uncomfortable and unattractive hand-built reed chairs to make the woman who enjoys creating them think people actually want them. A friend proclaims that he is smart for buying her creations: "Every woman has her chairs; something she needs to put herself into."[2] In *How Stella Got Her Groove Back*, Winston encourages Stella to spend less time in the office and more time with her woodworking hobby, which she abandoned because of career pressures. As a gift, he cleans up her messy workshop and readies it for her return, which is accomplished by the end of the film. In *The Notebook*, a woman gives up her love of painting when she becomes involved with an intellectual socialite, but the carpenter she ends up with gives her the gift of a fully stocked art studio, and she promptly begins to paint again (and in the nude, at that, linking the gesture to sexuality). In *Henry & June*, Henry encourages and inspires Anaïs to write and publish her work. George Baines in *The Piano* falls into this category, as well. Like *The Piano*, all the above films privilege the woman's romantic involvement with the body guy over her creative endeavors. The man of the earth's sensitivity, which is part of his appeal, remains secondary and doesn't displace the primacy of his sexuality. The radical potential of the outsider male artist is contained by turning him into a body guy with a stellar sex style. A related strategy is at work here. The body guy appears sensitive and benevolent by nurturing the woman's artistic impulses, but this ultimately functions to make his sexuality even more attractive.[3]

Fur: An Imaginary Portrait of Diane Arbus (2006) is a rare film that foregrounds a connection between artistic creativity and sexuality: the two go hand in hand. An unconventional body guy encourages the woman to act on her interest in photography, and that is exactly what we see her doing in the film's frame story. Granted, the empowering man eventually dies, but his concern was always that the woman develop her art, as well as her sensuality, the sexual arena in many ways subordinated to the woman's need for creative expression. Indeed, the woman eventually turns her creativity into a career. The movie is based loosely on the biography of famed photographer Diane Arbus, written by

Patricia Bosworth (1995), with major characters and family relationships largely fabricated. The setting is New York City in 1958. As the daughter of a noted New York furrier, Diane (Nicole Kidman) is stifled by her socialite status and her role as mother and assistant to her husband, a commercial photographer. Diane's malaise is laid out in an early scene at a party sponsored by her parents to plug her husband's work. During a promotional presentation, Diane admits that she does no photography herself but instead helps her husband and his models with mundane tasks. When someone then asks her for fashion tips about proper fingernail length, she breaks down and tearfully leaves the room. Diane is clearly not comfortable with the body-oriented lifestyle to which 1950s American society expects her to adhere. Like other women-in-between, Diane's melancholy lies partly in the sexual arena. After her tearful departure, she goes onto a balcony and opens the front of her dress, exposing her corseted torso to the neighboring buildings. Later she tries to seduce her husband, but he giggles and brushes her off.

During the party, Diane notices a man moving into her building. Though his face and body are shrouded in robes and masks, their eyes meet and, in the usual fashion, the man, Lionel (Robert Downey Jr.), sees Diane's sadness and deciphers her needs in an instant. Lionel literally looks like a lion from a debilitating genetic condition that causes his body and facial hair to grow at an excessive rate, thus establishing his outsider status. The two meet, and in Diane's first foray into Lionel's exotic apartment, he prods her to talk about her sexual fantasies and exploits as a teenager and stimulates her sensuality with fragrant tea and a dip in a warm pool.

Diane's decision to meet Lionel follows soon after a photo shoot in which her husband photographs six models posing behind ironing boards, their hands identically poised on irons, their make-up perfect, aprons nicely starched, smiles expertly held: the epitome of the femininity that 1950s America wanted to sell its women. Diane comments, "It's all so predictable." Lionel introduces her to a polar opposite world. Diane meets giants, dwarfs, people with physical deformities, prostitutes and their kinky johns, and drag queens (the subjects of Arbus's actual photographs). Lionel gives Diane an entrée into a world she has always wanted to explore: "I planned on going so many places . . . a doll hospital, the city morgue, the insane asylum, dumps, flop houses . . . and instead I was my husband's assistant." Diane's increasing involvement with Lionel is explicitly opposed to stereotypical family scenarios. She leaves husband and daughters gathered around the dinner table to go out with Lionel; she is not there when her daughter loses her first tooth. Even though she loves her daughters, Diane ends up leaving the family altogether to begin her career in photography, so great is her drive to create and express herself.

Figure 13. *Fur: An Imaginary Portrait of Diane Arbus*

We see Diane making love to both her husband and Lionel. Although neither scene is particularly graphic, the differences are significant. Her husband
takes her from behind and at one point rather roughly pushes her down and
pins her head with his arm. With Lionel, Diane is on top, and at least visually
there is a sense of freedom, space, and control in contrast to being trapped and
immobilized by her husband's body. Lionel also liberates Diane's creativity in
the manner of other body guys described above. Her husband purchased a
camera for her, but for ten years she never used it until she meets Lionel. He
wills Diane to pursue her photography by giving her a portfolio album with
each page blank but ready for her insertion of a photographic plate: Plate One:
Lionel by Diane Arbus; Plate Two: Untitled by Diane Arbus ... Plate Fifty:
Untitled by Diane Arbus.

Fur contains frontal male nudity, but the penis on display differs significantly
from the good-sized ones that are par for the genre. The plot about Lionel is a
flashback framed by Diane visiting a nudist colony to take photographs. She is
greeted at the gate by the camp's owner, whom we see nude in a frontal shot for
several seconds as he walks toward the gate (figure 13). His penis shows little
shaft when flaccid, and when he stops at the gate, we see just the head resting
entirely above the scrotum, a penis size and shape generally elided from representation. We see this man frontally nude two more times after they move
indoors; once while he's standing and again after he sits down in a relatively
close shot that is held for at least ten seconds. Both times his penis shows little
or no shaft. *Fur* is a story about unconventional bodies that initiate the narrative and take the protagonist, Diane, on a journey from stifling conventional

normality to liberation, both sexual and creative. The fact that the nude male at the film's start has a nonnormative penis is significant, heightened by the fact that before we even see him, we see another nudist mowing the lawn, his flaccid penis also showing little shaft, thus doubling a sight seldom seen in representation. The normative display of the "impressive" penis signals a fixed masculinity precisely of the kind that Diane must reject in order to embrace the kinds of people to whom she is attracted. Rejecting the normative allows Diane to create the photographs that celebrate unconventional bodies, freeing her from the role of assistant to her husband who reinforces and repeats the worst gender norms of their culture and time in the same manner that the body-guy genre and its filmmakers do in our time.

Contrast this liberating inclusion of nonnormative bodies and penises in representation with the quite different visual and thematic development in *The Piano*. The latter has two progressions: Ada must redirect her displaced passion from the piano to a man with a good-sized normative penis, and that man must move from his initial unconventional erotic explorations that involve looking and limited touching to culturally sanctioned, penile-centered penetration intercourse. At first he merely watches Ada from under the piano, touching with one finger a patch of her skin exposed through a hole in her stocking. He even "makes love" to the piano in Ada's absence by caressing it with his nightshirt while naked. But these alternative scenarios gradually move toward predictable intercourse.

HYPERMASCULINE / FEMININE

For a genre that strives so hard to present the preferred men as hypermasculine studly sex machines, however, this subgenre of body guys who appeal to some other aspect of what women want—a creative outlet—is curious. The connection between the body guys, art, and female desire returns us to *Box of Moonlight*, a movie that dissociates the penis from masculine mastery and links it instead to an assault on class difference. We demonstrated that the Kid's association with frenetic childlike play and intuitive knowledge support reactionary beliefs that ultimately maintain class inequality, but the Kid's radical potential can be defined in a number of ways. Although the Kid is a body guy, he is in many ways feminine, crying onto Al's shoulder after being beat up by a town thug. His "femininity" is even more strongly suggested in another rather shocking gesture. At the swimming quarry, Kid finds a pair of women's underpants, picks them up, assesses them ("Uh, huh. Size five. 100 percent cotton"), and sniffs them. He then announces to Al, with the calculated hesitation of a psychic medium, that they belong to a fifteen-year-old girl who's a redhead and either a cheerleader or swimsuit model. He encourages the reluctant Al to smell the panties, too. When Al doesn't smell anything, the Kid says, "Kind of dry mustard smell mixed with, like, bubble gum." When Al again can't smell anything the Kid says, "Your senses are gone, man. To my nose it's overpowering. You see, that's called sensory attunement, you should try that sometime." In another context, this might be offensively "kinky," but the Kid is not interested in having sex with underage girls. His gesture, instead, demonstrates that he knows women in intimate ways that delight rather than repulse him. Not coincidentally, this is one of the scenes in which the Kid strips in front of Al and we see his penis, not as a conventional marker of his impressive masculinity and sexual promise but as a sign of his threat to the regulation and control of the penis in support of such normativity.

Across the genre, body guys are paradoxically marked as feminine. As a working-class man, even George Baines in *The Piano* is, like women of the time, a second-class citizen in the eyes of the ruling class. George feels more comfortable with "the Other"—the indigenous Maoris—than with the arrogant white imperialists in New Zealand. Both George and Ada are language-impaired outsiders—one cannot read, the other cannot speak—but their class and sex also mark both as Others. Their common position as outsiders creates a bond between them; George identifies with Ada. And George is feminine in other ways, displaying symptoms historically linked to femininity. He longs so intensely for Ada that he cannot eat, sleep, or even get out of bed. Heroes in this genre commonly exhibit such "male femininity"; they cry and express other emotions demonstrably instead of stoically. They're exhibitionists: they wear jewelry and adorn their bodies with paint and tattoos; they dance, do tricks on horses, and pose nude for the woman's gaze. Their best friends are Native Americans, Maoris, whores, panhandlers, or circus sideshow freaks—in short, Others.

Therein lies the larger cultural threat of the outsider, working-class body guys: they have the potential to form an alliance with women and myriad groups of Others to challenge the authority and power of the dominant classes. The working class, close-to-the-earth, body guys must be recast as the exemplars of "proper" masculinity, thus masking the otherness they truly share with women and people of color. And that masculinity is best demonstrated by the display of the penis—the privileged signifier of masculinity and male sexuality—and a vivid demonstration of what it can do. And what it does in representation is control and define women and female sexuality. But, what if what some women want is the collapse of conventional sexual difference and its privileged signifier? What if they desire the body guy for the radical threat he poses to dominant culture rather than for the false promise of a good fuck contained in the sight of his good-sized penis and a fixed, highly limited sex style?

THE RETURN OF THE FEMME FATALE

The need to attribute hypermasculine qualities to mask potential femininity in body guys occurs at a point in history when women begin to display character-istics traditionally labeled masculine. The revival of the film noir genre and its seductively dangerous femme fatale addresses in popular culture the male fear of the loss of respect from and control over women. "Neonoir" began with *Body Heat* in 1981 but took off in the 1990s with *Basic Instinct* (1992), *Malice* (1993), *To Die For* (1995), *Devil in a Blue Dress* (1995), and *L.A. Confidential* (1997). *The Last Seduction* (1994) perhaps best depicts the fear of beautiful, intelligent, independent women. The brainy woman does not have her sexuality awakened by the body guy. Sex, for her, is something fun along the way to big-ger payoffs. Bridget (Linda Fiorentino) is a sophisticated manager of a telemar-keting business, married to Clay (Bill Pullman), a physician. The film establishes her dominance over men in the opening scene when she berates her male phone salesmen, calling them "eunuchs and suckers" as they literally sweat to make sales, looking up with fearful expressions at the commanding Bridget who is filmed from a low angle. Bridget conspires with Clay to sell medicinal cocaine to drug dealers but then flees with the $700,000 they earn in a deal. Knowing Clay will be out for revenge, Bridget goes on the lam and takes an executive job for an insurance company in a small town in western New York, where she adopts the alias Wendy Kroy.

While there, she meets Mike (Peter Berg), who tries to pick her up in a bar with a line about his large penis. When he says he's "hung like a horse," Wendy responds, "Let's see," then opens his pants zipper and reaches in to verify his claim (figure 14). She decides to date him but refers to him as her "designated fuck." Mike conforms to type in a variety of ways: he not only passes the penis-size examination but also plays hockey, wears plaid flannel shirts and a blue-jean jacket, drinks heavily at the local working-class bar, and performs admirably as a body-guy lover. At one point, in a reversal of the usual sex-against-a-wall position, we see Mike standing outside a bar with his back to a chain-link fence while Wendy "rides" him, her hands and feet hooked into the fence links. Mike is such a skilled lover that he maintains an erection after they pause to avoid being noticed and is able to immediately resume fucking—or being fucked, as it were.

As a lover, Mike may conform to the genre's hero, but he is not in control. In fact, his entire relationship with Wendy is essentially a role reversal. He says

Figure 14. *The Last Seduction*

he feels like a sex object, and she responds, "Live it up." She just wants "to fuck"; he wants to get to know her. He confesses to Wendy that he is insecure:

MIKE: You've been out there. You came here and you chose me.
WENDY: So?
MIKE: So, I was right. I'm bigger than this town.
WENDY: So, what's wrong?
MIKE: You can't stop reminding me that *you're bigger than me.*

The big penis can be supplanted by more significant abstract ways of being "big." Symbolically, Wendy tells Mike, "Mine is bigger than yours," after he initiates their relationship by bragging about how big *he* is. Indeed, Wendy is literally Mike's superior at the insurance company where he holds a low-level white-collar job, but her "bigness" comes from her urban sophistication, self-confidence, goal clarity, decisiveness, and intelligence.

Wendy uses her knowledge of male preoccupation with penis size to her advantage in another instance. To locate Bridget/Wendy, Clay hires Harlan (Bill Nunn), an African American private detective. Harlan confronts Wendy at gunpoint in her car and demands that she take him to the money. Although Harlan is depicted as savvy and sophisticated, Wendy outsmarts him when she looks at his groin and asks, "Is it true what they say . . . you know . . . size," and then playfully demands that he show her his penis. When he refuses at first, she teases him about his "shortcomings," and he eventually consents. As he undoes his pants and seat belt, she deliberately speeds up the car and crashes into a tree. Harlan is thrown through the windshield and killed. Instead of being impressed with the big penis, Wendy uses it to her advantage, leaving him "caught with his pants down" to be found dead in a humiliating position with his big penis, which was useless to protect him, on display for all to see. Harlan is even dishonored after death. When a law officer asks Wendy why Harlan was found with his pants down, she replies in a pretend childlike way that he was going to rape her ("He was going to impale me with, you know, his big . . .").

Mike's big penis also does not insulate him from feeling small in other ways. We learn, as does Wendy, that in his one attempt to leave the small town he despises, Mike moved to Buffalo and impulsively married a woman who, he later learned, was a male cross-dresser. Once again, a penis lies at the center of this interpersonal transaction. Mike, who feels so secure in the importance of his big penis, fails to see that the woman he marries also has one. Mike is not "big enough" to read through the surface appearance of his cross-dressing wife or of Wendy, who is really Bridget, the manipulative "actress." Wendy further exploits Mike's naiveté when she decides to eliminate her husband, Clay. In an elaborate plan, Wendy kills Clay and successfully frames Mike for the murder. Ironically, Wendy is able to frame Mike by taunting him to "rape" her, and as he pounds away, she secretly dials 9–1–1 to secure a witness to his aggression. Wendy / Bridget, who has no penis, is bigger than Mike because of her superior intelligence. Wendy is not impressed with the body guy's big penis and athletic sex style, nor is her sexuality awakened by them. True, if Wendy really wants and likes forceful sex with a big man (and even that is not clear), Mike is able to deliver, but all it ultimately gets him is life in prison. Bridget outsmarts her mind-guy doctor husband, the mind-guy / body-guy detective, and the body-guy hockey-playing claims adjuster. No man has the advantage. As the film's title suggests, with her $700,000, she may never even need a man in her life again—no more seductions, regardless of how big the man's penis is.

The Last Seduction critiques the cultural strategy of the body-guy genre. Bridget, the new woman of the late twentieth century, is not in awe of any man, nor does she care for any man in a traditional romantic way, and that is part of her strength. In fact, she feigns romantic love, which she knows Mike wants, to manipulate him. To deceive Mike about her feelings, she leaves a notepad for him to find with his name and "I love Mike" doodled on it, plus a drawing of a cupid's heart with "Mike and Wendy" in the middle. Bridget thinks romance is for schoolkids, and she correctly surmises Mike's maturity level. *The Last*

Seduction speaks to the 1980s–90s phenomenon of real American women earning good salaries and not necessarily needing men for financial security. Smart, independent women making money and not needing or wanting men: what is a traditional man to do?

ABSTRACT IDEAS / PEOPLE

The Last Seduction is an anomaly in that the body guy awakens nothing in the beautiful, intelligent woman, and she gets what she wants in the end. Oliver Stone's *Any Given Sunday* (1999) also features an intelligent, powerful career woman who eschews the body guy, but she is punished excessively. As owner of a professional football team, Christina Pagniacci (Cameron Diaz) holds a key position in one of the last strongholds of male dominion. She battles with the coach, Tony DiAmato (Al Pacino), over who will ultimately control the team, and her efforts are specifically linked to Tony's failing masculinity; he drinks too much, resorts to a prostitute for sex, and has mismanaged his money. The film depicts an intelligent, Ivy League–educated, wealthy, self-confident, beautiful woman in the workplace as a problem. To contain this threat, the film places the transgressive career woman on a narrative trajectory toward exclusion from the male world, while Tony is on a path toward restoration of conventional masculinity.

Christina's incursion into the previously all-male space of the locker room threatens the masculine realm. Equaling or exceeding many of the men in height and surpassing them in status, Christina is comfortable around them in their space. She is not embarrassed, intimidated, or impressed by an extremely well-endowed black player who makes no effort to cover his genitals when she enters the locker room, his penis also clearly positioned for the film spectator (figure 15). She checks him out and walks on. She actually jokes with another

Figure 15. *Any Given Sunday*

naked player about his penis ("Don't stiffen up on me"), to his astonishment. Her foray into the male space ends with the film's principal body guy, the team's star quarterback, Willie Beamen (Jamie Foxx), at which time he asks her for a date. As we see her look downward, the film cuts to her point of view as the camera tilts to Willie's formidable bulge covered only by a jockstrap. She replies, however, that it wouldn't be professional to date players; this is a woman who is interested in her work of running the team, not in being wowed by a body guy and his impressive package. Immediately after Willie is rebuffed, a player throws a snapping alligator into the shower room where naked athletes of massive size begin screaming and wildly running around, symbolically representing the threat Christina poses to masculine privilege. Female indifference to the spectacle of the penis is castrating. What is left if awe and envy is not instilled by what has been so insistently asserted as the one thing men have that women don't?

Casting Cameron Diaz is significant in that her extreme conventional beauty implies that she can have any man she wants, and, indeed, we see this with Willie. Such women are the trophy of the body culture in two related ways: their beauty makes them the prize catch for the body guys and also privileges their perspective in that they can attract the best lovers and speak from experience. When a beautiful woman turns down the body guy's package and promise of a special sexual performance, it has an extra sting, and that is precisely what happens when Christina turns down Willie. She is interested in her career as a businesswoman, negotiating with the mayor of Miami for a new stadium, or lobbying the commissioner of football for an executive position. She has other, more important, things that give her satisfaction and excitement in life than cavorting with a body guy and his big dick.

The linchpin to restore male dominion in the workplace lies with Christina's and Tony's differing views of football. For Christina it's all economics: football is a business, and winning games is good business. For Tony football is a symbol of larger abstract ideas—history, teamwork, loyalty, sacrifice—to which winning is subordinated. Christina considers trading a player because he's aging, injured, and is no longer worth the money they pay him. Tony sees the symbolic importance of the player and barks, "He helped build this franchise. He's the goddamn hero to the working people of Florida." Christina's situation is doubled through the character Willie Beamen, who is also in conflict with Tony. Like Christina, Willie is ultimately concerned with winning and sees "Coach Stone Age" (his nickname for Tony) as an anachronism. Neither character views the team in terms of its larger symbolic social value—Christina wants to sell it because of declining revenue, and Willie randomly changes plays, keeping the ball for spectacular plays. Unlike Christina, however, Willie develops a full understanding of Tony's position.

In a pep talk, Tony compares football to life: life is ultimately a series of moments, as football is a series of inches, and the team must fight for one inch at a time. This is the moment when Willie learns to think metaphorically and symbolically, a realization emphasized by way of a dramatic slow zoom into him. He learns to love the game and the team more than himself and goes on to excel on the field. Indeed, the film begins with a quote by Vince Lombardi that equates football to a social or political cause that one can fight for: "I firmly believe that any man's finest hour—his greatest fulfillment to all he holds dear—is that moment when he has worked his heart out in a good cause and lies exhausted on the field of battle—victorious." The androcentric quality of Lombardi's words points to the film's portrayal of the love of work and the larger understanding of its abstract importance as a "guy thing."

Christina comes to see the team's value to Miami and doesn't sell, but the decision is not based on an understanding of football's symbolic importance. Her realization occurs after a series of father figures chastise and embarrass her. She is clueless about the way business is done between men. The commissioner of football admonishes her for an owner's violation, a gesture that occurs after she unsuccessfully lobbies him for a position on the football commission, thus doubling her humiliation. The commissioner's rejection follows a nearly violent argument she has with Tony when she enters the locker room during a game's halftime to berate him, her second disruptive intrusion into the sanctified male space. Christina's problems with the male world are traced to the fact that she doesn't really love the game of football, unlike Tony and Willie. She inherited her position from her father, and if she appears to love anything, it's filling her father's shoes. The film formally reinforces the notion of doing well for daddy by repeatedly juxtaposing Christina with her father's ubiquitous portraits that loom over her, and by showing her sitting at her father's desk, the only time in the film she appears small (figure 16). Not even the football player's massive penis can do that.

The film opposes the love of work vis-à-vis football to the family. Christina's mother complains that the game took her husband and daughter from her. The football commissioner (played by Hollywood's ultimate patriarch, Charlton Heston) couches Christina's aggressive professionalism in terms of family dissolution: "I honestly believe that woman would eat her young." For Tony, work and family are an irreconcilable dichotomy, and he concedes that football (work) has won, an attitude that allows the restoration of his failing masculinity by the film's close. He dramatically realizes his career's importance in his life. Tony first looks at a picture of his family from whom he is alienated, then, through a photo montage, we see various images of his father during World War II and himself at football games. Tony ultimately concludes that like the

Figure 16. *Any Given Sunday*

worthy sacrifice his father made at Normandy for a "larger cause," his sacrifice of family for football was worth it. Christina, however, at the moment she realizes that her tactics with men are not working, reconstitutes what is left of her family and apologizes to her mother for her unfeminine aggressive behavior. This is an ironic gesture in that her mother, played by former sex-kitten Ann-Margret, has admittedly done nothing in her life but be a trophy wife, drink booze, and fawn over her Pekingese. Though the film stops short of representing Christina on the arm of a boyfriend as they shop for a baby carriage, a team executive actually says to her, "You're still young, start over, start a family."

Christina ultimately reconciles with Tony, but at the film's end she is a punished woman, entirely on the side of loss, shunted to the margins of the narrative. In a surprise public statement with a stunned Christina in the audience, Tony announces that he's leaving to coach another team and taking his star player, Willie, with him. By *Any Given Sunday*'s conclusion, the career woman's trajectory through the narrative ultimately excludes her from the strong body, the penis, and the ability to understand the abstract concepts associated with the phallus—the film's three privileged signifiers of the world of men and patriarchal power. Tony is taking Willie to another team, where presumably women are excluded, and the game is played by men—as it was meant to be played.

In essence, *Any Given Sunday* sets up an opposition between "people" and abstract "ideas." A problem arises, however, in how it engenders that opposition. When a woman or man invests time and money in education and training, it signals a certain commitment to the abstract ideas that a given field stands for: practicing the law responsibly, establishing public policy, educating a populace for responsible citizenry, designing public space to enlighten and stimulate a populace. Body-guy films, however, often function to privilege "people" over "ideas." This project is particularly devious in that women have traditionally been conditioned to be "*people* persons": mothers, nurses, secretaries, and teachers. It's rational to believe that a well-balanced person needs to care about both people and ideas, but movies usually structure the opposition as an either/or option, with "people" being the favored option.

Oliver Stone's treatment of the work/family (ideas/people) opposition in *Any Given Sunday* recalls a theme in many of Ron Howard's films. By consistently depicting work as invigorating in films such as *Gung Ho* (1986), *The Paper* (1994), *Apollo 13* (1995), *A Beautiful Mind* (2001), and *The Da Vinci Code* (2006), Howard reveals the other side of the coin: women who focus principally on home and family find themselves in a comparatively dull and stifling environment. In *The Paper*, Michael Keaton's character has a near psychotic breakdown trying to concentrate on dinner with his pregnant wife and parents while he wants to be somewhere else on a work-related matter. His nearly full-term pregnant wife misses her job as a reporter and, though on leave, interviews an important source on her own initiative. She's alive on the job but shows disdain for domestic tasks such as sending thank-you notes for baby gifts. Similarly, the engineers and scientists in *Apollo 13* display energy and teamwork that far outshines the sentimentalized and moribund waiting of the astronauts' homemaker wives. In *A Beautiful Mind*, a friend says to John Nash, a brilliant but schizophrenic mathematician who's upset about not being able to work, "You know, Nash, you should go easy. There are other things besides work." Nash replies, "What are they?" after which we hear the sound of Nash's infant son crying. Howard sets up the notion that children are the "other things," but when we see Nash in the next scene actually holding his own baby, he is bereft of emotion, totally uninterested, unmoved, and literally immobile. Nash's indifference to his infant son is attributed to his mental illness, but since the baby as psychic savior has been mentioned two times prior, the film sets up expectations that Nash's indifference to his son will be countered with an image of a mentally healthy Nash who receives joy from holding a baby or interacting with his child. We see no such image, however; Nash's detachment is never redeemed. In fact, it is reinforced when the only other time we see him with his son, more than a decade later, they are filmed in a high-angle, extreme long shot walking in opposite directions. The son yells, "Bye, Dad," to which, without breaking stride or turning around, Nash simply replies, "Bye," as he eagerly heads off to work. The animation that he lacked while holding his baby, however, is very present when he teaches and interacts with students. His colleague even summons Nash's wife to see him surrounded by enthusiastic students at a library table.

Work, not fucking, invigorates Nash. Films such as *Any Given Sunday* and *A Beautiful Mind* that valorize the vitality of the workplace, however, typically engender it in such a manner that only men are invigorated and, indeed, some-times saved by their work, even if they are literally mentally ill, as is John Nash. Women, by contrast, who work with such intensity and devotion like Christina Pagniacci are seen as having something wrong with them, almost as if they *are* mentally ill. Instead of worrying about the alleged distinction between being fucked like a cop or a lawyer, these woman want to *become* cops and lawyers—or CEOs.

CHAPTER 4

"Brain Work Isn't Much of a Spectator Sport"

In *From Reverence to Rape*, Molly Haskell writes of early Hollywood films: "A woman's intelligence was the equivalent of a man's penis: something to be kept out of sight" (4). Ironically, the second edition of Haskell's book was published in 1987, on the cusp of the body-guy genre's emergence. This was the very moment educated and professional women reached historic "visibility" in America, and the penis came into sight in movies. Haskell and the body-guy genre point to the same thing albeit from quite different perspectives: the power and threat of an intelligent woman. Prior to this time, keeping the penis hidden helped maintain the awe and mystique of the powerful phallus. In contemporary cinema, however, good-sized penises signal desirable masculinity and promise a good sexual performance—the essence of phallic power in the sexual arena. Although on the surface it appears a profound shift, ironically, hiding the penis and dramatically displaying it in such a carefully regulated manner serve the same purpose. The penis is made to seem awesome and powerful, the locus of masculinity and male sexuality and the focus of female desire and fulfillment. Forget the mind; the "dick" is what it's all about. A woman's intelligence is still kept out of sight, but now the penis is what keeps it there.

How do we bring women's intelligence into view? In cinema, women's bodies are the site of sexiness, but how do we make their heretofore hidden intelligence sexy? Patt Morrison of the *Los Angeles Times* observes, "Unfortunately, the daily stuff of brain work isn't much of a spectator sport. You can't sell 50-yard-line tickets to watch someone think" (Morrison A-21). This observation applies to cinema, as well, but it only partly accounts for the absence of the sexy mind in representation. In the body-guy genre, denigrating the sexuality and personality of intellectual male characters further enhances the appeal and sexual prowess of the men of the earth. Intellectual women do not fare much better. In *I.Q.*, a brilliant woman is so clueless as to the "real" source of her potential happiness that her uncle—*Albert Einstein*—and his academic cronies coach the film's body guy on how to pose as an intellectual to get the woman away from her professor fiancé. For an anti-intellectual ideology to succeed, cultural groups that esteem the mind, intellect, and education must be policed in representation in a manner equivalent to the regulation of the penis. We have identified several strategic categories that point to the nearly diabolical nature of the mind-body narratives, making it imperative to find a way to represent intelligence and intellectuals as sexy.

NUTTY, NAUGHTY, AND NERDY PROFESSORS

Although the mind is denigrated in many ways in the body-guy films, perhaps no group of intellectuals is more eviscerated than college professors—the embodiment of intellectual pursuit. The sexually incompetent psychology professor's beautiful fiancée leaves him for an auto mechanic in *I.Q.* In *Junior* (1994), the clinically cold college scientist must have romance and children in his life for completion; the same goes for the brilliant but klutzy professor he ends up marrying and impregnating. The writing teacher in *The Squid and the Whale* (2005) is self-centered, insensitive to his wife and children, overly competitive, lacking in self-control, conceited, and narcissistically self-deluded—so his wife leaves him for an affable tennis instructor. The professor in *What Lies Beneath* (2000) turns out to be a philandering murderer, similar to the chemistry professor in *The Vanishing* (2003), who has a loving wife and daughter but acts on his fantasy of abducting and murdering a woman. Professors: antisocial, sexually repressed, pathologically unbalanced, or homicidal at worst, or, at best, comically harmless and lovingly inept in the tradition of *The Nutty Professor* (1963) or its predecessor *The Absent-Minded Professor* (1961).

Good Will Hunting (1997), written by Ben Affleck and Matt Damon (who won screenwriting Oscars for the film) and directed by Gus Van Sant, reveals many of the strategies used to devalue the intellect vis-à-vis the figure of the professor. Will Hunting (Damon) is a body-guy custodian in a math building at MIT. He's a former abused foster child who resides in a rundown working-class neighborhood in Boston, but he's also a genius. Mathematics professor Gerald Lambeau (Stellan Skarsgard) discovers Hunting's mental talent when he observes him solving a difficult equation posted on a public blackboard. Lambeau wants to mentor the young genius but only if Hunting agrees to see a psychologist to get control of his anger and repeated troubles with the law. Hunting ends up in the office of Sean Maguire (Robin Williams), a former Harvard classmate of Lambeau's who teaches at a local community college. A mind/body or ideas/people battle ensues: Lambeau wants to help Hunting develop his mental acumen; Maguire wants him to learn to trust and be intimate with other people. Thus the film establishes fundamental oppositions: university versus community college, professor versus teacher-helper-friend, ideas versus people.

Lambeau and Maguire embody the opposition as well. Lambeau is an award-winning university mathematician, passionate about and dedicated to his field, whereas Maguire is an underachieving community college instructor who loves his counseling work but is even more passionate about his deceased wife, who has been dead for some time and for whom he still mourns. Several other related oppositions contribute to stereotypical beliefs about intellectuals: upper class versus lower class, university students versus "townies," formal education versus "natural" or self-taught intelligence. One scene establishes all this when Hunting and his construction-worker friends go to a bar in Cambridge and are callously insulted by a Harvard student who assumes the working-class guys are ignorant. Hunting then displays his superior knowledge, simultaneously putting the arrogant student in his place and getting the attention of Skylar (Minnie Driver), a beautiful Harvard pre-med student. Hunting eventually is torn between taking a high-paying position in a think tank or going to California to pursue a relationship with Skylar, who will attend medical school at Stanford. Per Maguire's example, Hunting chooses people over ideas. He turns down the think tank to literally drive into the sunset after Skylar in the final image of the film. According to Hollywood logic, if you value the world of ideas you are deficient and must learn to value people more.

The incredible importance of people is presented through Maguire and Skylar, then reinforced by Will's best friend, Chuckie (Ben Affleck). Chuckie thoughtfully and unselfishly encourages Will to get out of the "hood" one way or another in an effusive diatribe:

> In twenty years if you're still living here coming over to my house to watch the Patriots games, still working construction, I'll fucking kill you. . . . You got something none of us have. . . . You owe it to me [to get out of here]. . . . Tomorrow I'll wake up and I'll be fifty, and I'll still be doing this shit. . . . I'd do fuckin' anything to have what you've got. So would any of these fuckin' guys. It would be an insult to watch if you're still here in twenty years. Hangin' around here is a waste of your fuckin' time.

Chuckie is a true friend who selflessly wants Will to fulfill his potential instead of bringing him down with a "misery loves company" attitude. He says that every day he hopes to knock on Will's door and have him be gone, and one time he is—in a car his *friends* rebuilt for him. He's off to pursue Skylar, leaving us to only guess about how he will develop and use his exceptional mental abilities.

Molly Haskell observes that "we have been sold a bill of goods by the Hollywood film, a bill of goods that has led us to expect love to be more beautiful and people to be better than they actually are" (27). *Good Will Hunting* tries to hawk this bill of goods. What is good for Will Hunting? Friends and a beautiful woman, not hard work and developing his mind in the workplace. It's an either/or proposition: people versus ideas, body versus mind.

The fact that Skylar, herself a bright student, is initially attracted to Will's intelligence opens a possibility that his mind could be linked to his sexiness, but, instead, his sex appeal is all on the side of the body. We don't see them making love, but we do see a satisfied Skylar in bed with Will, who is garbed only in boxer shorts, his sculpted biceps, pecs, and abs openly displayed. His brain may have gotten Skylar's attention, but his body is what the bedroom is all about. They even discuss sports during their postsex repartee. Will's mental acumen is distanced from sexuality in other, more subtle, ways. He goes to the local bar with Chuckie, who immediately banters with other patrons about sex. Will soon leaves the bar to go home and work math equations on his bathroom mirror. The spaces associated with sex and Will's mental activities are kept totally separate, suggesting that one cannot be associated with the other.

The penis is not shown in the film, but it is talked about several times. In Will's presence at the local bar, Chuckie shouts at a woman, "Why didn't you give me none of that nasty little hoochie-woochie you usually throw at me?" The woman replies, "Fuck you and your Irish curse, Chuckie. Like I'd waste my energy spreading my legs for that Tootsie Roll dick? Go home and give it a tug yourself." A friend of Chuckie's embarrasses him when he laughingly chants, "Tootsie Roll, toot, toots." It is soon after this that Will goes home to do math problems, leaving Chuckie alone and looking distraught. Instead of linking Will's big brain to a sexy mind, the opposite occurs. The failure of the small penis associated with the "loser" Chuckie, who stays in his dead-end job, is accentuated, while Will, with a presumably good-sized penis, goes to California and gets the beautiful woman. In other words, the big brain works in the service of the penis, abandoning mathematics to win the beautiful woman. Skylar even utters: "If you're not thinking with your wiener, then you're acting directly on its behalf."

The depiction of community college in *Good Will Hunting* intersects with other cultural discourses that circulate in American society, such as the idea that community college instructors are not encumbered by research and publishing, so they can be there "for the students." Another discourse suggests that university professors care more about research than teaching, to which they devote half-hearted efforts, sometimes relinquishing the classroom to inexperienced graduate students (who often have "foreign" accents) in favor of release time for their scholarly pursuits. Many community college instructors directly or indirectly support the "people versus ideas" opposition in that they are hired for their practical work experience instead of their training in pedagogical methods, as if experience automatically includes the ability to be a good teacher and trumps a theoretical understanding of a field. In addition, community colleges often subordinate academics to vocational training—a problem if learning a practical skill displaces the concurrent development of critical thinking.

In their detailed history of community colleges, published in 1989, Steven Brint and Jerome Karabel contend that "junior colleges" were once liberal arts–oriented but transformed to a vocational focus against the actual preferences of students. The change allegedly occurred to meet the needs of big business in America but also in response to the "management of ambition" (7), a concept that presumes "the number of individuals who aspire to privileged places in the division of labor . . . tends to surpass, often by a considerable margin, the number of such slots that are available. . . . In the United States, the management of ambition is a particularly serious dilemma, for success . . . is supposed to be within the grasp of every individual, no matter how humble his (and, more recently, her) background" (7). Brint and Karabel conclude that the management of ambition is a structuring principle that underlies the community college system, working to reinforce existing inequalities of class, race, and gender. In our terms, successfully controlling ambition in this manner empowers the body (people) more than the mind (ideas).

Good Will Hunting could serve as a textbook of strategies to manage ambition. Will Hunting transcends his existence, but what about the rest of his working-class friends who could benefit from finding the joy of the sexy mind? Hunting is a born genius, but his friends aren't; therefore he gets out, and they don't. Chuckie hates his work ("I'll still be doing this shit"), but the film suggests he will get some satisfaction living vicariously through Will, his friend who moves to California—an interesting reference to the real-life American obsession with the lives of celebrities, especially movie stars. It's almost as if people have given up on their own lives, preferring to see themselves through ersatz representatives either onscreen or in other positions of power that they believe unattainable for themselves. The film totally effaces the possibility that Will's pals might get out of their situation. They *could* go to community college and benefit from it in some way, but even that option is undermined in the film. The person who represents the potential of community college, Sean Maguire, takes a sabbatical at the film's close. He's traveling to India and China to get in touch with his spiritual, not intellectual, side.

Maguire and Lambeau literally battle for Hunting's heart and mind throughout the film, but they reconcile in the end. In their final shot together, the two men walk *away* from the community college, while Maguire puzzlingly takes a lottery ticket from his pocket and proclaims that he's got the winning numbers. Lambeau, ever the mathematician, then playfully starts talking about the terrible odds of winning the lottery as the scene fades out. This image and gesture perfectly encapsulate the workings of power in culture: two gifted, Harvard-educated men (which refers to the film's writers and stars Damon and Affleck in real life) with opportunities to do work that they love and to do it well, *walk away* from the institution of learning while reinforcing the importance of people, friendship, and luck—actions and attitudes that keep real people with less education and opportunity in their place, illustrating the management of ambition.

Good Will Hunting disparages the mind orientation of the university compared to the people-oriented world of the community college, and this putdown is particularly disturbing in that Lambeau is not a mean-spirited ogre; he just cares about abstract ideas and is not as sensitive and nice as Maguire. Lambeau's teaching assistant poignantly says to Hunting: "Most people never get to see how brilliant they can be. They don't find teachers that believe in them. They get convinced they're stupid. I hope you appreciate what he's doing, because I've seen how much he enjoys working *with* you . . . not *against* you." This gets to the heart of what many real people who achieve career success in the United States understand: it helps to have a mentor, to establish a network of connections, and to take advantage of available opportunities and resources. But Will Hunting applies this advice to Sean Maguire and the message he stands for. We are therefore in a position to conclude that the "smart" thing for Will to do is pursue the beautiful, intelligent woman—who just happens to be independently wealthy. Will's genius, and what it could get him with some guidance, practice, and experience, is subordinated to a romantic relationship and the notion of easy money. The management of ambition.

THE JEWISH MALE BODY AND MASCULINITY

Jews, like professors, have historically esteemed education and the intellect. Bluntly stated, the stereotypical body guy is not Jewish. Indeed, if anything, the Jewish male is the mind guy associated with professional careers such as academia, medicine, law, business, and science. David Jacobson's *Down in the Valley* (2005) dramatically enacts the difficulty of even imagining the Jewish male as a virile man of the earth in contemporary American society. A precocious, sexually active teenage girl named Tobe (Evan Rachel Wood) lives with her younger brother, Lonnie (Rory Culkin), and her single father, Wade (David Morse). In a chance meeting, Tobe initiates a relationship with Harlan Fairfax Carruthers (Edward Norton), a modern-day cowboy who says he's from South Dakota, dresses in a cowboy hat, boots, and shirt, and speaks with a midwestern twang. In that the cowboy is perhaps the quintessential American body guy, Harlan seems archetypal: he rides horses with ease, is an expert marksman with a handgun, has a buff body, and sexually satisfies Tobe.

Both Tobe and Lonnie are children with growing pains and are out of Wade's control. Harlan, as an outsider and a romanticized anachronism, appeals to both kids, befriending the timid Lonnie, a thirteen-year-old who is still afraid to sleep in the dark. He gives both kids a kind of confidence with his straightforward "cowboy" wisdom: "You can do anything you want to do. You can even be anybody you want to be. You just have to decide on it. And then just do it." Harlan's heroic body-guy status slowly breaks down, however. He takes Tobe riding on what seems to be his own horse, but when they return to the stable, the real owner awaits them with a gun. We also see Harlan enact scenes from western movie shoot-outs while he's alone in his apartment, talking to himself loudly enough to disturb neighbors. His monologues in front of a mirror become increasingly violent and disturbing, reminiscent of Travis Bickel in *Taxi Driver*. Later, Harlan's psychotic break with reality reaches a dangerous level when he threatens Tobe, then accidentally shoots and seriously wounds her for refusing to run away with him. When the police investigate the shooting, we learn that Harlan is really Martin Lassen, a young Jewish man from Los Angeles, not South Dakota, who has done jail time for robbery.

Before we learn his true identity, the film dramatically emphasizes the extreme nature of Harlan's cowboy persona as a fantasy far removed from his actual life. In his cowboy attire, he enters a synagogue where Orthodox Jews are praying and says that he's looking for someone later revealed to be his father. The congregants, clothed in prayer shawls and other traditional garb, encircle him and force him from the premises when he threatens to get violent— graphically presenting the split between who Harlan *is* and who he would like to be. His desired identity as the quintessential body guy is available to him only in "make-believe," a fact that infantilizes him and causes his complete loss of self, first in psychosis then death.

Down in the Valley literalizes the difficulty of representing the Jewish male as a body guy. In retrospect the lovemaking scene is telling. The very fact that the thirty-something Harlan is sexually attracted to Tobe, a relatively vulnerable high school girl, implies a lack of sexual security on his part. Classic body guys have self-confidence in their sexual performances and awaken and fulfill sexual desires in experienced women. Not only are the women experienced; they are involved with someone when the body guy comes along, and so his visible self-confidence is part of the allure. Furthermore, Harlan's lovemaking scene itself differs markedly from the genre norm. Nothing suggests that he can perform all night or pound, pound, pound. On the contrary, we see a brief scene dominated by Tobe on top of him as he sits still. He is not the active partner, nor is the scene sweaty and vigorous. In the classic montage sequence, the woman rides the man, but that image is intercut with shots of him in highly active positions. Even the teenage boy who does it all night long, banging the headboard into the wall in *Dead Presidents*, is the real thing in comparison to Harlan, a grown man who takes advantage of a teenage girl's immature fantasies and who performs neither long enough nor hard enough to be a true body guy.

How, then, are Jewish men represented in relation to the body and sexuality? A seemingly simple question like this quickly becomes entangled in a nexus of related questions about race and ethnicity since the answer lies in part in comparisons to other groups within specific historical and cultural contexts. At the moment, for example, the United States and much of the rest of the Western world has constructed a paradigm with well-endowed hypersexual black men at one end of the spectrum, undersexed Asian men with small penises at the other, and white men embodying the average penis in the middle, all of which suggests an invisible norm whereby blacks are excessive and Asians lack sexuality. As *Down in the Valley* makes clear, for a Jewish boy growing up in late twentieth-century America, the desire to *embody* the western hero is not the same thing as for a white Christian boy of the same age. The Jew is, as it were, out of reach of the ideal, and as we will see, the same holds true with other central aspects of male sexuality, including the cherished ideal norm of the penis.

While much critical attention has been paid to black and Asian masculinity and sexuality in film, little has been devoted to Jewish masculinity, the Jewish male body, or the Jewish penis. We turn our attention to the representation of Jewish men in films, not only to remedy this oversight but because the cultural positioning of Jewish males as intellectuals and professors makes them central to this book—they are the ethnic embodiment of the mind guy. And as we will see, even Jewish filmmakers have succumbed to disturbing ethnic stereotypes. Nobody emerges unscathed in this pervasive and dangerous environment.

Undoubtedly, one of the most disseminated images of the Jewish body since World War II has been that of mounds of naked corpses in concentration camps. Unlike images of the lynching of blacks in the American South, which have only recently begun to permeate the entire nation, these images of dead Jews were seemingly authorized from the very beginning as images of taboo

Figure 17. Jews facing execution during the Holocaust (anonymous photograph)

subjects that could and should be shown for a greater good: lest we forget. Yet as with the images of blacks circulated in, for example, the recent photography exhibit and book, *Without Sanctuary: Lynching Photography in America*, these images are more complex than the context of good intentions implies. On the one hand, they serve to remind us of the atrocities committed against Jews and blacks in the past, but on the other hand, they may have additional unintended consequences.

Consider for example this image of naked Jewish males about to be executed (figure 17), which circulates widely on the Internet on Holocaust Web sites. In addition to documenting the intended unspeakable atrocities, the photograph may be read by many as a narrative of failed masculinity at several levels. Questions may arise in the viewer's mind: "Why are these men meekly marching to their death?" "Why did they compliantly remove their clothes before doing so?" "Why don't they resist and make a run for it?" "Wouldn't it be better to die in a last effort of defiance, shot in the back, than to stand meekly before a grave waiting to be shot?" In addition to posing such questions about the victims, viewers may also be deeply affected by the specific bodies and framing of those bodies in the image. Two things jump out immediately: the man in the center covers his genitals as if in shame or humiliation, and in the right rear we see a young boy. While emotionally overwhelming, these particulars may suggest that these grown men march to their deaths like a little boy and that these humiliated men so lack the culturally sanctioned outward signs of masculinity that one goes to his death hiding his humiliation from the camera, the onlookers, and history. Meanwhile the fully clothed Nazi executioners stand with long rifle barrels, prominent as they prepare to slaughter these men and the boy.

Jewish masculinity in international cinema since World War II has been profoundly affected by documentary images of seemingly passive, weak, starving, naked men on the verge of death or, in fact, dead: their naked bodies a testimony to a very public, failed masculinity. Ever since the publication of John Berger's *Ways of Seeing* in 1972, the distinction between the naked and the nude has been widely accepted within the world of art, photography, and cinema. Naked people are people without clothes, whereas nude people have their bodies displayed to-be-looked-at. As with many such categorical distinctions, such as the one between art and pornography, this distinction may be too convenient. Much "art" contains elements of sexuality and eroticism similar to and at times identical with elements in pornography, and if one simply accepts the basic distinction, those elements of art may go undetected and unanalyzed. After Berger, nearly all scholars working on the representation of sexuality and eroticism have focused on the category of the nude, but the category of the "naked" is in some manner as sexual as that of the nude. One single voyeuristic gaze underlies both, oscillating between the poles of the naked and the nude.

Heather Kravas, a dancer and choreographer, discusses what she identifies as dancing "naked": "We can't help but sexualize bodies. We put our own against others, or we rate them in terms of desirability" (Kourlas). We suspect Kravas uses the word *naked* because she refers to herself as dancing "without clothes." Yet she quite rightly notes that even within that context and within a serious work of art, being naked does not somehow turn off the sexual component of the look. Both of her points are perceptive and crucial. All looks at bodies include a sexual component and an evaluative one, and disturbing as it may be, that includes dead bodies, especially within the voyeuristic gaze of cinema, art, and photography—the look at those dead and dying Jewish men includes a look at their penises.

The constant circulation of these images of dying and frequently dead and naked Jewish men for nearly sixty years makes it difficult, if not impossible, to imagine those pathetic bodies as vibrant, erotic spectacles that promise sexual fulfillment.[1] In a sense, they have failed not only in the social, political, public arena but also in the private arena of the bedroom. Just as surely as with choreography, we sexualize those bodies and place them against more desirable ones. In fact, we seem to have done this so successfully that the notion of the sexually desirable Jewish male body has become something of an oxymoron, even for such Jewish male comics as Woody Allen, who jokes that he's the only man he knows who suffers from penis envy. Funny as the joke may be, he may have it wrong—far from being the only one, he may be speaking about western Jewish masculinity in general. In other words, a representation of a naked body is seldom just a naked body—it also contains an element of display and invokes a voyeuristic, even sexual, gaze. Although cinematic images of Jewish male bodies are always seemingly "naked" and never "nude," this has had profound implications on the representation of Jewish masculinity, sexuality, and intellectualism. The naked and the dead are not as far away from the nude and the dead as we think.

Sunshine (1999), a German-Austrian-Canadian-Hungarian coproduction directed by Hungarian filmmaker Istvan Szabo, closely examines three generations of Ashkenazi Jews in the same family during the twentieth century, with Ralph Fiennes playing the principal male character from each generation. The film contains what may be the quintessential image of the naked, dead Jewish male body. After Jews have been rounded up by Nazis in Hungary and taken to a camp, they are forced to watch the torture and death of one of their members (played by Fiennes). The crowd includes the teenage son of the stripped and tortured man. During the first part of the humiliating torture, the naked man is bound upside down to a horizontal pole with his penis visible (figure 18). Then the film moves to a level of insight almost too painful to watch as the tortured, naked, body is hung vertically by the wrists, the victim still alive. In the freezing cold, a Nazi guard sprays the man with a hose, his body slowly icing as he freezes to death on public display, invoking the common association of the

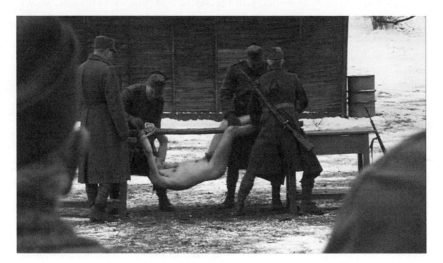

Figure 18. *Sunshine*

penis retracting in cold water. In a later segment with Fiennes, playing the son now as a man, a rhyming scene occurs when communists break in to confront him while he showers in a completely open area. Once again his nakedness is a sign of his powerlessness and humiliation, the shower water falling on him in contrast to the water sprayed on his father.

Frontal male nudity abounds as an image of humiliated, vulnerable Jewish masculinity. Steven Spielberg lingers on images of pathetic-looking Jewish men in a concentration camp in *Schindler's List* (1993), their emaciated, skin-and-bones bodies foregrounding their genitals even more. In Spielberg's *Munich* (2005), a Jewish man, Carl, is the victim of a female assassin's seduction. When his compatriot, Avner, discovers the dead body, Carl is lying naked on his back in bed. His body position contains several layers of humiliation. The beautiful assassin had earlier propositioned Avner, who declined with some hesitation. When Avner passes near Carl's room, he catches a whiff of the assassin's perfume and comments to himself that he saw her first, suggesting some jealousy of Carl's sexual exploit. But when he enters Carl's room, he finds him lying dead, completely nude, his penis visible. Sex was more than deadly for Carl. Instead of using his penis for the intended masculine sexual performance, he was killed by a woman who left him exposed, knowing that Avner would find him in that humiliating condition.

In Agnieszka Holland's *Europa, Europa* (1990), we see the central Jewish character's penis in three scenes: first, when he frantically exits a bathtub and runs outside to hide in a barrel during a Nazi assault on his home; again when he tries to hide his penis from a Nazi soldier who is playfully attempting to see it; and yet again when he inspects his blackened and infected penis after trying to camouflage his circumcision in order to masquerade as a Nazi. In all cases the boy is vulnerable. In an episode of the HBO TV series *OZ*, a Jewish prisoner is murdered and his naked body is hung upside down with the word "Jew" written on it in blood, eerily recalling the image in *Sunshine* (figure 19). The Jew has a small penis, further highlighted by the extensive use of male nudity throughout the *OZ* series, which generally features noticeably larger men. Furthermore, in a later rhyming shot, we see the dead, naked body of the Aryan who killed the Jew filmed in a manner that more clearly displays his larger penis for the spectator. This is underscored and replicated in a bizarre manner on the Web site *The Men of OZ: Nude Scenes from HBO's TV Series "OZ,"* which shows images of male nudity from the series organized around the actors. Fred Koehler, playing the Aryan who kills the Jew, is included, and a montage of images of him nude includes two frames from the shot in which he lies dead on his back, his penis prominently displayed resting on this thigh as the camera moves up and away. Yet the Jew whom he killed is missing from the site, the

Figure 19. *Oz*

dead Jewish penis and the actor who played the part not even memorable enough to be included, erased from the penile spectacle parade of the series, which, according to the site, "developed an enormous gay fan base." The reference to gay fandom makes explicit the site's assumption about the sexual component and eroticism of the display of the penis in *OZ*.

The Jewish penis in these films is always shown in situations of humiliation, vulnerability, and death—never sexuality—never as potent, always as impotent. Even in films, like *Sunshine*, that grant sexual potency to Jewish males, that potency is always separated from the naked body. It is as if the mounds of dead bodies and naked "living corpses" of the concentrations camps—whether in documentary photos and newsreels or in the cinema—have contributed to the cultural attempts to fix the sight of the Jewish penis, thus profoundly affecting the perception of Jewish male sexuality. Indeed, this notion is actually represented in *Europa, Europa*. Near the end of the war, the Jewish boy masquerading as a Nazi surrenders to the Russians, revealing that he is Jewish and only in the German army to protect himself from persecution. A disbelieving Russian officer pushes his head toward a pile of photographs of concentration camp victims. One by one, the officer throws the pictures in front of the boy, saying that if he was Jewish, he would look like the men in the pictures—emaciated and dead.

All the concentration camp images invoke a sexual look in several senses of the word: there is something inherently pornographic, in the truest sense of that word, in looking at these images. In an oft-identified pattern, the desire to look away in horror is countered by the desire to stare in fascination, and, of course, sex and death have been strongly linked by many, including the well-known works of Georges Bataille. Within this pattern the common distinction between naked and nude is worse than useless since it obscures what connects the nude (erotic) body with the naked (merely unclothed) body. They become horribly intermingled in these films, leading to deep disturbances in the representation of the sexuality and masculinity of Jewish men.

A subset of films depict the "failure" of the Jewish male in terms of another body-guy characteristic: rhythm. Rhythmic physical coordination is directly connected to the body guy's sex style and is even reflected in the terms used to describe this kind of performance: jackhammer sex, pounding, pumping. A number of films such as *Dirty Dancing* literally enact the cliché that Jews don't have rhythm by contrasting the awkward moves of brainy Jewish men with Patrick Swayze's sensuous and masterful dancing. Swayze's working-class character ends up awakening the sexuality of a sheltered Jewish woman, winning her from a physically klutzy Jewish suitor who brags about his money and success. Learning to move rhythmically is also central to *A Walk on the Moon* (1999), directed by Tony Goldwyn. The film suggests that even when a Jew is a body guy, he still doesn't have the "stuff" to sexually satisfy a woman. Marty Kantrowitz (Liev Schreiber) has many classic, man-of-the-earth characteristics: he's fairly buff, wears sleeveless undershirts that emphasize his biceps, and works as a TV repairman. But this is never the kind of guy he wanted to be, giving up college to marry his wife, Pearl (Diane Lane), whom he had gotten pregnant. He is a faux body guy, setting the stage for the appearance of the real thing.

Marty, Pearl, and their two kids routinely vacation at a summer bungalow colony for Jews in upstate New York. One night Pearl asks Marty if they can experiment in bed. Marty agrees and goes into another room. He then makes a joke of the request, however, by emerging in their young son's too-small cowboy hat and gun holster while doing a John Wayne impression, a gesture that distances him from the quintessential body guy, the cowboy. Like Harlan in *Down in the Valley*, Marty can only pretend to be a cowboy; the role does not fit him. It's implied that they then have sex in their usual manner, something Pearl wants to change.

While Marty is back in the city working, Pearl meets Walker (Viggo Mortensen), a hippie who sells blouses from a bus (this is 1969). Walker is the "true" body guy, and we see him bring Pearl to sexual ecstasy per the genre: he enters her immediately and effortlessly, they engage in intercourse repeatedly, she experiences cunnilingus for the first time, and they have sex up against rocks under a waterfall. Walker and Marty are directly contrasted via the motif of dancing. Marty and Pearl slow dance stiffly at the resort club, but Walker joyously cavorts with Pearl in his arms at the Woodstock festival. After Marty finds out about the affair, he goes back to their home in the city and grieves in his teenage daughter's room. He eventually turns on her record player, which is cued to Bob Dylan's "Subterranean Homesick Blues," and surprisingly begins to dance, though his movements are rigid and out of sync with the rhythm of the music. When Marty and Pearl decide to reconcile in the film's last scene, reggae music is playing on their radio. Pearl switches the station to Dean Martin singing "When You're Smiling" and says, "Dance with me." The two begin to slow dance, and we presume it will result in a romantic embrace or kiss to celebrate their reconciliation. The film could easily have ended at this point. Marty, however, changes the station once again to find Jimi Hendrix playing "Purple Haze" and begins to bob his head with the beat, saying, "I'm not very good at this." The two then begin to fast dance, and although Marty still looks awkward doing the outdated "Twist," he attempts to get rhythm in order to please Pearl's desire for something different. The film ends with them dancing to Hendrix, as if the issue of rhythm and coordination is literally the root of their marital problems—and also the antidote.[2]

The denigration of Jewish intellectuals vis-à-vis rhythm masks the fact that there can also be a pleasurable movement of the mind as Richard Hofstadter described it. David Brooks even discusses the mind in terms of rhythm. In his *New York Times* article on the impact of personal environment on I.Q., Brooks writes: "Speed and strength are part of intelligence, and these things can be measured numerically, but the *essence* of the activity is found in *the rhythm and grace and personality* [of intelligence]" (emphasis added). None of the body-guy films suggest that the intellectual male's mental activity and rhythm can be sexy in itself—the rhythm of intelligence and the mind. Why can't that rhythm be as exciting as physical movement? And why do we presume that if one possesses the former, he lacks the latter? Ironically, this combination of being intelligent and lacking rhythm describes a cultural stereotype of Jewish men.

As if these disturbing ideas about the Jewish penis and body were not enough, some films even find a way to negatively portray the Jewish mind, a stalwart aspect of Jewish identity. The Jewish mind fares little better than the Jewish body, further complicating the imagination of a vibrant Jewish masculinity. In *Enemy at the Gates* (2001), a U.S.-U.K.-German-Irish coproduction directed by French filmmaker Jean-Jacques Annaud, a Jewish intellectual who is also a Soviet military officer competes with a sharp-shooting, provincial

Figure 20. *Enemy at the Gates*

shepherd for the affection of a beautiful, intelligent Jewish woman. The Jewish male flirts with the woman by emphasizing their shared background: their Judaism and love of books, education, and Marxist ideology. He points out how vastly different the two of them are from the illiterate shepherd. The woman's response, of course, is to initiate sex with the shepherd, an intensely satisfying experience for her. The film cannot imagine that happening with the Jewish intellectual. The Jew ultimately commits suicide by taking a bullet in his "useless" brain, as he calls it, to reveal the location of a Nazi sniper for the shepherd (figure 20). His decision to die coincides with his loss of the woman to the peasant shepherd and his disillusionment with communist ideology, which he had previously embraced with gusto. His death denigrates the world of ideas and political activism, thus laying waste to the notion that a sexual relationship can develop from intellectual and ideological pursuits and passions. In addition, the woman's seduction of the uneducated, non-Jewish shepherd obliterates in an instant her cultural heritage and connection to men of her past—a connection that the intellectual was certain he could exploit to his advantage. In effect, the film literally adds the image of the dead Jewish brain to the dead Jewish penis.

SEARCHING FOR THE SEXY MIND

How does one visually represent the sexy mind? The 2004 movie *Sideways*, written and directed by Alexander Payne, is a good place to begin. The film features a mind-guy writer-teacher, Miles (Paul Giamatti), and his body-guy actor friend, Jack (Thomas Hayden Church). The friends take a road trip through California's central coast to commemorate Jack's last days as a bachelor. Miles, a wine connoisseur, wants to hit all the major wineries in the region for some

Figure 21. *Sideways*

quality tasting. Jack, a notorious womanizer, wants to hit on any tasty woman he can find before his marriage. Miles reconnects with a waitress, Maya (Virginia Madsen), whom he met on a previous trip, and a double date is soon arranged, pairing Maya's friend, Stephanie (Sandra Oh), with Jack. After a wine-soaked dinner, the four go to Stephanie's house, where she and Jack soon go to her bedroom for sex. Miles, still pining for his ex-wife, opts for conversation with Maya. The initial chat between Miles and Maya is interrupted by Stephanie's lusty moans from the bedroom, so they move to the quiet of an outdoor patio to continue their discussion. This scene establishes the basic opposition between the Jack/Stephanie and Miles/Maya pairings; a dichotomy centered on conventional sex versus unconventional eroticism.

We see just how conventional Jack's sex style is later when Miles accidentally catches him in the act. Stephanie is lying on a bed with her legs in the air, one leg resting on Jack's shoulder. Jack is leaning over her from a push-up position at the edge of the bed. He pumps away as she audibly and rhythmically pants (figure 21). In contrast, the only sexual moment we see between Miles and Maya is characterized by stillness and lyrical language rather than hyperactivity and inarticulate grunts. After the two move to the patio, their conversation centers on wine; Maya is also a connoisseur and a grad student in horticulture. Both Miles and Maya express what they love about wine, and erotic moments present themselves in ways that surprise and disconcert Miles (and possibly the film spectator, as well). The scene is filmed in warm golden light, first in alternating two-shots and then in separate close shots as the scene progresses, emphasizing the intense interest each person has in what the other is saying. Adding to the erotic mood, soft piano music also begins in the background. Maya asks Miles why he has a "thing" for Pinot Noir, and he replies passionately:

> It's a hard grape to grow—as you know. It's thin-skinned, temperamental, ripens early. . . . It's not a survivor like Cabernet, which can just grow any-where, and thrive even when it's neglected. . . . Nah, Pinot needs constant care and attention. In fact it can only grow in these *really* specific little tucked away corners of the world. And only the most patient and nurturing of grow-ers can do it, really. Only somebody who *really* takes the time to understand Pinot's potential can then coax it into its fullest expression. And, I mean, ah, its flavors; they're just the most haunting and brilliant, and thrilling and sub-tle and . . . ancient on the planet.

Miles then asks Maya why she's into wine, and she replies:

> I discovered that I had a really sharp palette, and the more I drank, the more I liked what it made me think about. . . . I like to *think* about the life of wine; how it's a living thing. I like to think about what was going on in the year the grapes were grown—how the sun was shining, if it rained. I like to think about all the people who tended and picked the grapes, and if it's an old wine, how many of them must be dead by now. I like how wine continues to evolve. Like if I opened a bottle of wine today, it would taste different than if I opened it on any other day. Because a bottle of wine is actually alive, and it's constantly evolving and gaining complexity, that is until it peaks . . . and then it begins its steady inevitable decline. And it tastes so . . . fucking . . . good.

As Maya pours her heart out to Miles, she places her hand over his which we see in close-up (figure 22). The moment is so intimate and intense that the con-flicted Miles breaks the spell by getting up to use the bathroom. The sexual component of their conversation is emphasized as Miles splashes his face with water—the metonymic cold shower—berating himself for ruining the moment. When he emerges, Maya is in the kitchen. He abruptly approaches and crudely kisses her on the lips, but she rebuffs his conventional lovemaking, the special connection and erotic moment created with language lost.

The film favors the sensual interaction between Miles and Maya over Jack's and Stephanie's pounding sex by its visual presentation and character develop-ment. Both Miles and Jack are flawed, but Miles, as the sympathetic protago-nist, is the character with whom we identify. Jack, though not unlikable, is ultimately narcissistic and immature, and he deeply hurts the highly likable Stephanie. The relationship between Miles and Maya, therefore, appears the favored one, largely because of the way they interact. The artistic and sensual lighting of the scene and background music highlight the manner in which

Figure 22. *Sideways*

language and conversation in themselves can be erotic. They find sexual intimacy through a shared interest. Both Miles and Maya have knowledge about their subject, but they also have enough self-knowledge and confidence to articulate their thoughts, opinions, and feelings about it. They've acknowledged their passion for something in life that gives them pleasure and have consciously contemplated it. Furthermore, they both have enough respect for education, the intellect, and language to poetically articulate their thoughts. Maya mentions that she became interested in wine because of her ex-husband, who had a "big show-off wine cellar." As she became more knowledgeable about wine and the subtleties of its tastes, she realized her husband was a fraud, caring only about the status and surface appearance of possessing the right wines. For Maya, the physical experience of tasting wine stimulates her mental faculties—her imagination—as well as her body. She likes thinking about wine, as well as tasting it. Maya is linked to depth, her ex-husband to surface appearances.

This scene lays out several components of what we call the sexy mind. When Maya asks Miles why he's into Pinot, he initially says he doesn't know, but then he takes a moment to collect himself and proceeds to articulate his thoughts, to Maya's delight. It's sexy to have the self-knowledge and confidence to precisely articulate one's thoughts and experiences. This scene succeeds in placing us at the fifty-yard line to observe two sexy minds in action; thinking *can* be a spectator sport. Contrast this with the mathematician in *Antonia's Line*, who contemptuously throws out the blathering intellectual for his inadequate sexual performance after we have heard him passionately express his ideas. Maya encourages Miles to express his thoughts and ardently responds to him in kind, clearly connecting sexual and intellectual passions when she erotically touches his hand.

A movie from nearly a decade earlier than *Sideways* has two people develop a sexual interest in each other from the work they do together, extending the notion of the sexy mind. *Angels and Insects* (1995) is a U.S.-U.K. coproduction written by Belinda and Philip Haas and directed by the latter. Like others in the pattern, the film sets up a mind/body opposition, but it uncharacteristically privileges the mind guy, actually depicting the body guy as repulsive, his penis and pound-cubed sex style as troubling. In 1860s England, the wealthy Sir Harald Alabaster, an amateur entomologist, hires biologist William Adamson (Mark Rylance) to help him write a book. William lost the records of his own work on insects in a shipwreck while returning from a research expedition to the Amazon. The film quickly establishes an opposition between the two women in William's life at the manor: Sir Harald's beautiful daughter, Eugenia (Patsy Kensit), and Matty Crompton (Kristen Scott Thomas), the dowdy-looking governess for Sir Harald's younger girls. Eugenia is bored with William's scientific endeavors and literally repulsed by insects, whereas Matty is fascinated with his work and understands it. William marries Eugenia, and she quickly becomes pregnant. As Eugenia withdraws to slouch in a chair eating pastries, Matty enlists William's help with science outings she conducts with the younger girls. Matty and William develop a mutual admiration around science and the intellect, and both find joy in exploration. William says, "You think a great deal, Miss Crompton," to which she replies, "It's my great *amusement, thinking.*" This is one of the rare instances where a film actually articulates Hofstadter's "play of the mind."

When William expresses discontent in the work he does with Sir Harald, longing to travel again in the Amazon, Matty suggests that he can earn money for the trip by writing a book on the natural history of the ant colonies they observe on their nature walks. As she imagines it, the book will both appeal to a general public and have scientific value. William replies that it might indeed be "interesting and fun," to which Matty repeats "fun," and they proceed to set up a regimen to observe and record a red-ant colony. The pursuit of knowledge as fun is both articulated and presented visually via telephoto cinematography that depicts the world of the ants and other aspects of nature in beautiful, play-ful, and extraordinary ways. The fun extends to others in that Matty and the girls create sketches to accompany William's text, and household servants happily contribute as well.

One day William intently watches Matty's wrist (significantly filmed in close-up) as she draws the ants; and her wrist becomes a kind of fetish for him. The image is so potent for William that he fantasizes the wrist while making love to Eugenia. A literal sexual component arises from his collaboration with Matty. As William and Matty work together, he becomes less interested in Eugenia, who is almost constantly pregnant; thus, the film establishes a children/work (people/ideas) opposition. Later, William discovers that Eugenia has been having a long-term sexual affair with her own brother, Edgar, who is the actual father of all the babies. His response is one of relief, and he says to Matty, "my most powerful feeling is that I'm free. . . . I can go now. . . . I can leave this house; I can return to my *true work*." The two, who have since published William's book, then profess their love for each other, leave babies behind, and head for the Amazon.

Eugenia's brother, Edgar, conforms to the body guy as brute category. Coarse and mean, he rapes a housemaid, and he is totally divorced from the mind as his father furiously berates him for not knowing about Darwin: "you would know if you ever took any interest in the important ideas of our time. . . . Think, Edgar, before you speak." Like other body guys, we see Edgar's penis displayed but with notable differences. In a highly melodramatic scene, William discovers Edgar having sex with Eugenia and orders him to get dressed and get out of the bedroom. As we see him jump out of bed to do as ordered, he stands facing the camera with an erection. The erection creates even more of a spectacle since the genre norm shows only the flaccid penis. The body guy's penis is generally one of the principal gifts he offers to the beautiful woman, but here it is only humiliating and powerless, rendering the empowered mind guy superior. Even the spectacle of the erect penis fails to impress, the sight of it linked to cruelty, shame, familial dysfunction, and possible incestuous ruin for the family. Here the sight of the body guy's penis frees the intellectual from a stultifying existence and from the woman who wants the kind of sex the body guy gives her.

Uncharacteristically, William, the scientist, is a good lover in traditional terms. He is not denigrated in the manner typical of other intellectuals in the genre; indeed, he outshines Edgar on all levels. In addition, the film smashes the markers of power for both genders. In the usual pattern, the woman-in-between's beauty works to endow the body guy with even more importance. He can win and control the woman who exhibits the culturally defined and sanctioned markers of feminine power, and she wants him in return. Edgar's impressive penis is useless, even destructive, and Eugenia's beauty is hollow. As she says of herself, "It has not done me any good to look pretty, to be admired. I would like to be different." The thinking person, Matty, prevails over the beautiful but shallow Eugenia. Power is associated with using the mind, being passionate about one's work, and finding a way to make a living from it in order to escape the trap of the ruling class. One must find the mind sexy in order to achieve this freedom, and a sexy mind in *Angels and Insects* is one that

Figure 23. *The Governess*

is curious, welcomes complexity and a challenge, and is persistent, mindful of details, and respectful of the interdependent web of existence.

The British-produced *The Governess* (1998), written and directed by Sandra Goldbacher, also features sexual passion arising from a work-oriented collaboration, but this film adds a dimension for the woman that ties the act of investigation to the realm of the erotic. To avoid an arranged marriage in Victorian England, a Jewish woman, Rosina Da Silva (Minnie Driver), takes a job as a governess for the family of a wealthy scientist, Charles Cavendish (Tom Wilkinson).[3] Charles primarily works in a laboratory that his family is forbidden to enter. One evening, Rosina sneaks into the illicit space with a lantern and peruses Charles's work (figure 23). Charles gleans that Rosina has trespassed, but is amused rather than angered, and makes her his assistant. Together they collect and classify fossil shells and experiment with photography, seeking to concoct the first fixative agent for photographic image preservation. The two then begin a torrid sexual affair, but only after a fertile intellectual and professional collaboration, similar to the scenario in *Angels and Insects*.

Rosina's passion for Charles arises from the work they do together, but his penis is not the focus of her interest, nor is it depicted as the magical center of a thrilling sexual experience that awakens her dormant sexuality. On the contrary, Rosina awakens Charles's sublimated libido with her seductions. She insists that he photograph her enacting the biblical tale of Salome who danced specifically to seduce. These creative scenarios as foreplay—orchestrated and controlled by Rosina—are much more exciting than the depiction of their actual intercourse, which they carry out fully clothed (although in contrast to other 1990s mind guys, Charles is portrayed as a sensitive, passionate lover, within the constraints of his time). Rosina's passion is not ignited from being penetrated by Charles's penis but by her penetration into the forbidden and private "male" space of the laboratory. This reversal of the usual meaning of penetration reconfigures the penis/brain opposition.

Defying Molly Haskell's observation about cinema quoted at the beginning of this chapter, *The Governess* shows us both a man's penis and a woman's intelligence. The film also defies the body-guy genre in that the penis ultimately destroys instead of empowers. Charles's penis is displayed but only when he is passive—passed out from too much alcohol. At this point, Rosina disrobes him and sees his penis for the first time. The sight of his penis, which is good-sized, nonetheless does not impress her, nor is she enticed to arouse it for her pleasure. What is aroused is her desire to photograph Charles, and she poses him in the aesthetic oil-painting tradition of female reclining nudes. She sees the penis, rejects it as the locus of her desire, and moves on to her more pressing interest: creating artistic works. She illicitly uses the camera Charles had previously forbidden her to touch, and in so doing she feminizes Charles's good-sized penis by posing him like a woman instead of succumbing to the normal phallic powers associated with it. In a reversal of the usual pattern, Charles is objectified instead of the woman. Indeed, this entire scene foreshadows Charles's eventual loss of control.

Rosina develops the picture while Charles continues to sleep, and she leaves the photo for him before exiting. When we next see Charles, he has a troubled look on his face as he examines the photo of himself with a magnifying glass, deeply troubled by Rosina's aesthetic representation of his body. He then instantly ends his professional and personal relationship with her, even going so far as to sadistically take full credit for their coauthored scientific research leading to the discovery of photographic printing. In retribution for his behavior, Rosina steals several of his camera lenses and presents a copy of the offending photograph to Charles's wife in the middle of a family dinner. Rosina then permanently leaves the Cavendish manor for her native London, where she starts and maintains a thriving photography business. In the film's final scene, Charles visits her studio and says, "I'm in your hands, Miss da Silva, do with me what you will." Rosina's response is to do nothing more than photograph him, after which he dejectedly leaves. The trajectory of Rosina's investigative journey leads her to reject the penis and the masculinity associated with it in favor of appropriating the camera lens to control representation. Rosina directly challenges the dominant male world and empowers herself by seizing both the opportunity to penetrate Charles's laboratory and the investigative eye of the camera. *The Governess* foregrounds the importance of investigation for women. It links erotic investigation to female empowerment and resists returning the woman to a traditional feminine role.

The scenario of women sneaking into a private space and then touching or surveying personal items recurs in cinema, often in scenes with sexual over-tones. In Alfred Hitchcock's *Psycho* (1960), Lila Crane enters the Bates home uninvited and searches several rooms. In Mrs. Bates's bedroom, she looks through her closet, touches her bedspread, and surveys ornaments and groom-ing items on her dresser. She does the same in Norman's room, noting his childhood toys, his unmade bed, and an album of Beethoven's "Eroica" Symphony on the record player. She even pages through one of his books. In Brian De Palma's *Obsession* (1976), the female protagonist secretly investigates what is revealed to be her dead mother's bedroom, looking through photo albums and trying on jewelry. The event occurs during an elaborate scheme in which the woman is seducing her own father (who does not know her identity). In Jonathan Demme's *Silence of the Lambs* (1991), FBI agent Clarice Starling peruses the bedroom of a serial killer's victim, noting various photographs, posters, and trinkets. She surveys a music box, finding a secret compartment with pictures of the victim seminude in a variety of poses. In all of the above films, the women gain the knowledge that they seek through their investigation as they intrude on forbidden spaces.

Zalman King's production *Lake Consequence* makes explicit the frequently implicit erotic charge in investigative scenarios. The central female character is erotically drawn to the body guy who is working on her property while her hus-band is away. Thinking she is alone, she sneaks into the gardener's trailer and begins to go through his personal belongings only to be startled when the vehi-cle begins to move. She finds herself trapped within as he drives off taking her with him. The entire plot of the film, which includes her intense sexual encounter with him, is thus literally set in motion by her transgressive investigation of his private space.

The above scenarios suggest an ideal or utopian vision of investigation that empowers women as investigators who dig beneath the surface and actively search for evidence. The perfect fantasy investigation would empower in a vari-ety of ways: good investigators resist superficial and simplistic explanations. They unearth evidence and interpret it objectively to draw creative connections and conclusions. They acknowledge that there are no absolutes—anything is possible. They take risks, do not fear the mysterious or the unknown, and accommodate to discomfort. They know how to use language and psychology to question and probe for the information they want. They go after the truth, even if it is elusive and challenges their own belief systems. Such investigators infiltrate, delve deeper and deeper into aspects of culture that may expose the disturbing side of institutions nations hold dear, such as monogamous marriage and the family. Going deep means something very different for female investigators than it does for body guys.

With that kind of empowerment, it is not surprising that men have historically dominated as investigators in representation. One recent film magnifies how strongly investigation is linked to the masculine domain. In David Fincher's *Zodiac* (2007), eight key male characters are intensely involved with trying to identify a serial killer who calls himself Zodiac. One man becomes so obsessed with his investigation that his wife and three children move out. When he reads the message from his wife telling him they've gone, he crumples the notepaper in frustration. He quickly notices, however, information he wrote concerning Zodiac on the back of the paper, and his frustration dissolves in an instant. The lure of his research outweighs the loss of this family. His wife is so excluded from the investigative process that she is even visually depicted as a menacing character—someone who threatens to disrupt the man's inexorable drive to solve the case.

By contrast, Steven Soderbergh's *Erin Brockovich* (2000) plays out exactly what is at stake if a woman investigates. Erin conducts extensive (at times illicit) research on behalf of her law firm's injured clients, but she does so while clothed in short-shorts, low-cut tops, tight short skirts, and/or see-through blouses and often has one or all of her three kids, including an infant, in tow. When her boss asks her how she can obtain additional sensitive documents they need for their case, Erin replies, "They're called boobs, Ed." Erin can investigate only if she's a walking advertisement for traditional femininity. Erin speaks other words, however, perhaps never before heard in Hollywood cinema, about the value of her investigative career and its relationship to mothering. When Erin's boyfriend asks her to quit her job, the conversation is intense:

ERIN: How can you ask me to do that? This job . . . for the first time in my life, I got people respecting me. Up in Hinkley, I walk into a room and everybody shuts up to hear if I got something to say. I never had that before, ever. Please don't ask me to give that up.

GEORGE: Well, what about what your kids are giving up?

ERIN: Look, I'm doing more for my kids now than I did living with my parents. One day they'll understand that.

GEORGE: Well, what about me?

ERIN: What about you? You think either one of the men who gave me those children asked me what I wanted before he walked away? All I've ever done is bend my life around what men decide they need. Well, not now. I'm sorry, I won't do it.

Could such a defense of feminine individuality that speaks to the empowering aspect of investigation have been spoken if the movie didn't feature babies, boobs, and a boyfriend?[4]

In *The Governess* and the other scenarios we have examined, the women's investigations are active penetrations into illicit spaces that result in knowledge and empowerment. Body-guy films would have us think, however, that empowerment for a woman comes from her being penetrated by a certain kind of man and his wondrous penis. In a sense, the body-guy genre tries to validate Freud's notion of penis envy, that from childhood on girls envy what boys have and they don't—the penis. The genre falsely conflates the penis and empowerment, however, and attempts to prohibit women from discovering this insidious ploy. Power has nothing to do with the penis. Power is attained through a penetrating mind, not from being penetrated by a big penis. There may be a good reason why male private investigators are called "dicks."

As we have seen, much of society's valuation of the body culture is way out of proportion to the actual power of the body and, by extension, the power other people or material things can bestow on an individual. Yet the body is privileged, to the denigration and even exclusion of the mind, ideas, or abstract causes as potential sites of power, pleasure, and fulfillment—a situation heightened in America with its long-standing anti-intellectualism. And it is particularly the at-risk groups in American culture—people of color, lower socioeconomic classes, and women—that are most damaged by this anti-intellectualism, the discouragement of the intellect as an avenue to power. *Sideways*, *Angels and Insects*, and *The Governess* show us the empowering and even erotic potential of intellectual activities involving language, meaningful work, and investigation.

CHAPTER 5

Hung like a Horse . . . or an Acorn

Within the body culture, people will pay money to see the sexy body but are not yet lining up on the fifty-yard line to watch the sexy mind at work. From this perspective, the undervalued brain is made up for by the overvalued penis. If we have trouble imagining the mind as sexy, we have equal trouble imagining sex without the thrusting good-sized penis. This model of lovemaking is so prevalent in representation that it now seems to dominate cultural notions about what sex—especially good sex—is. It is ridiculous, however, to measure all men against one model of "correct" and superior lovemaking performed with a correct and superior penis. Individual men cannot be categorized as good or bad lovers apart from their sexual partners. To assess men by such a standard is just as ridiculous as defining entire races with abominable stereotypes, such as those that claim Asian men have small penises, are undersexed, and are bad lovers while black men have large penises, are oversexed, and are good lovers. A range of lovemaking skills and abilities exists among men of all races, just as a range of penis sizes does.

In contemporary America all adults, and even teenagers for that matter, have heard penis-size jokes or slang terms such as "pencil dick" for men with thin penises or "hung like a horse" for men who are well-endowed. Indeed, when the central male character in *The Last Seduction* attempts to impress a woman in a bar by telling her how big his penis is, he remarks that he's "hung like a horse." Radio shock jock Howard Stern frequently talks about his small penis and has remarked that he's "hung like an acorn." Phrases like "pencil dick" and "hung like an acorn" are precise and graphic in relation to a general term such as "small penis." The former invokes an image of an extremely thin penis and the latter of one that does not hang at all. "Hung like an acorn" is an oxymoron, and Stern's funny, incisive language reminds us that not all men do hang—some men in fact resemble acorns with just the head of their penis visible above their scrotum with nothing hanging down. As such, they're not just *not* "well hung"; they're not hung at all.

In contrast to this world of omnipresent graphic language in the media and everyday society, we find nearly the opposite situation in film and all other visual and even performing arts where a polite silence reigns regarding various penis sizes and shapes. As if by unspoken agreement, society, critics, and spectators don't notice or comment on the array of different penis sizes and shapes when looking at male frontal nudity in movies, photographs in art museums, or naked actors in the theater. But such "polite" silence does not mean that assumptions about size, virility, sexuality, and race are not operative. Ironically, it is precisely when important assumptions about gender, sexuality, and race are implicit rather than explicit that they may be most powerful. What kinds of penises we display and represent, and how we look at them is certainly as important as how we joke, talk, and write about them.

How is it possible that such an extraordinary emphasis could be placed on the penis from D. H. Lawrence's origination of the body-guy genre through its current popular reincarnation in the movies without critics discussing the specific penises they see? It is important to carefully consider how the penis is represented in that it is a highly privileged sign of masculinity. The representation of the penis is crucial and unique for the following reason: all other parts of the male body are to some extent on display on a daily basis. Men and women alike can see that some men are tall and some short, some fat and some thin, some muscular and some not. Even with more eroticized and "covered" parts of the body such as the buttocks, everyone can see that some men have much more pronounced, rounded buttocks than others. But the penis remains relatively hidden away because of fashion and clothing, even in the Calvin Klein era. Except for when and how they are represented, penises are a mystery.

In his groundbreaking work on race in his book *White*, Richard Dyer introduced the concept of the "invisible norm." In the western world people speak about race in terms of people of color (blacks, yellows, browns, reds). White is colorless—the invisible norm. But once we recognize that white is a color, it ceases to be invisible; it ceases to be the unquestioned norm against which others are judged and measured and becomes one more color, like the others, that must be analyzed and understood. But first it must be *seen*. Until what has been invisible is made visible, and what has been excluded is included, we are in a situation similar to the 1950s and early 1960s in which white people constituted all the major characters of most Hollywood films and network television series. Although black characters were excluded, most white people did not scratch their heads every night when they turned on their TVs and wonder where they were. They simply accepted the white world that was offered to them as the normal or "real" world. And when blacks were represented, it was crucial to ask how they were represented. It was not enough to simply note that there was a black character or an Asian character in a movie or a TV show.

Something similar has happened with the penis: we have adopted an invisible norm against which some penises are judged small and others large. To understand the cultural assumptions about masculinity and male sexual performance represented through the body guy and the genre that celebrates him, we must understand all the implications of the normative penis. As the penis becomes more and more commonplace in movies and on television—as it has—it does not mean that we have put the issue behind us. On the contrary, it is now imperative that we understand what *kinds* of penises are represented and in what contexts. It is also vital that we notice what kinds of penises are excluded. How do these representations of the penis contribute to our ideas about male sexuality and virility? In a world without an invisible norm, a man couldn't joke with great humor and insight that he is "hung like an acorn." Stripped of its comic context, the description "hung like an acorn" applies to commonplace perfectly "normal" men.

The Demand for a "Normal" Penis

We will detail how "normal" penis size was established, but in brief, after myriad studies the statistical norm is now accepted as four inches flaccid and six inches erect, meaning that the flaccid penis hangs completely or nearly completely over the scrotum. A humorous anecdote widely circulated in the media demonstrates the excessive "need" to always see this normative penis when the penis is publicly visible or represented. An exact replica of Michelangelo's *David* was displayed in the Appian Way shopping area of Caesars Palace Hotel and Casino in Las Vegas. The statue was temporarily removed, however, when tourists regularly laughed at the smallness of David's penis, which, in fact, does not hang down far enough to cover his entire scrotum. The statue was replaced for public viewing after a couple of inches were added to the penis, thus defiling one of history's greatest artistic masterpieces. This obsessive need to perceive the penis as impressive is a twentieth-century phenomenon, and it all begins with Sigmund Freud. A widely circulated story about Freud has him remarking, "Sometimes a cigar is just a cigar." Before the twentieth century, sometimes a penis was just a penis. Since the twentieth century, however, it is never just a penis. Freud writes, for example, "little girls . . . notice the penis of a brother or playmate, *strikingly visible* and of *large proportions*, at once recognize it as the superior counterpart of their own *small* and inconspicuous organ" (quoted in Heath 53; emphases added). With his notions of penis envy and castration anxiety, Freud theorizes that our formation as gendered beings all comes down to that strikingly visible organ. Girls envy it and boys fear losing it. By the latter part of the twentieth century, not only is the penis still central to masculine identity, but the issue of specific size becomes integral as well, a phenomenon succinctly summarized by David R. Reuben in his extremely popular 1969 sex manual *Everything You Always Wanted to Know about Sex (but Were Afraid to Ask)*. The first question the book poses is, "How big is the normal penis?" The answer begins, "That is the question of the century" (5).

By the time we get to the twenty-first century, the notion of establishing a penis-size norm reaches an almost desperate level. The evidence of this curiously brings us back to Michelangelo's *David*. In 2005, two Italian art historians, Massimo Gulisano and Pietro Bernabei of Florence University, actually attempted to explain David's "smallness" utilizing a modern notion of scientific measurement, assuming his unusual penis size demands an explanation. One of them remarked about his penis, "David is not really highly gifted, but he is totally normal. His penis measures 15cm which, considering the height of the statue, corresponds to 6–7 cm in an adult [2.4 to 2.8 inches]. . . . Here we have a naked man who is about to fight. He has an orthosympathic activation consistent with the combined effects of fear, tension, and aggression. A contraction of the genitals is totally normal in such conditions" (Lorenzi). The assumption here is that David is only normal if we view his penis as being retracted owing to fear of battling the giant Goliath! In other words, in a more relaxed state he would hang further down, fulfilling our expectations for a "normal" if not "gifted" man. Without such contextualization he is indeed small. The art historians assume that the penis has always and only been perceived in terms equivalent to that of medical measurement and judged by a fixed historical norm and that a physiological response to the unusual context explains the sculpture's small penis. They do not, however, even consider as an option that there are many men whose usual flaccid size is in the two and four-tenths and two and eight-tenths range and even smaller, and that such men are perfectly "normal." What if Michelangelo's model was one such man? What if it simply didn't matter to Michelangelo, or what if he preferred it to the four-inch flaccid norm?

In the analysis of the art historians, we see the influence of two additional developments that occurred after Freud: the twentieth-century history of medical measurement of penis size to define the "normal" penis and a new emphasis in evolutionary biology and psychology centered on the evolution of the penis from the chimpanzee to the human male. In *Running Scared: Masculinity and the Representation of the Male Body* (1993), Peter Lehman detailed the shift in the medical literature that took place between the nineteenth and twentieth centuries in regard to penis size. In the nineteenth century the issue of normal penis size was absent, both within medical and popular literature. Doctors did not dwell on the size of the normal penis in inches or centimeters, let alone measure penises in such a manner. Penis size usually comes up with reference to extreme clinical abnormalities. The normal penis seems to be a given, something that doesn't need to be carefully studied, investigated, measured, or talked about. Indeed, in the marriage manuals of the time, every other part of the body but the penis seems subject to such scientific measurement.

The twentieth-century medical and sexological obsession with measuring penis size began in midcentury. In the preface to the 1949 second edition of his book *Human Sex Anatomy*, sex researcher R. L. Dickinson comments on a study of the erect penis: "Very exact measurements on 1,500 white males . . . yield an average penis length of 6 ¼ inches or 16 cm . . . and it corresponds with the 3,500 self measurements obtained by Kinsey" (vi-a). In the 1933 edition, which is reproduced unaltered in the 1949 edition, Dickinson had noted, "Elaborate search of medical and other literature has brought to light no published series of measurements of the erect penis; nor, with one exception, do the few writers who give figures state their sources of information" (73). The sole documented study was conducted in 1899 by Heinrich Loeb in Germany and measured only the size of the flaccid penis for purposes related to administering medicine for treatment of gonorrhea, something totally unrelated to the twentieth-century discourse of sexual norms and penis size. Although the Kinsey Report, as it came to be known, was published in 1948, it did not include the penis-size data to which Dickinson refers.

In 1969, the same year as *Everything You Always Wanted to Know about Sex* was published, William H. Masters and Virginia E. Johnson published *Human Sexual Response*, nearly raising sexology to the level of a media circus. Size plays an important role in the book, but, like Kinsey, Masters and Johnson did not publish their actual data but report that it confirms the average flaccid and erect penis size presented by Dickinson and Loeb. In 1979, a decade after Masters and Johnson's book, *The Kinsey Data* was finally published, marking the first massive public documentation on penis size, which coincides with the rise of the body culture. Suffice it to say, it would not be the last. Indeed, the twentieth century ended with a very important penis-size study, relating to a new context for such measurement: penis enlargement surgery. The study, "Penile Length in the Flaccid and Erect States: Guidelines for Penile Augmentation," by H. Wessells, T. F. Lue, and J. W. McAninch, found that the mean flaccid length was three and a half inches, and the erect length was five and one-tenth inches. Predictably, by the late twentieth century this kind of measurement would be the determinant of whether a patient was a candidate for penis enlargement surgery.

As if Freud and medical science weren't enough, the last decade of the twentieth century gave rise to yet another discourse that placed an enormous
emphasis on penis size: evolutionary biology and its application in the social
sciences and humanities, including psychology. Remarkably, the 1990 publication of Maxine Sheets-Johnstone's *The Roots of Thinking* marked the first book
to address crucial aspects of the evolution of the human penis. Evolutionary
theorists had been oddly silent about the fact that one of the marked distinctions between male chimpanzees and male prehominids and hominids was the
dramatic increase in both the length and girth of the penis, as well as the evolution of a more flexible penis. Sheets-Johnstone argues that female mate selection drove this difference based on pleasure-giving rather than reproductive
criteria. Longer, thicker, more flexible penises enabled different sexual positions
such as face-to-face intercourse, which in turn enabled pleasurable thrusting
with tactile, genital stimulation as well as embracing and touching.

The evolution of the penis, in turn, played a key role in the evolution of
humans. Past attempts to explain the move to standing upright were based on
the utilitarian benefits of being able to see further over the horizon, to hunt and
defend against aggressors, and to the use of hands to carry objects. Sheets-
Johnstone argues, instead, that humans evolved this way so that males could
display their large penises in order to attract females who would choose them
for copulation. Such penile display served also as a dominance signal to intim-
idate other males, similar to the manner in which deer use their antlers. Males
adopted a continual upright position to constantly display the penis to both
females and males—and bigger was always better.

Versions of Sheets-Johnstone's formulation quickly appeared in other
books, including Geoffrey Miller's widely read *The Mating Mind: How Sexual
Choice Shaped the Evolution of Human Nature*. Miller points out that Darwin's
legacy has overemphasized natural selection and all but ignored sexual selection. Sexual selection hinges on male display for the purpose of attracting
females for mating. Bluntly stated, males are on display, and females make their
mating choices based on a number of fitness factors, choosing males with the
best genes to pass on to their offspring for perpetuation of the species. Miller,
in many ways, extends Sheets-Johnstone's argument, tying past evolutionary
behavior to present human behavior. Miller places a great deal of emphasis on
the penis as chimpanzees evolved into humans: "The large male penis is a
product of female choice in evolution. If it were not, males would never have
bothered to evolve such a large, floppy, blood hungry organ. Ancestral females
made males evolve such penises because they liked them" (236). Interestingly,
this comes in a section entitled "Size Mattered" (232). While this, of course, is

a pun on the current popular expression "size matters," it points to an important consideration of all such arguments about penis size in female mate selection: if this account is accurate, was it accurate only at a key moment in the
ancient evolutionary process when prehominids evolved from chimpanzees, or
is it still accurate now? What exactly is the connection between the evolutionary past and the present? If a large penis was a "sexual signal," as Miller terms
such displays, is it still one? And if it still is, is it for the same reason? Does it still
signal the same thing?

These are very complicated questions that get at the heart of the issues
briefly outlined above. It's important to note that Sheets-Johnstone's work and
the work that quickly followed correspond exactly to the emergence of the
body-guy film genre. During the same time that these movies were celebrating
the appearance—or, perhaps more accurately, the return—of the sexually
gifted man of the earth with a penis of seemingly magical powers, these scholars were celebrating the evolutionary importance of the penis in female mate
selection centered around the pleasure-giving capacity of the newly emergent
large penis and the much greater possibilities for lovemaking that it offered. Is
there a relationship between these developments, and if so, what is it?

Although the research of Sheets-Johnstone and Miller, as well as that of others, has significant differences, questions about the central thread of their arguments must be raised in that their work presents a glaring omission: if the penis
is such an important sexual signal in driving evolution, why did it evolve in
such a manner that the flaccid penis is not an accurate indicator of the size of
the erect penis? Miller repeats Sheets-Johnstone's claim that males stood
upright continually so as to display their penises. If female mate selection was
based on the pleasure-giving capacity of the larger penis, and that was the basis
of their choice since bigger was better, why didn't the penis evolve in such a
manner that they knew what they were getting when they looked at the display?
If size was so important, why wasn't there an accurate indicator? The penis,
which is the most important signifier in evolution from chimpanzee to prehominid and hominid is a false signifier: what you see is not what you get.

According to scientific medical data, the correlation between flaccid and
erect size is low—so low in fact that a new dilemma has arisen for urologists:
how do they evaluate potential candidates for penile augmentation surgery to
determine whether they have a true physiological condition or simply a psychological problem? It is a dilemma because simply looking at the patient's
flaccid penis in a clinical setting doesn't tell them what they need to know.
Test after test has concluded that men with very short flaccid penises commonly expand to a full normal erect size. There are now three standards of

measurement: the flaccid penis, the stretched penis, and the erect penis. Clinical stretching refers to a doctor measuring the flaccid penis after fully stretching it out. In clinical tests, erections are induced with the administration of drugs and then measured. The stretched penis, while somewhat smaller than a full erection, enables the physician to accurately estimate the erect size. The flaccid penis is clinically unreliable for that purpose, and most studies now recommend using stretched size to make a determination.

So the human penis has evolved in such a manner that urologists with special training and diagnostic skills cannot accurately estimate its erect size from looking at it flaccid. Where does this leave our hominid female ancestors, who were not even "pre-med," lusting after the pleasures of the big penis? And a second related question arises here: why did the penis evolve in ways that are dramatically different visually? In the words of Alex Comfort, author of *The Joy of Sex*, some men have flaccid penises that "reveal no penile shaft at all, but extend to full size equally" (90–91). Other men have a long shaft. The former have short penises that rest entirely above their scrotum while the latter have long penises that hang down in front of their scrotum. This distinction becomes important as we analyze the significance of representations of the penis, including within the body-guy genre. These representations rigorously exclude men who "reveal no penile shaft at all" before erection but always, instead, show men with prominently dangling penises. Significantly, *The Joy of Sex* itself fits this very pattern in that all the illustrations conform to such penises even as the text stresses the normalcy of the alternative that shows no shaft.

It seems Miller has made some scientific errors here. At one point, he cynically urges the reader to forget the "nonsense" of poststructuralists like Michel Foucault and go to the zoo, where we can learn much more about bodies. Using his logic, we urge him to return to the locker room where he might observe that it is not true that all human males evolved large, floppy organs. Some human males have large floppy organs, but others have short organs that do not hang, flop, or do anything as dramatic as Miller presumes this flopping spectacle to be. Nor can he explain this by claiming that some men are small, or it would not be a meaningful choice for mate selection. Our point is precisely that those men are not "small" in the usual way the word is used with negative connotations but, rather, that their penises have just evolved in a different manner in terms of visual display. Indeed, since Miller's claims about the importance of penis size are 100 percent contingent on the alleged stimulus from penetration during copulation, only erect size is of significance, and his hegemonic large, floppy fantasy does not correspond to anything real about how the penis has evolved in that regard. There are other things for penises to do besides flop.

STANDARDIZING "GOOD" SEXUAL PERFORMANCE
AND THE "NORMAL" PENIS

The phrase "size matters" has permeated American culture, including advertising and media, to the point of banality. Despite his clever punning variation "Size Mattered," implying it was indisputable in the distant evolutionary past, Geoffrey Miller falls into a trap of his own devising. He argues that the oft-noted mismatch between men who easily achieve orgasm and women who do not makes perfect sense within his theory of sexual selection. If it were easy for men to give women orgasms, then the ability to do so would be useless as a fitness indicator. It is only because it is difficult that men with the right genes can demonstrate their fitness by performing well enough to bring their partners to orgasm. Miller assumes that women have orgasms "when an attractive man provides a lot of foreplay and deep, slow copulatory thrusting" (240). At one point, Miller highlights the fact that he has no use for bringing ideology into his work, which is ironic in that he is totally unaware of the manner in which he is bound to that old unscientific figure of the early twentieth century, Dr. Sigmund Freud. Freud overvalued the penis in his psychoanalytic theories in a manner parallel to Miller's overvaluation of it in his scientific account of the relation of evolution to current human behavior. Indeed, it's amusing how Miller's formula for female orgasms seems to answer Freud's famous question, "What do women want?" Handsome men, lots of foreplay, and deep, slow thrusting.

Miller creates a false opposition between the "nonsense" of poststructuralists and the presumed objective observation of scientists. Susan Bordo succinctly summarizes the problem of this false dichotomy in a chapter aptly titled "Does Size Matter?" She is sophisticated enough to realize that merely asking women about whether size matters is inadequate, because even if they do have a preference, it may be based on much more than physiology:

> We don't have to choose between physiology and fantasy. In fact we do so at peril of radically misunderstanding the *kind* of physiology we have—one that is tremendously suggestive to the "cultural superstructure" of ideas, associations, images. . . . Whatever our nerve endings, orgasm and sexual excitement are never simply a matter of touching the right buttons. . . . A lot may depend on just *what* you imagine you have inside you. We could thus poll a hundred people, gay or straight, and probably get a pretty wide range of answers to the question of whether or not size matters to pleasure. Some preferences would undoubtedly reflect differences in anatomy and physiology. None of them, however, would be describing a "purely" physiological or anatomical set of facts. (30)

How can we simply trust as accurate women who report that they need a good-sized deep-thrusting penis that lasts for a long time for orgasmic bliss when for decades now this has been the overwhelming cultural and media message to them? The body-guy genre and its intensely romanticized hero is an important part of that highly suggestive culture-generated and media-circulated fantasy. The close-to-the-earth working-class man who awakens and then fulfills intense sexual desires in women has a suggestive power that shapes desires and responses in actual lives. In short, the fantasy becomes a self-fulfilling prophecy.

We're encouraged to accept one model of penis, lover, and sexual perform-ance as the right one, but what about those who are excluded from the range of possibilities that could fuel fantasies? Clearly in 1506, the biblical David, who slew the giant Goliath with a slingshot, had what it took to be a body guy. But as the frantic Italian art historians and the giggling hordes of Bermuda shorts–clad tourists in Las Vegas indicate, his penis is too small for him to fulfill the role of the body guy today; he no longer has what it takes. Similar to Geoffrey Miller, the art historians seem to presume that human males have large, floppy penises. They show the same bizarre belief in one norm for determining what a "nor-mal" penis looks like, and, clearly for them, how long it is and how much of the shaft it displays is crucial. But it never occurs to them that this expectation is really about what they are used to seeing in paintings, sculptures, and photo-graphs, and how they've been influenced by twentieth-century medical studies of penile measurements. Remarkably, it also never occurs to them that the real question is about representational practices rather than actual penises. The world is full of men who are regularly much smaller than David without having "contracted" out of fear and in preparation to do battle with a giant.

Dominant culture believes that only certain kinds of penises can bear the burden of representing masculinity and male sexuality. Such beliefs, however, negatively limit our ideas about desirable masculinity and sexual performance. A single norm such as the "large floppy penis" or the six-inch erection is the genital equivalent of the elevation of the body guy in current media narratives: a representational strategy highly invested in maintaining a belief in the impor-tance and near magical powers of one type of man and penis, neither of which in reality possess the power representation attributes to them. The two are strongly linked in several ways. The body guy's stellar sexual performance is penile-centered in a manner close to that envisioned by Miller.

The body-guy films have a telling feature: they inordinately display the hero's penis, explicitly demonstrating the belief that his special powers are in some ways tied to it. We have just demonstrated that this phenomenon must be seen within a larger historical context. Indeed, the penis is so important to the genre that even when we don't see the body guy's penis, it's displaced onto another character or onto a male nude in a work of art such as in *Two Moon Junction*, *Sideways*, and *Asylum*. One way or another, penises abound within the genre. And in some films, owing to the requirements of the rating system, instead of seeing the penis, we see the body guy's sexual performance, which is always tied to the sustained thrusting intercourse that Miller claims is necessary for all women's orgasms.

But the body guys can't just have any penis, and the exceptions prove the rule. Body-guy penises conform to or exceed the four-inch medical norm, dangling prominently in front of the scrotum, displaying the shaft. The few exceptions of men who are noticeably shorter or smaller than this norm are characters whose masculinity is marked as disturbed, as, for example, in the psychotic violent manner of *Twentynine Palms*. Normative masculinity is tied to the normative penis.

Urologists acknowledge that men with short, fully above-the-scrotum penises are normal, and we would all agree those are not large floppy organs. There is nothing wrong with those men. The problem is with singular notions of what a flaccid penis is. The same is true with Michelangelo's David. The art historians were in a near panic to explain how, because of fear of battle with a giant, he could be considered normal even though he was only about two and four-tenths to two and eight-tenths inches. In fact, two and eight-tenths inches is nearly double the size of some of the normal men in a recent urological study who were measured several times, presumably far from the battlefield (Shamloul). In that study, a number of men who were only one and six-tenths inches flaccid were considered "normal." Indeed, this study tells us in medical terms what anyone would see in our suggested visit to the locker room. Even if David had a one-and-one-half-inch penis that rested entirely above his scrotum, showing just a head and no shaft, there would be nothing to explain. We only think something is wrong because we expect to see something that conforms to a norm. The real question is why aren't there more, not less, men with one-and-a-half-inch penises in the world of art, photography, and movies, because such men are everywhere in life?

CHALLENGING THE FLOPPY NORM AND DEEP THRUSTING

In the animal world, much male display is about change and action as opposed to static ornamentation. The famous peacock feathers to which Miller repeatedly refers are a perfect example. As anyone who has followed Miller's advice and visited a zoo knows, the moment that the tail opens up and spreads out in front of our eyes is the most dramatic and visually arresting moment. Might there be a similarly impressive moment in watching a one-and-one-half-inch penis expand to five or six inches, more than tripling in size, in comparison to watching a four-inch penis similarly expand by only increasing half as much or less to the same five or six inches? When Miller refers to the fact that chimpanzees have a one-inch penis, he conveniently forgets to mention that they do not expand in the manner that most humans with a penis that size do. Alex Comfort, as we mentioned, notes that men with a penis that shows no shaft before erection easily expand to equal the size of men who display their shaft, an observation borne out by extensive scientific documentation. In current language, some men are grow-ers not show-ers. In other words, there is no comparison between a man with a one-and-one-half-inch penis and a chimpanzee, even if the length of their flaccid penises is similar.

Second, if one focuses on male genital display, there is something other than the penis on display: the scrotum. Men who show little or no shaft before erection are not all on the side of deficit: their short penises enable a much more prominent display of their scrotum, which can also be big and, within common terminology, impressive. Indeed in 2001, Joann Ellison Rodgers directly challenged the Miller line of reasoning. She claims that despite what many women think, "studies incontrovertibly confirm that female pleasure is *independent* of penis length or circumference" (99, emphasis added). She goes on to argue that the size of a man's testicles, however, do provide an estimate of sex drive since they produce key male sex hormones. Remarkably, Rodgers fully agrees with Miller that female mate choice drove evolution, but with an entirely different conclusion: "And succinctly if rudely put, females selected the men with biggest balls because that meant they would get relatively, albeit, probably unnecessarily, more sexual stimulation and pleasure" (99). It is also possible that the proportionality and symmetry of the penis and scrotum, as well as their relation to the groin area, have a total visual appeal. In contemporary language, maybe the female making her mating choice evaluates the package, not the penis or the scrotum in isolation.[1]

Gary Taylor also considers the issue of the penis in relation to the scrotum but from a cultural rather than evolutionary perspective. In his remarkable book, *Castration: An Abbreviated History of Western Manhood*, he shows that beginning in the twentieth century, a profound shift took place in the meaning of castration. Prior to that, the word meant cutting off the testicles, but in the twentieth century it shifted to cutting off the penis. This shift relates directly to Freud and the newfound importance that the penis and castration anxiety played in his psychoanalytic theories that, in turn, can only be understood in relation to the historical shift in population from the countryside to the city, a shift that we also think is crucial to understanding the appeal of D. H. Lawrence's gamekeeper in *Lady Chatterley's Lover*, as well as the emergence of the body-guy film genre later in the century. The Freudian emphasis on the now all-important penis and the romanticizing of the man of the earth as the supremely gifted lover with a pleasure-inducing penis is directly related to industrialization—the loss of the connection to agrarian, rural life. Versions of Freud's account of castration in the psychoanalytic development of boys and girls have so widely permeated Western culture that even people who have never read a word of his writings link it to the fearful spectacle of the castrating woman cutting off a man's penis, the biggest dread of all. Yet Taylor points out that Freud could only think of castration this way because he was far removed from its dominant previous meaning within rural culture: cutting off livestock testicles. It had nothing to do with the penis.

Indeed, historically, the same was true of human castration, which centered on removing the testicles of boys so that they would become eunuchs for various reasons, including being trusted by powerful men around their women in court and singing with voices that were unchanged by puberty. Taylor points out that the actual dimensions of men's penises between Michelangelo's time and our time could not have changed significantly. Instead, he argues that Michelangelo lived at a time when the scrotum was the focus, not the penis, and, indeed, if one looks at the scrotum from that perspective, the shorter penis foregrounds the prominent scrotum. Taylor documents through extensive analysis of literature and art that the scrotum, not the penis, was the centerpiece of defining male sexuality. In the vernacular, a good set of balls was of more importance than what in the twentieth century would be known as "the big dick." Penis size did not matter; the testicles and scrotum did.

Contemporary viewers, however, expect the flaccid penis to hang at least to the bottom of the scrotum, if not further. The criteria have shifted for evaluating how male genitalia define proper, desirable masculinity and sexuality. But the penis can be evaluated and judged in a manner quite different from Miller's. He privileges one aspect of penis size in an overly insistent manner, indeed, in a manner inconsistent with the complex realities of penis size. In this regard, Miller's errors and blind spots resonate within the ideology of the body-guy narratives and with how the penis is represented in films, media, and the arts. Miller fails to recognize one of the central features of the evolutionary model he employs. Yes, there was a significant and important increase in penis size as hominids evolved from chimpanzees; yes, this is tied to female sexual pleasure and mate selection; and yes, if females had not continually made choices in favor of bigger, more flexible penises, this evolution would not have occurred. But once it did occur, it was over. It's over in several senses. First and foremost, the hominid penis evolved in such a manner that nearly all hominids and humans were big enough to give females the pleasure afforded through the new copulatory model. Aside from rare medical abnormalities such as micropenis, all men are now in the range of the evolved bigger penis that can bring women to orgasm, if in fact those women want or are responsive to penetration for their orgasmic pleasure.

In other words, as a species, all males now possess a much bigger, more flexible, penis than all chimpanzees. The reason for the growth and change is over. It is not part of a never-ending process moving further and further along toward more gloriously bigger penises, except in the minds of those caught up within the cultural obsession with big penises, including some filmmakers and scientists. The display of a big penis was important when females were evolving away from chimpanzees, but it is no longer important in a way that is even similar to that prehistoric context. It is also worth noting that evolutionary display is tied to novelty, and in the late twentieth and early twenty-first centuries, the display of a big penis is anything but novel; indeed, the search for novelty may very well lead us away from it.

And with the beginning of culture everything changed in yet another dramatic manner. The male genitals were covered rather than displayed, and representations and cultural discourses began to shape and determine human response in complex, historically shifting ways. Again, Miller's arrogant assumption that writers like Foucault and his historical, cultural theories are all nonsense and we can learn more from a visit to the zoo blinds him to the manner in which the media-saturated contemporary world plays a significant role in perpetuating certain ways of looking at and thinking about the penis and scrotum, as well as styles of lovemaking and the men who hold out the promise of fulfilling women sexually.

As for Miller's assumption about good sexual performance, he is talking about contemporary men and women, not prehominid or early hominid males and females. And he presumes that there is one single model of sexual performance that works for all women and will bring them to orgasm. The three things that all women need are an attractive man, lots of foreplay, and deep, slow thrusting. This is presumptuous in the worst and most literal sense of the word. The term *deep* speaks for itself, of course, and goes back to Miller's insistence on the importance of long penises. It never seems to occur to him that penetration of any kind, deep or otherwise, may have little or nothing to do with what some women want or need for an orgasm. Penetration may be something in which they engage for their partner's pleasure rather than their own. For other women, deep thrusting is uncomfortable and even painful, especially when it is done by a big penis. And why should all women have orgasms with the same speed when being penetrated by these perfect penises? For that matter, why should they all prefer lots of foreplay?

For some women a little foreplay may be desirable; for others a lot of fore-play may be boring. And who and what determines what makes a man attrac-tive? This one-size-fits-all mentality is a male fantasy of what constitutes female pleasure, and it is a total ideological product of the late twentieth century—the exact same ideology that produced the body-guy narratives, with their notions of precisely this kind of lover: handsome, savvy to the needs of women, and a masterful control of deep thrusting that ordinary men, including mind-guy lovers, lack. In fact when reading Miller's highly prescriptive account of what women need for orgasm, we hear echoes of Zalman King speaking with us about body guys; King and Miller have almost identical views on the kind of sex women need for orgasmic pleasure. Miller's fantasy isn't just obsessively focused on his idea of what all women want and need for their pleasure, but it is also like that of the filmmakers lost in a romantic revelry about men close to the earth who magically perceive, awaken, and then fulfill the sexual desires of women whose successful, educated lovers are clueless.

The clueless, educated mind guys in the mind-guy / body-guy genre could, of course, be represented as sexy, creative lovers. Miller himself acknowledges this in relation to evolution, but he turns out to be another champion of missed opportunities. Miller devotes entire chapters of his book to arguing that the development of the intellect in all its manifestations from art to science was driven by male evolutionary display, men showing off their mental and moral fitness to women who would select them as their sexual partners to pass on their genes. Nevertheless, at the precise moment in time when the penis is no longer necessary for anything, including procreation, he heroically strives to make it the centerpiece of orgasmic female pleasure, overlooking the implica-tions of his own observation that human evolution has, in fact, been focused on the mind, not the body. It is odd therefore that for him, sexual pleasure and orgasm remain centered on the big penis and fitness as demonstrated in inter-course. Of equal importance to us is Miller's stunning admission that "during human evolution sexual selection shifted its primary target from body to mind" (10). Is he consistent with his own observation in outlining human sex-ual behavior? And if Miller is right, why have movies and popular culture resis-ted the shift from body to mind, making the mind guy an unappealing figure of sexual incompetence in comparison to the potent sexual allure of the body guy?

To be sure, Miller grants that the brain and intelligence can rival the penis and sexual fitness as the basis of female mate selection, but why not think of sexual pleasure as evolving new avenues opened up by the evolved mind? Rather than seeing one as compensating for the other, why not expand our repertoire of models of orgasmic pleasure in ways unimaginable either in a long-ago evolutionary past or even a more recent historical past when the demands of procreation restricted the range of sexual activity for many? The sex lives of many people in many parts of the world today are devoted to pleasure rather than reproduction, yet Miller privileges a certain kind of penis and thrusting technique that he thinks evolved to make reproductive sex pleasurable and to enable females to evaluate their partner's fitness.

RETHINKING THE "NORMAL" PENIS

Even if one accepts the notion that some men will be good lovers and some bad lovers separate from their partners (and we don't), why would we think that looking at their penis size would tell us which is which? And even if we thought penis size would tell us about the quality of a man's lovemaking, why do we put so much emphasis on the size of a flaccid penis since there is little correlation between flaccid and erect sizes? In short, there is something wrong with this picture. And we mean *picture*.

In chapter 3 we discussed *Fur*, a film with images of a man whose penis rests above the scrotum with just the head visible (figure 13)—a sight seldom seen in films. The character is totally comfortable with his nudity, and his penis size and shape actually mark the female protagonist's entry into a world of sexual and creative liberation. We turn now to three other examples of such men with totally above-the-scrotum penises: two from the Internet and one from the world of art photography. A number of Internet sites celebrate public nudity in a variety of locales, such as nude beaches, naturist resorts, the annual Naked Mile Run at the University of Michigan (begun in 1986), and gay pride parades. Such public nudity events are reminiscent of the defiant counterculture of the late 1960s and 1970s. In a photo of a Naturist Society gathering a young, attractive man stands nude and appears entirely comfortable (figure 24). His penis conforms exactly to what we have described as one that shows no shaft before erection and rests entirely above the scrotum; it does not hang down. This is precisely the kind of man normally excluded from representation, not just in movies but also in art, photography, and even medical illustrations, including those with multiple images that claim to show a range of "normal" penises. Indeed, based on the history of representation, one would hardly know that men with such penises exist, let alone are quite ordinary and certainly normal. These men are not chosen by directors for acting roles that emphasize frontal male nudity or by photographers and artists as their nude models, and their images are not published by editors.

Figure 25 shows the same man in a public setting, this time with two women and another man, all of whom are naked with a large crowd behind them (figure 25). The same man from the naturist meeting stands at the left, smiling

Figure 24. Speaker at a nudist gathering (anonymous photograph)

and once again appearing totally comfortable. His genitals look almost identical in both photographs, indicating that he was not nervous or cold in the previous image—this is his normal resting state, showing no shaft, the head protruding rather than the penis dangling. He is clearly much smaller than David's two and four-tenths to two and eight-tenths inches so carefully calculated by our art historians, but there is no evidence that he is terrified from the prospect of doing battle with a giant. On the contrary, he's having a good time. And so are the three other people with him, all of whom are smiling. As the "Clinton" campaign sign in the photo shows, this event takes place in the era when the body-guy genre became popular, ironically underscoring the absurdity of affirming the body guy's masculinity as the privileged, desirable one. There is a social, communal aspect to this picture that shows this man happily integrated with his group. There is no hint that anything about him is deficient, that he lacks anything or need be ashamed or humiliated. Yet we do not see men like him in mainstream representations, implying that he cannot be the representative of proper masculinity, virility, and sexuality like the body guys of the then-emerging genre.

Figure 25. Nudists at a public rally (anonymous photograph)

Figure 26 comes from the same public nudity Web site with a series of photos devoted to a gay pride dance (figure 26). We chose this image because, once
again, the man in the center conforms to the repressed image we have identified: his flaccid penis shows very little shaft and rests above his scrotum, which
is prominently displayed. And once again, he is attractive and seems completely at ease. Indeed, he stands next to a man on the right who fully conforms
to the ideal norm of representation. Their proximity to each other creates a
striking contrast. Yet all the men seem entirely at ease with their bodies and
each other and nonjudgmental about their differences. This image also flies in
the face of stereotypes about gay men and the alleged emphasis they place on
size. In this social setting, this man is comfortably integrated within the group.
Their difference is primarily noticeable because the smaller man in the middle
is usually not represented. But their difference actually signifies nothing.
Indeed, such discourses as penis-size jokes and medical measurements actually
create the significance of the difference.

Penis-size jokes ask us to laugh at small men, but what exactly is a small
penis? What are we laughing at? None of the men whose penises show little or
no shaft in the above images have what we consider a small penis in the pejora-
tive sense of the word. Clearly, if one uses a ruler and thinks of the medical
norm of four inches or even a range of two and three-quarters to four inches,
they are strikingly smaller. But these perfectly ordinary men (and others just
like them present in nearly all the group photos on the naturist and public

Figure 26. Nude men at the Toronto Gay Pride Dance, 2002 (anonymous photograph)

nudity sites, including three at this one dance) clearly also lie outside the so-called normal range of penises as measured in inches or as illustrated in medical texts. Just as noticeably, they lie outside the normal range of images in art. But this tells us nothing about these men and everything about these norms: they are constructed and enforced, indeed policed, in the service of an impressive masculinity that connotes power and virility, and also flaunts the one thing contemporary Western culture still believes men have that women don't.

In contrast to the above snapshots that capture a moment at social gatherings, figure 27 shows a male model with a strikingly similar above the scrotum penis that shows no shaft before erection. The model is posing for Robert Flynt, perhaps the most important photographer working on the male nude today. Flynt constructs profoundly complex and ambiguous images about masculinity that frequently include nudes along with various cultural grids, representations, and artifacts such as charts of scientific measurements, classical sculptures, and found photographs loaded with specific meanings both historical and cultural. Flynt's work often minimizes the traditional normative display of the penis as spectacle, and one way he accomplishes this is by using a variety of models with differing body types. His works are multilayered, so the image

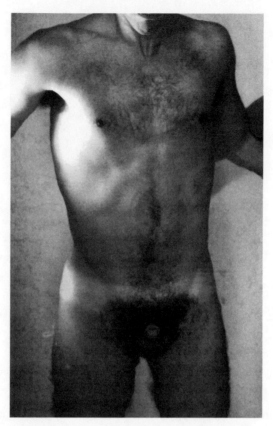

Figure 27. Detail from the base layer of photomontage (Robert Flynt, 1990)

presented here is simply a building block (see Lehman 223 and robertflynt.com for the finished image and a discussion), but it is a very important one in that Flynt is open and responsive to underrepresented aspects of the male body, such as fluidity, roundness, softness, and gracefulness, offering a possibility for new forms of beauty, sexuality, and eroticism to emerge. Flynt is far removed from the anonymous photographers of the public nudity events, but the men of our analysis could easily be models in one of Flynt's groundbreaking photographs, and that connection is profound since it shows the need to acknowledge such men both in the world of art and in the world at large.

   Kinsey (Bill Condon, 2004) is a film that provides a mature representation of a character with a small penis. The biopic-style film tells the story of the well-known twentieth-century sex researcher Alfred Kinsey (Liam Neeson). In the scene with frontal nudity, Kinsey's assistant, Clyde Martin (Peter Sarsgaard),

Figure 28. *Kinsey*

disrobes to sexually arouse Kinsey in a hotel room the two share on a business trip, revealing a shorter than average flaccid penis (figure 28).[2] Indeed, he succeeds in seducing the bisexual Kinsey. Sarsgaard's penis directly challenges cultural assumptions about the desirability of the big penis, in that early in the film we see Kinsey and his newlywed wife visit a doctor to discuss their sexual problems, whereupon they learn that Kinsey's large penis is the source of her pain and their difficulties. The doctor asks Kinsey how large his erect penis is— "how long from the scrotum"—and holds up an eight-inch ruler. The doctor points to the three-inch mark and asks, "Here?" When the Kinsey's do not respond, he moves his finger to the five-inch mark. When they still do not respond, he moves his finger close to the eight-inch mark, at which time Mrs. Kinsey points to an area off the ruler at what would be about the nine-inch mark. The doctor then says it's a wonder she didn't pass out. He initially assumes that the problem is caused either by an abnormally small three-inch erect penis or a five-inch erection, which lies at the very low end of the normal range, as if he cannot imagine that an average or large penis could be the cause of such a sexual problem.

Sarsgaard's flaccid penis, on the other hand, is not only noticeably smaller than the four-inch normative flaccid penis of medical measurement but also of representation. He is at the far extreme of Kinsey, who is unusually well endowed, yet his character is highly sexual and attractive, seducing both Kinsey and later his wife. He in fact turns out to be bisexual, like Kinsey, but his small penis does not mark him as deficient, unattractive, or pejoratively deviant. Indeed, he is marked as confident in that during his seduction of Kinsey he never projects a sense of embarrassment about his body or that he will fail in his seduction—which he doesn't! He is self-assured throughout.

THE RADICAL POTENTIAL OF THE ABOVE-THE-SCROTUM PENIS

Much is at stake here. Consider the widespread use of the term *well-hung*, to characterize ideal masculinity, and related language such as "How's it hanging?" In 2009 HBO premiered a TV show titled *Hung*. Why do we want to see that four-inch hanging norm—the "big floppy organ"—so strongly that we exclude so many men? What comfort does that visual spectacle offer? What's our hang-up about hanging?

The norm underpins masculinity in at least four ways. It makes a visual spectacle of the penis, presents a flaccid penis that closely resembles an erection, clearly differentiates the fully developed adult penis from that of the undeveloped child, and demarcates male from female. Above-the-scrotum penises that reveal no shaft threaten all four functions and, in doing so, reveal the desperate cultural need to pin so much power and importance on what is always comparatively a small and perilous organ. A very short penis that is nestled in or slightly protrudes from the pubic hair does not provide a spectacle. In a sense, there is little to see. The normative penis not only dangles prominently but also closely resembles the culturally valorized erection: it gets bigger, harder, and changes positions but the erection resembles the resting state. The normative flaccid penis of representation is an advertisement for its intended sexual use—penetrating a woman's vagina. The very short above-the-scrotum penis that reveals just a head does not resemble what it will be like erect, and we are not just talking about size. The shape of such a penis is primarily all head and no shaft and is not long and straight. When it becomes erect it will be mostly shaft with a much smaller head. Observing it in its flaccid state does not in any way suggest penetration; it is short and round. Thus, one of the primary functions of the invisible norm is to always present the flaccid penis as a spectacle that closely resembles the allegedly powerful, desirable erection necessary for female pleasure.

But that spectacle has an even more basic function. The normative penis not only supplies a spectacle that resembles an erection, but it also clearly displays the cultural imperative to distinguish boy from man and male from female. In the late 1960s, during the streaking era, conservative radio talk-show host Paul Harvey reported on a public event as follows: two women streaked the event and were taken into custody by the police. When they were booked at the police station, authorities discovered one was a man. Harvey followed the report with a characteristic, "Page three," indicating the story was self-explanatory and that he was moving on to the next one. In the late 1960s many men wore long hair, and it was a common complaint among conservatives and older people that they couldn't tell men from women. In a streaking context, for example, this was true even in the nude, where a man with a short, above-the-scrotum penis and long hair could easily be mistaken for a woman. An impressive spectacle would, of course, reduce the likelihood of such an error. Harvey's manner of reporting the story was meant as the ultimate humiliation for that man and even for the woman with him—there was no need for comment. A naked man being mistaken for a woman was the ultimate humiliation.

Similarly, standard sex-education books for children such as Peter Mayle's "What's Happening to Me?" commonly illustrate normal male sexual development with a series of images of a naked, standing boy maturing from childhood into adulthood. In each image his penis gets longer and hangs further down until in the last one it reaches the bottom of his scrotum or hangs below it—the normative hanging penis showing proof of fully developed manhood. What's Happening to Me is unpaginated, but the page in question appears opposite a page entitled "Boy's Guide," and it shows five images of a boy with his age written above each one, progressing from a picture labeled eight to ten years old to one labeled seventeen to eighteen years of age. The eight-to-ten-year-old boy has a very small penis, showing little shaft, but by the time he is fifteen to sixteen years old his long, thick penis dangles down with the tip reaching the bottom of the scrotum, and in the final seventeen-to-eighteen-year-old image it has grown noticeably thicker and longer, the tip extending below the bottom of the scrotum. The books shows that even a boy who starts out with a small penis revealing little shaft will progressively develop and that when he is fully developed he will display a long impressive penis, in marked contrast to one that is above the scrotum. The all-important visual images in this book and others like it, in other words, lead all boys to expect they will develop such a penis and that they will do so in a precisely regulated manner. Likewise, all girls are taught to expect to see such a penis when they are grown and sexually active, acknowledged by the fact that girls are included in the drawing, looking upward at the images of the maturing boys. Implicitly, short, above-the-scrotum penises appear childlike or not fully developed.

Terry McMillan articulates this assumed distinction between the childlike and fully developed adult penis in an extraordinarily explicit passage in her novel How Stella Got Her Groove Back. Recalling conversations and memories about the big penises of Jamaican men, Stella then remembers a related incident with her son as he is reaching puberty. She notices hair on various parts of his body and wonders about his penis:

> I asked if I could see an example [of bodily hair] and he said no way and I said please you don't have to show me your *unit* although I did want to see if he was going to be as *lucky* as his daddy. . . . Then I heard him say well I'll

only show you the top part and I was suddenly in shock because first of all showing me the "top" meant there was something *separate and apart* from the "bottom." . . . When he was little it all seemed to be *in one little cluster* but now there was a top and a bottom . . . and I heard myself ask How big is your little unit now? (47, emphases added)

Here a mother literally thrills at the realization that her son's penis has a top that is separate from the bottom, and she opposes this sign of development to the childlike package of the small above-the-scrotum penis that reveals everything at once. She also emphasizes "the unit" (the penis) to the point of totally excluding the scrotum, even implanting the importance of size in her son's mind by asking him how big his is. Developing into a man (and if he is "lucky," a big man like his father) is totally tied to a penis that develops and displays itself a certain way: a top totally separate and apart from a bottom.

Within such a context it is no exaggeration to say that some adolescent boys undergo a psychological process analogous to Freud's description of how little girls develop penis envy. If their penis does not grow in the normative manner as they mature during adolescence and they have a short above-the-scrotum penis, they may find themselves in locker rooms surrounded by their peers who have "strikingly visible" penises of "large proportions" in relation to their "small inconspicuous organ." We have carefully chosen the term "above-the-scrotum penis" to precisely emphasize that when looking at such men, one cannot separate the penis from the scrotum; it is indeed one cluster. But we interpret that much differently than either the character Stella or author Terry McMillan, who valorizes big penises throughout the novel. When above-the-scrotum penises appear in representation, they often incite disparaging remarks or laughter, making penises like that abject. The actual reason to repress such men from representation, however, is that far from being inadequate, their penises reveal a truth about all penises: they are all comparatively small and insignificant, just inches away from retracting and disappearing from sight. Woody Allen's joke of being the only man he knows with penis envy not withstanding, men with small penises do not necessarily suffer from penis envy. Nor do they have to become hypermasculine or in some manner overcompensate for their supposed deficiency, or become losers with low self-esteem. They can use their perceived difference to reject the "superior" status of the norm and find alternative definitions of masculinity and sexuality.

It is thus the ultimate irony to refer to the normative penis as the invisible norm of representation since the function of the norm is to guarantee that the penis is, indeed, always strikingly visible and fully on display (what we have called throughout this book, a good-sized penis). In a sense much of the history of the representation of the penis betrays a kind of penis envy; it is a history of policing to ensure that small, above-the-scrotum penises are excluded. Artists, editors, and casting directors all seem to embrace, perhaps at times unconsciously, the Freudian psychodynamics of the strikingly visible penis of large proportions on the assumption that it is indeed superior to a small, inconspicuous penis. Penises are usually large and larger. Pornography nearly always makes that clear. The exclusion from visual representation occurs at the other pole: it is difficult, indeed, to find the men who are "hung like an acorn," despite the fact that Alex Comfort assures us in writing of their normalcy and Howard Stern proclaims to the world over the radio that he is one of them. Men whose penises do not conform to the cherished norm can use that difference to question and redefine the norm rather than envy and emulate it. So, too, can artists stop honoring the plentitude of the striking visual spectacle of the big penis through endless repetition. They can represent such difference to empower alternatives.

Art historians can learn much from Gary Taylor. Do we have any reason to believe that Florentines in 1506 stood around wondering why David was so poorly endowed? Or might they have accepted his "package" as perfectly normal, indeed attractive and impressive, requiring no explanation? For Miller, this would require returning from the zoo to the library, but it is a trip we highly recommend because the real questions underlying both the early twentieth-century emergence of the body guy à la the gamekeeper in Lawrence's *Lady Chatterley's Lover* and his reemergence in the latter part of the century in such movies as *The Piano* and *Legends of the Fall* cannot be separated from the nonstop medical and scientific discourses about the importance of the penis that have defined and redefined the twentieth century: Freud's emphasis on the penis, castration, and the phallus in understanding psychoanalytic development; the midcentury medical and scientific measuring of the penis in an effort to define what is "normal" in this all-important sexual organ; and finally the fixation on the role of the evolution of the large human penis as a way of understanding current human behavior and sexual practice. All these medical-scientific discourses share something in common: they make the penis the central aspect of their subject, be it psychoanalytic development, sexual pleasure (the question of the century), or even the origins of modern humans.

One cannot exaggerate the stakes. For Freud the foundations of psychoanalytic development for both men and women revolved around the penis (having it, not having it, fear of losing it, envying it); for the popular sexology movement and within the medical profession penis size was measured and remeasured flaccid, stretched, erect, both by the subjects themselves and by medical professionals; and for evolutionary biologists the penis became the speciating event between chimpanzees and hominids and the foundation of all human culture as hominids stood up to display what they had for females. How can Geoffrey Miller begin the twenty-first century without a trace of irony about the similarity between the prominent place he gives the penis in relating the evolutionary past to the present and the place that Freud, one of his unscientific enemies, gave it at the beginning of the previous century? Only by ignoring the entire issue of discourse shaped by ideology.

We believe there is much value in psychoanalytic theory, empirical medical studies about the penis, and in evolutionary accounts of how male genitalia evolved from the chimpanzee to the human male. Like all science, none of this is outside ideology: the twentieth century *was* the century of the penis. Clearly all these things are intertwined: were it not for the medical and sexology movements' preoccupation with measuring and determining normal penis size, we wouldn't have art historians running off and doing the same thing with statues. Without Freud we wouldn't have the modern era and D. H. Lawrence and his ilk challenging the Victorian silence on sex, the body, and the penis in "serious" literature as opposed to "pornography." Is it pure coincidence that our art historians are driven by the same notion of the penis that drives Geoffrey Miller's work: large and floppy or there must be something wrong with it—there must be some explanation for it? They all sound uncannily alike. And the return of the body guy in movies of the late twentieth century is accompanied by precisely the valuation and display of this kind of penis and the sustained, thrusting sexual performance style described and prescribed by Miller for female orgasm as if he was the evolved lover of our narrative imaginations.

REAL-SEX FILMS: THE BIG PENIS REIFIED OR REJECTED?

Given the emphasis on the penis and penetration sex in the body-guy films, perhaps it was inevitable that the desire to see the penis in action would lead to a new group of international films that we call "real-sex" films, including *Romance* (France, 1999), *9 Songs* (England, 2004), *Lie with Me* (Canada, 2005), and *Shortbus* (U.S., 2006). Several of these films, including *9 Songs* and *Shortbus*, have won critical acclaim, and Catherine Breillat, who directed *Romance* and several other "real-sex" films, is now recognized as a major director. Traditionally, "real sex" was the exclusive domain of hardcore pornography, the element that distinguished it from soft-core porn: films were hardcore if the actors actually "did it;" soft-core if the sex was simulated. Seeing the penis in action supplied the crucial distinction. Within this frame of thinking there was a clear-cut distinction between "art" or "entertainment" and hardcore porn. Not so in the above films and others like them.

Figure 29. *9 Songs*

9 Songs highlights several of the key assumptions in this new subgenre of films. The film tells the story of Matt (Kieran O'Brien) and Lisa (Margo Stilley), two lovers who meet at a rock concert and spend a summer together. We see them attend the nine rock concerts from which the film takes its title, and much of the rest of the time we see them at home making love. Since the rock concerts appear to be documentary footage from actual concerts, a heightened reality effect is cast over the entire film. The reality of the sex scenes is demonstrated around the penis, which is frequently on display and which we see "in action" to verify the film's sexual authenticity. We see Matt receive oral sex from Lisa, and we see him penetrate her during intercourse. There is much nudity emphasizing Matt's strikingly large penis, including for example a medium close-up where it lies on his belly with the tip almost reaching his navel before Lisa begins oral sex (figure 29).

Shortbus interweaves the stories of a number of young people who frequent a sex club in Manhattan named Shortbus, after the little bus that takes challenged and gifted students to school—in contrast to the big yellow bus that carries "normal" students. *Shortbus* is a world of big penises and bigger penises. Indeed, the entire film begins with a man so large that he is able to fellate himself. The film focuses on three gay men who at one point are all seen erect in a sexual threesome, a scene that is central to the film's "real-sex" status. Throughout the film, however, there are many shots of both of the men in the main gay couple (James and Jamie) flaccid. All the men are strikingly large, both flaccid and erect. There are also many shots of an orgy room at the club with much heterosexual penetration, some of which is graphically "authenticated" with dramatic thrusting.

Lie with Me tells the story of a totally physical sexual relationship that begins between David (Eric Balfour) and Leila (Lauren Lee Smith) before they even know each other's names. The film establishes its "real-sex" credentials during their first lovemaking scene, when we see Leila hold David's erection before performing oral sex. During the following lovemaking scene we only briefly glimpse his erect penis as she rides him. His penis, however, is fully on display in several scenes in the film, including one where he dances nude with Leila.

These real-sex films reveal profound and contradictory attitudes toward the penises and sexual performances that they display. On the one hand they are driven to show us the real thing that has come to mean so much in the early twenty-first century, while on the other hand the narrative trajectories of the films work to contradict the near awe they inspire around the male spectacle that authenticates them. *9 Songs* is framed by an image of Matt in an airplane flying over Antarctica. He is a scientist en route to a workstation, and his relationship with Lisa, which constitutes most of the film, is a flashback. His fling with Lisa is one of a summer of love before they go their own ways. But all is not the idyllic, simple pleasure it seems to be. Their relationship becomes distanced and troubled as Lisa withdraws. At one point she hurts him by biting his lip and drawing blood; when they go to a club together, Matt gets upset and leaves when Lisa becomes involved with an erotic dancer in a scene with bisexual overtones; and Matt is visibly disturbed when he comes upon Lisa masturbating with a vibrator, suggesting his penis and sexual performance are not enough for her. At the end of the summer she has no problem going her own way as originally planned, but Matt is devastated by the personal loss, and the film returns to the frame story with imagery of Antarctica from the plane and Matt at the research site. Antarctica appears as a vast, cold wasteland wherein Matt is a small, almost inconsequential, being. D. H. Lawrence wrote about phallic sexuality in terms of the mighty phallus filling the female "void," and, indeed, the representation of the penis and phallic sexuality earlier in the film seemed to fit that description; but by the end everything is on the side of loss and emptiness for the man and far from filling the void, Matt appears lost within it.

Shortbus is caught within a similar contradictory movement. On the one hand all the characters seem happily, and at times enviably, busy with their penis-centered fucking, be it gay or straight (lesbian sex is very much at the margins), but once again there is trouble in paradise. In an opening montage sequence, for example, we see James in the above-mentioned self-fellatio scene intercut with scenes of a female sex therapist having wild, Kama Sutra–style sex with her husband. Both scenes are shot in the real-sex style. Before long we learn, however, that the sex therapist has never had an orgasm and has been faking it with her husband. He has the requisite big penis and certainly knows how to perform pound cubed in every imaginable position and then some, but it doesn't work for her. Similarly, James, who has such a strikingly large penis that one commentator on CNDB.com blurts out that he judges it eleven inches long, is so unhappy that after taking antidepressants that fail, he attempts suicide. The scene is particularly interesting from this perspective since he attempts to drown himself while naked and several shots reveal his penis. What good is his big penis? What pleasure or power does it bring him in the end? What good did the big penis do Matt in the end in 9 *Songs* as he laments the loss of the woman he loves in the frozen emptiness of Antarctica? What good did the big penis and Kama Sutra–style pound-cubed sex do the "preorgasmic" sex therapist in *Shortbus*, who finally has her first orgasm at the film's finale in a bisexual threesome that does not show and may not even include penetration?

Lie with Me is extraordinary within this context. Once again the film draws the spectator into the world of real sex as a physical paradise, at times literalizing what all these films hint at, the image of a sexual playground. Quite unexpectedly, the film then introduces an old man who lives with David. After a while it becomes clear that the man, who is in a wheelchair and requires constant attention, is David's father. In one scene, Leila, who does not know of his presence, walks in on them as David is bathing his father. As the old man stands up in the tub she looks right at him but David slips a bathrobe on him before he turns around. The way in which Leila looks emphasizes the expectation that he will turn around and that she and we will see his penis. When the view is denied, it appears that the purpose of the scene has been to simply pass the specter of the aging male body before her and our eyes in contrast to the seeming plentitude of the youthful, virile son in whose body, penis, and sexual performance she and perhaps we as the audience have invested so much.

If it stopped there, the use of the old man in *Lie with Me* would be quite amazing in how the image of that body troubles our overinvestment in the youthful sexed body within the current body culture. But that moment is just the beginning. In a later scene, David cleans his father after he has urinated in his pants. We see the man lying on his back as David cleans him with a washcloth. Once again it appears that his positioning will block a view of his penis when David unexpectedly tells him to roll over, which he does, fully revealing himself (figure 30). He lies with his groin facing the bed but then when he rolls back on his side, we once again see his penis (figure 31). This is one of the most profoundly mature moments of frontal male nudity in the history of cinema. First, the earlier denial of frontal nudity and the manner in which this scene begins lull spectators into the belief that they will not see his genitals, giving the shot a riveting impact that will focus nearly everyone's eyes on the penis. Second, the context of the old man having lost control of his bladder already

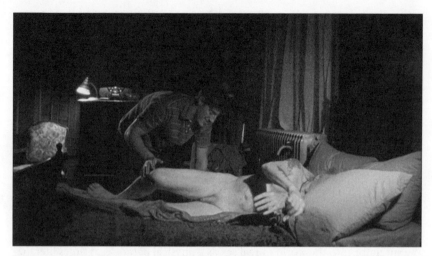

Figure 30. *Lie with Me*

Figure 31. *Lie with Me*

tinges the scene with sadness about the loss of masculine control associated with the penis. As the old man rolls over and we see his long penis hanging use-lessly between his legs, we see what most of these films repress: a direct acknowledgment that the penis is really powerless and that all these body guys, with their seeming sexual potency and vitality, will end like this. What good will it do them in the long run? But the film goes even further since in the single take when the old man rolls back his long penis has retracted to nothing more than the head. The manner in which it almost disappears in front of our eyes also emphasizes the point we have made about the careful regulation of the penis to ensure the proper visual spectacle. Even that is literally deflated in front of our eyes. The scene could easily have been reshot or edited in such a manner as to eliminate the contrast, but this moment fits in perfectly with everything that the film has been leading up to about using the father to undermine the naive overemphasis of the body culture's definition of phallic sexuality. Does the penis have the power to prevent aging and death? The old man is found dead in the next scene, the culmination of this pattern.

Paradoxically, then, the real-sex films seem both the logical end point of body-guy sex by seemingly showing us the "real" thing as opposed to fantasy simulation and at the same time betraying an ambivalence that the real thing may not be all that it is cracked up to be. For all the psychoanalytic theorizing about the striking visual drama of the penis, for all the medical measuring to reassure men about the adequacy of their penises, and for all the evolutionary accounts of the evolved large human penis for sustained deep-thrusting intercourse for female orgasmic pleasure, these films betray a profound ambivalence. Why would Lisa leave the well-endowed Matt in 9 Songs? Why give us the image of the father's large penis retracting to near invisibility before ours eyes in Lie with Me?

In the next chapter we go to the opposite extreme and look at a group of films that at least open the door to thinking about sex in alternative ways that do not hinge on the centrality of the big penis and the pound-cubed sex style. They suggest a world where the penis and penetration are marginal or even irrelevant.

CHAPTER 6

Unmaking Love

Mae West once famously remarked, "Sex is emotion in motion." Her statement is uncannily reminiscent of the way many people speak of the medium that made Mae West famous: the movies. Many see motion as the essence of movies, and much bad filmmaking and film criticism has followed from accepting simplistic assumptions about this essentialist nature of cinema. In order to be "cinematic" movies should have action and not rely too much on dialogue. But what about Yasujiro Ozu, the Japanese director who many critics, us included, consider among the greatest filmmakers of all time? His films are known for their stasis, not their movement or action. In his nearly three-hour-long masterpiece *Tokyo Story*, the camera moves once, and there are no action scenes, fights, or car chases. Characters spend a great deal of time talking, walking, and sitting but none physically fighting or blowing things up.

In a related manner Linda Williams subtitled her groundbreaking academic book on the porn film, *Hard Core: Power, Pleasure, and "the Frenzy of the Visible."* The *frenzy* of the visible. Frenzy of course is just another word for a hyperkinetic concept of motion, here presumed to lie at the heart of filmic sex. Sex is emotion in frenzied motion, to extend Mae West's famous quip. And even though Williams is quoting a concept that she recognizes is part of an ideology, in some ways her book nevertheless succumbs to it, confining itself to the history of this filmed frenzy. And then there's "the visible." Well, if we're going to have frenzy, it has to be visible, right?

Remarkably, many who rightly scoff at the essentialist notions that good cinema means lots of action seriously accept the equally limiting notion that good sex is one thing: motion, frenzy of the visible, and the centrality of the penis. Throughout this book we have shown that the body guy is aligned with the promise of that kind of sexual performance: he has the motion, he has the penis, and he can sustain the frenzied performance (ratings permitted, of course). Why shouldn't some good sex like some good cinema tend toward stasis rather than motion, toward language rather than action, toward inward "invisible" pleasures rather than visible frenzies? Why shouldn't some good sex have little or nothing to do with the penis or penetration of any kind, let alone the exact same kind endlessly repeated? And why shouldn't the history of filming sex include the Ozus of such notions of eroticism as well as the Michael Bays? Why shouldn't there be a wide variety of sex styles just like there is a wide variety of movie styles? Just like some people prefer an Ozu film to a Hollywood action blockbuster, why shouldn't some people prefer an alternative sex style to that of the dominant twentieth-century spectacle of sex epitomized by the body-guy genre, the blockbuster version of sex, as it were?

What does it mean to make love? It has long been noted that films in general, and Hollywood in particular, frequently include heterosexual love stories. Indeed, this is so obvious and common that without the benefit of scholarly analysis, critics and those in the filmmaking industry alike speak of the "romantic subplot" or the "love interest" in film. For David Bordwell the classical cinema comprises two sets of goals: public and private, the latter frequently consisting of heterosexual romance. And with romance, there's lovemaking. Upon hearing the phrase "making love," most people immediately imagine a fairly predictable scenario, presumably heterosexual and involving some foreplay followed by intercourse. The word *love* implies that both members of the couple (for it is always a couple) have some special feeling for each other that presumably sanctions and gives meaning to the act in which they engage. In this regard, the movies have little more imagination than the general public. Substitute the phrase "making love" with the common filmmaking phrase "a lovemaking scene." Immediately on hearing those words, nearly every filmgoer conjures up a similarly predictable and narrow range of images and sounds that vary slightly depending on the rating. While much work has been done by many scholars such as Virginia Wright Wexman on the nature of film couples in various genres and time periods, surprisingly little has been done on the particulars of how lovemaking is represented in films.

It's ironic that the only place scholars have even hinted at the potential value of such a project is in the analysis of pornography, where the appropriate term is styles of "fucking" rather than styles of lovemaking. Linda Williams, among others, has commented on the centrality of the "big dick," the vigorous style of sex whereby the male performer penetrates his partner fast and hard in a variety of positions, the liberal use of the meat shot (the close-up of the penis thrusting in and out of the vagina) and the money shot (withdrawing and ejaculating upon her body). In such porn films, the ideology of fucking assumes that what women need and want is the big dick (for which they frequently articulate a desire by their moaning and groaning) that will stay hard a long time while their partner penetrates them in a variety of positions. Many contributors to the Voyeurweb RedClouds, a division of a user-generated adult site, call this kind of sex "a good pounding." We have referred to this kind of sexual Olympics as "pound, pound, pound (or pound cubed)," and Susan Faludi calls it "jackhammer sex." The idea underlying this style of fucking assumes that after being "nailed" by a big dick long enough in a variety of positions, a woman's ecstasy will somehow reach its climax just when the man ejaculates upon her, sometimes as she asks or, indeed, begs for it. Suffice it to say, the ideology of good sex here is totally dependent on the large penis and the duration necessary for the performance demanded of the male.

Ironically, Hollywood's idea of good sex is not all that far from porn's: a little foreplay followed by intercourse in various positions (including the nearly obligatory woman on top with her head thrown back in ecstasy), followed by everyone being perfectly exhausted and sated. In place of the meat shot, Hollywood displaces the image with the entire male body, which slides up and down the female body in exaggerated motions of thrusting, the body standing in for the erect penis that cannot be shown. And the bodies are always straining, sweating, contorting, and screaming in a combination that is the Hollywood version of the sexual Olympics and a good pounding (see our discussion of *Legends of the Fall* and *Dead Presidents* in chapter 1). Depending on ratings, such scenes are more or less graphic, but they share a similar message: lovemaking is a fixed and limited thing, endlessly repeated.

Hollywood and the porn industry both herald the centrality of the big penis and deep thrusting heterosexual intercourse as the very essence of making love. But once in a while we find films that, intentionally or not, reveal a much larger world of sexuality that the concept of normalcy attempts to keep out. These cracks in the concept of normalcy betray the atrocity on which the phallic fantasy of filmmakers and producers rests. *40 Days and 40 Nights* (2002), a teen comedy of all things, plays out in graphic detail a creative, alternative sexual scenario in which a sexually obsessed young man takes a vow of celibacy not to have sex for forty days but, soon afterward, falls in love. At one point, as he and his girlfriend talk, she strokes him with a long stemmed flower, getting the idea that he can make love to her with the flower since it will break none of the rules—he won't even touch her. The scene is quite unorthodox in that it shows the woman build toward and reach an intense orgasm only from the way the man uses the flower. At one point, he erotically blows a fallen petal along her body (figure 32). After her climax she seems totally fulfilled. The scene does not leave her begging for conventional sex. The flower is not foreplay to the main event—it clearly *is* the main event.

If, however, it takes extraordinary circumstances like a vow of celibacy for Hollywood to imagine such an alternative scenario in the first place, the end of the film goes a step further and reinstates traditional intercourse with a

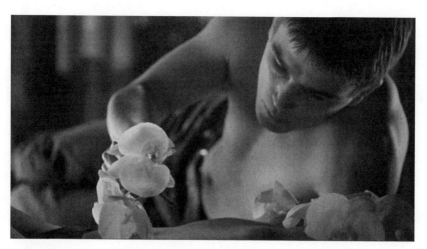

Figure 32. *40 Days and 40 Nights*

vengeance. The young man's friends, who originally had an office betting pool for how long he would remain celibate, now have a pool on how many hours he can last making love with his girlfriend. They sit in his apartment while the sounds of lovemaking emanate from the bedroom. We learn they have been at it for thirty-eight hours. When the young man finally emerges it is only to go to the refrigerator for snacks and drinks before returning to the bedroom. The film ends with the friends changing their bet as to whether or not the young man will die having sex. All this hyperpenile-centered normative sex serves to both make up for the "penis-less" orgasm the woman has had earlier and ensures that the audience knows that these are really "normal" lovers who want exactly what, presumably, the majority of viewers want—to fuck. Despite all this, the remarkable flower scene demonstrates that eroticism can be some-thing much different than what is transpiring offscreen in the bedroom at the film's conclusion.

Alternatives to the Big Penis and Penetration Sex

Some films represent a range of options to normal lovemaking from the neces-sary (films with a paraplegic hero) to the alternative (telephone-sex films) to the bizarre (films involving necrophilia). Collectively, these films acknowledge that sex can be about something quite different from the penis and penetration and reveal our desire to see such scenarios. Telephone sex is in some ways the least extreme form since it does not involve dire circumstances and unusual activity. People have easy access to this alternative since they talk on the phone all the time. Given this context, we might think that telephone sex would be used to explore the erotic potential of language and conversation as an extension of what we saw in our analysis of *Sideways*. In that film, the two people are together in the same space, and this, of course, works to contain their conversation and pull it into the realm of potential conventional sexual interaction. Phone sex involves disembodied voices and offers the participants neither the opportunity to look at each other's facial expressions during the conversation nor the possibility of quickly moving on to conventional body sex; it forces them entirely into the realm of language and imagination.

Perhaps predictably, most people can only conceive of this use of imagination in phone sex as doubly degrading. First, the disembodied language is deemed inhuman, in the most depraved sense of the word, and, second, the dominant manner of representing phone sex invokes the cliché of the pathetic and desperate customer who must pay for anonymous human contact. This cliché even appears in the 1991 Aerosmith music video "Sweet Emotion," in which a man imagines making love to a beautiful woman as he talks to her on the phone but the video ends by showing the actual unattractive "housewife" to whom he has been talking. Something similar happens in several scenes of Robert Altman's *Short Cuts*, where Jennifer Jason Leigh portrays a 1–900 phone-sex operator fulfilling someone's sexual fantasies while disinterestedly sitting at home in the presence of her husband, flipping through pages of a magazine, or changing her baby's diaper. All these films and videos imply that there is a sad, pathetic quality to the delusions involved in phone sex. The usually male clients imagine they are talking to beautiful, romantic women, and the discrepancy between their fantasy and the actuality is pathetic. The whole thing is sordid at best, and telephone sex is reduced to a base business transaction for presumably desperate men who can't get what they want and need in their actual sex lives.

TELEPHONE SEX

Spike Lee's *Girl 6* (1996), a film about phone sex, also complies with this basic cliché, though because it is a feature-length film, it expands and complicates the basic scenario contained in these briefer scenes. The film tells the story of an out-of-work actress who, desperate for money, takes a position in a phone-sex company where she is the girl number six of the film's title. Throughout the film, we see a range of customers who are represented in varying degrees as pathetic, comic, and pathologically dangerous. On the comic end of the spectrum, one man's fantasy involves having his pubic hairs removed with a monkey wrench one by one; another involves a man who stands in a room surrounded by wall-size photographs of a baseball stadium filled with spectators who watch him as he bats wearing only a jockstrap, a helmet, and baseball shoes, while talking to Girl 6 on a speaker phone and imagining the roar of the crowd. On the more "kinky" side, one caller's fantasy involves group sex, and we see Girl 6 and one of her colleagues both "ooohing" and "aaahing," talking dirty in unison. In a variation we see a Latino married couple using Girl 6 to form their threesome. With a hint of pathological behavior, we see a millionaire businessman who wants to be masochistically humiliated by Girl 6. At the far extreme of pathology, we repeatedly see a return caller who gets abusive and finally threatens to enact a snuff fantasy by actually coming to her apartment and killing her. He then terrorizes her by revealing that he knows her address.

Girl 6's main customer, however, is a man identified as "Bob from Tucson," who repeatedly calls to talk about his relationship with his dying mother. Finally, he asks to meet Girl 6, and she agrees to meet him on the boardwalk at Coney Island. She goes there in anticipation that this customer is really interested in her as a person rather than merely as an erotic fantasy object. She waits a long time, increasingly disheartened as she realizes that he is not going to show up. This sequence further reinforces the pathology element by implying that no man who engages in telephone sex is capable of a "normal" loving relationship and shows the dangers inherent in breaking down the line between phone sex and reality, something that Girl 6 seems incapable of resisting. Indeed, a close male friend (played by Spike Lee) calls her clients perverts and deviants and even warns her that she is beginning to enjoy her work. To varying degrees, all of these scenarios reinforce stereotypes of phone sex as comically pathetic, sadly desperate, and varying in degrees from mildly to severely pathological.

Whereas Spike Lee does not see or imagine any valid erotic potential in the wide range of scenarios he represents, another film in the telephone sex genre, *1–900* (1994, Theo Van Gogh, Netherlands) has this imagination. *1–900* tells the story of an architect and an art historian who develop a sexual relationship with each other entirely over the telephone. They have never met before, and they never meet during the course of the film. Each scene in the film consists entirely of separate erotic telephone conversations between the two, and at the end of the film we see a final shot of each person hanging up after what is presumably the last conversation they will ever have. As such, the film bears comparison to the novel *Vox*, by Nicholas Baker, in which every chapter is structured around a series of erotic telephone conversations between two people who have never met and never meet during the course of the novel. Both these works are noteworthy simply because they pursue telephone sex as something other than a distasteful, pathetic, one-dimensional activity in which desperate people pay someone to fulfill their presumably sordid fantasies. These works take those fantasies seriously even while using humor to acknowledge the unconventional aspects of the scenario.

...Greek pillars linked to the house,
but with light material.

Figure 33. *1–900*

In *1–900* the fact that the man is an architect and the woman an art historian already challenges the stereotype of the desperate loser. Furthermore, the film challenges the basic anti-intellectual assumptions of the body-guy genre that mind guys lack sexuality. In contrast to the conventions of the body-guy genre, the mind guy in this film is attractive. The film chronicles a complexly developing relationship in which each participant describes erotic scenarios they presume will help the other achieve orgasm through masturbation: at times their descriptions are true and at other times they lie about what they are doing. Occasionally they exhibit genuine concern for each other's pleasure, while at other times they seem to simply use the other person. Sometimes they get along perfectly and please each other, and at other times they fight and incite anger. In short, their sexual relationship is as complex as the supposedly conventional, "healthy" model of sexuality.

This film even has the imagination to realize that phone sex can take place without the topic of the conversation having anything to do with sex. In a remarkable sequence, the architect talks passionately about his work and his philosophy of architecture while, unbeknownst to him, the woman erotically caresses her body with a feather, reaching a powerful orgasm (figure 33). The man is surprised and happy to learn that she reached orgasm from listening to him talk about his work, illustrating our earlier analysis of the erotic potential of intellectual and creative work—the sexy mind. Indeed the art historian is comparable to Rosina in *The Governess*. Her secretive, erotic entry into the architect's workplace in her imagination is much like Rosina's actual illicit investigation of Charles's laboratory.

For all its complexity, *1–900* somewhat contains its radical premise that phone sex can be a very creative form of erotic gratification. The ending of the film qualifies much of what we have seen in two ways. As they develop their phone sex relationship, the man accidentally discovers the woman's identity. When the man relates this knowledge during one of their phone sessions, she becomes extremely upset, rebuking him for breaking one of the central rules of their relationship—that they remain totally anonymous to each other and never meet. In the last sequence of the film, we see her call him only to have the architect's father answer the phone, explaining that his son has been killed in a car accident. She is simultaneously distressed with the news of her phone partner's death and disturbed when she learns that the son's biographical profile is far removed from what he had told her. Just when she has been fully drawn into this scenario, the voice suddenly shifts back to that of the architect, who reveals that he has tricked her to hear how she would respond to the news of his death. Furious, the woman declares that she never wants to talk to him again and slams the phone down. The final two shots of the film show each of the phone sex lovers isolated. What started out as a mutually gratifying set of erotic conversations has ended badly as a result of the inability of the two to separate their phone-sex lives from their "real" lives.

Paraplegic Sex

Given the cultural emphasis on sexual normalcy, it is not surprising that it takes extraordinary, usually catastrophic, events to motivate and explain why someone would engage in a form of sex that is not penis centered or does not culminate in intercourse. War and horrible accidents that result in paralysis usually supply just such a context. The best-known examples in Hollywood cinema are *Coming Home* (1978), *Born on the Fourth of July* (1989), and *The Waterdance* (1992) (all made after the new rating code, when it was commonplace to graphically represent lovemaking).

Coming Home may be the first R-rated film to deal with a paraplegic soldier's sexuality. After developing a relationship, the paraplegic, Luke Martin (Jon Voight), and a woman, Sally Hyde (Jane Fonda), make love. Luke first emerges from a bathroom naked in his wheelchair, a towel covering his groin. Sally then helps him onto the bed, and the film cuts to her, nude, sitting astride him. The conversation is sensitive as she asks him things such as where she can touch him and what he can feel. She expresses frustration that he can't feel being inside her but the film then cuts to her lying on her back as he performs oral sex. Her moans and facial expressions indicate the intensity of the sexual experience for her, and after finishing he rises up to her upper body and she says, "That's never happened to me before." The scene exposes as a fraud the widely held belief that female pleasure depends on penetration or an athletic model of pounding intercourse. The paraplegic man not only brings the woman to an intense orgasm but one that she has never experienced before through normative sexual intercourse. Indeed, the scene rhymes with an earlier one in which we see her hypermasculine military officer husband on top of her performing conventional thrusting, but her face reveals boredom and disappointment instead of orgasmic bliss.

In a *Vanity Fair* article (2008), Peter Biskind writes of producer Jerome Hellman's observation that the original idea of the lovemaking scene from *Coming Home* was premised on the fact that paraplegic vets could perform cunnilingus, something Fonda's character had never experienced: "She's had a traditional guy who jumps on and pumps away until he comes and gets off. But manliness wasn't necessarily related to a big stiff dick. This big macho guy with his medals was a total wipeout as a husband and lover. And the vet who had only half a body, he was the real man" (Biskind 275). Hellman notes that to underscore this point, they added the lovemaking scene between Fonda and Bruce Dern, who plays her husband. Fonda agreed with Hellman's interpretation and wanted to focus on oral rather than penetration sex as the source of her character's sexual pleasure. According to Fonda, when director Hal Ashby heard a vet's girlfriend remark about the unpredictable manner in which paraplegic men would get erections, sometimes lasting for four hours, he changed his entire approach to the lovemaking scene in the film. He eliminated the oral sex and shot the scene as penetration sex using a body double for Fonda. When Fonda saw the rushes, she was horrified, "'It was real clear that she was riding him'" (275). According to Biskind, Fonda realized that "Ashby had won the first round of what she referred to as 'the battle of penetration'" (275).

Fonda became determined to undermine the footage Ashby shot with the body double by enacting the remainder of the scene in such a manner that he could not use the riding footage. Indeed, at one point Ashby became so frustrated that he yelled at her, "'Ride him, goddammit, ride him!'" (275), but she refused to do so. When they did a close-up, Fonda defied Ashby by not moving her body in a manner consistent with a riding motion. Fonda remarkably concludes, "'Maybe he [Ashby] was just resistant to my wanting to make a point that good lovers don't necessarily have to have erections . . . which has become even more important to me now that I'm 70!'" (275–76). As a much younger woman in 1978, Fonda articulated what was at stake in resisting Hollywood's insistence on the standard lovemaking scene with its emphasis on the erect penis and penetration sex. Big penises are not important for men to be good lovers; in fact, erections are not even necessary for good lovers. In short, Fonda embraced the value of alternative scenarios as early as 1978 and recognized the need to develop alternatives to the dominant movie sex scene.

In a highly memorable line from Oliver Stone's *Born on the Fourth of July*, the central character, Ron Kovic (Tom Cruise), angrily declares, "I gave my dead dick for John Wayne." The line's intended meaning is crystal clear within the context of the film: the idealistic young Kovic, motivated by a John Wayne brand of American patriotism, enlists in the Vietnam War, where he is wounded in action. His experiences in Vietnam leave him a paraplegic (that is, with a "dead dick") and also disillusioned with his country (that is, John Wayne) and what it stands for. In accordance with normative masculinity, Kovic here equates his sexuality and his masculinity with his penis. A dead penis means no "real" sex (that is, penetration intercourse), and no "real" sex means no real masculinity.

As is typical within this genre, the issue of the presumed loss of "normal" penile-centered sexuality is confronted in the film. Kovic goes to Mexico, where he has sex with a prostitute. As he lies in bed she removes her clothing and asks him why he isn't removing his. He tells her of his paralyzing war wound, but as she lies nude next to him, she seductively asks him to let her see as she slides her hands toward his groin. He becomes upset as he tells her that his spinal cord was totally severed, "I have no movement, no feeling. There's nothing down here at all. Nothing happens." This emphasis on the words *no* and *nothing* indicates how traditional notions of masculinity and sexuality are centered on the penis. The prostitute then assures him: "We're going to have a good time." A dissolve to a shot of the moon suggests the passing of time, and when we return to them, she sits astride him and moans in pleasure, repeating that she is coming as he continues to fondle her breasts and stroke her body and hips. Afterward she gently kisses his nipples, and we see him near tears, presumably agonizing over his lost manhood or now realizing that it is, in fact, not all lost. Either way, the scene shows her and him getting pleasure. He tells the woman how beautiful she is as he caresses her, and clearly the acts of looking and touching are erotically fulfilling for him. The film also suggests that although the woman is a prostitute, her moans of ecstasy and sexual fulfillment are authentic and not an act for her client. Even though he doesn't perform oral sex on her, before he goes to the whorehouse, another paraplegic soldier obscenely uses his tongue and says to him, "If you haven't got it in the hips, you better have it in the lips." In other words, there are alternatives to the penis.

Necrophilia

The last category of alternative-scenario films is necrophilia. In some ways, obviously, this is the most extreme of the alternative scenarios we survey here in that, unlike telephone sex and alternatives to intercourse necessitated by physical injury, it can only be explored as cinematic fantasy rather than real-life alternative. In the real world, necrophilia is both a criminal and pathological act, but in the fictional world of cinematic and literary representation it can function in quite creative, if sometimes horrific, ways to dramatically illustrate just how deep the desire for escape from sexual normalcy is embedded in some individuals. The Canadian film *Kissed* (1996, Lynne Stopkewich) and the short story on which it is based, Barbara Gowdy's "We So Seldom Look on Love," supply a concise illustration.

The film's central character is a woman who derives her sexual pleasure from male corpses. Many reviewers at the time of the film's release complained of its ambiguous representation of necrophilia. For once, it seemed, critics were frustrated that a film was not graphic enough. How does a woman have sex with a dead man? The film does not make this clear. In contrast, Gowdy's short story is somewhat more explicit: "I drew back the sheet. This was the most exquisite moment. I felt as if I were being blasted by white light. Almost blinded, I climbed onto the table and straddled the corpse. I ran my hands over his skin. My hands and the insides of my thighs burned as if I were touching dry ice. After a few minutes I lay down to kiss his mouth. By now he might be drooling blood. A corpse's blood is thick, cool and sweet. My head roared" (180–81). Notably absent from its explicit account of the corpse is any reference to the penis. This contrasts sharply with another passage describing a repressed homosexual necrophiliac's practice: "He would take a trocar, which is the big needle you use to draw out a cadaver's fluids, and he would push it up the penises of dead men to make them look semi-erect, and then he'd sodomize them" (176). The contrast of these passages makes explicit what is implicit in the critical response to the film: those who want to know more about necrophilia are assuming that it somehow involves the penis. How can you make love to a man with a dead penis? The novel also makes this explicit: "For fifteen years, ever since Matt died, people have been asking how a woman makes love to a corpse. Matt was the only person who figured it out. He was a medical student, so he knew that if you apply pressure to the chest of certain fresh corpses, they purge blood out their mouths" (177). Instead of mounting the penis, the woman sits over the cadaver's mouth and the blood flow stimulates her orgasm.

And while the homosexual man with the trocar provides a different answer to that question, the woman neither needs nor wants the trocar because her erotic use of the male body in death is intimately tied to the fact that she doesn't have to concern herself with the penis in any manner. For her, the dead male body is a nonphallic body in contrast to the rephallicized body of the man's desire. In a remarkable passage, Gowdy writes of her central character's relationship with her boyfriend: "With Matt, when we made love, I was the receiving end, I was the cadaver. When I left him and went to the funeral home, I was the lover" (181). The place of the woman within the phallic economy of male sexuality is the "receiving end" or being the "cadaver" while the necrophilia enables her to become the active lover who need pay no attention to the penis. She uses death imaginatively to find an alternative to normative sexuality in contrast to the man with the trocar: his perversion deviates far from the norm but remains centered on the penis.

Gowdy's representation of necrophilia is eerily similar to that of Karen Greenlee, an actual necrophiliac who reminds an interviewer, "People have this misconception that there has to be penetration for sexual gratification, which is bull! The most sensitive part of a woman is the front area anyway and that is what needs to be stimulated. Besides, there are different aspects of sexual expression: touchy-feely, 69, even holding hands. That body is just lying there, but it has what it takes to make me happy" (Greenlee). Greenlee even recounts an anecdote about a male mortician who, in contrast to her, uses a trocar to create erections.

Although *Kissed* avoids explicitness about how the woman achieves her pleasure with the male corpses and avoids the trocar penis imagery, it does contain a somewhat surprising moment of frontal male nudity. After getting a disturbing phone call from her boyfriend, the central character rushes over to his apartment, where she finds him standing on a chair naked with a rope around his neck. At this point, we see his body in a full frontal long shot. When he kicks the chair over and hangs himself, however, the action occurs offscreen, and we do not see his penis after his death. Although the film is silent on the dead man's erection, Gowdy's description of the scene in the short story is once again notable: "There was a loud crack, and gushing water. Matt dropped gracefully, like a girl fainting. Water poured on him from the broken pipe. There was a smell of excrement. I dragged him by the noose. In the living room I pulled him on to the green shag carpet. I took my clothes off. I knelt over him. I kissed the blood at the corner of his mouth" (186). Gowdy totally ignores the cultural fascination with the erection a hanging frequently produces and, instead, refers to the loss of control of the bowels that also occurs at that moment. Furthermore, she returns to the image of blood coming from the mouth, the alternative to the penis as the source of erotic gratification. The dead man may have an erection, but it is of no interest to the female character in the story nor to Gowdy, who describes the scene without reference to it, nor to Stopkewich, who elides the entire subject. None of these women have any interest in the penis. This film—directed by a woman, based on a short story written by a woman, and narrated from a female protagonist's point of view—indicates the all-pervasiveness of dominant culture's insistence on a penile-centered male-controlled penetration model of sex. To get outside that model, these creative women—both artists and characters—are driven to extremes. Far from being erotically fulfilling, engaging in conventional sex is like being a lifeless corpse.

All of the above scenarios are so alternative to big-penis and pound-cubed penetration sex that there is no place for them within the body-guy genre. This is true even for Clifford Chatterley, the paralyzed husband in the novel on which the entire genre is founded. His paralysis is never used to explore alternative ways in which he can give or receive sexual pleasure. It serves merely to explain and motivate Connie Chatterley's need for and receptivity to the body-guy gamekeeper, whose sexuality is profoundly penile-centered. Glimpses of or films devoted to radical alternatives require a willingness to question the assumed primacy of the body guy's lovemaking style and in a sense unmake love before proceeding to imagine alternative ways of making love.

BODY-GUY FILMS AND ALTERNATIVE SEXUALITY

Sexuality in the body-guy genre is highly normative, but one alternative scenario occurs with some frequency, though it is not centered on the figure of the hero—bisexuality. Such classic mind-body narratives as *Two Moon Junction*, *Henry & June, Lake Consequence, Wide Sargasso Sea* (1993), *Sirens*, and *Head in the Clouds* (2004) contain bisexual scenes. *Sirens* is a paradigmatic mind-guy / body-guy narrative, but it enables us to explore the radical potential of bisexuality within the genre. Hugh Grant plays Tony, a klutzy and socially awkward Episcopal minister/scholar who travels from Sydney to outback Australia in the 1930s with his cultured wife, Estella, to convince a bohemian artist to remove his so-called blasphemous paintings from a public art exhibit. The artist, Norman Lindsay (Sam Neill), resides in a rural estate that is effectively an artist colony inhabited by his sexually liberated family and his models.

As is typical of the genre, the literate and eloquent Tony is boring in bed, his wife staring at the ceiling as he bobs up and down atop her. Immediately after sex with her husband, Estella goes to a buff handyman, Devlin, and he excites her passion with his first touch. Although her experience with the handyman is exciting to her, Estella also has an erotic experience with three female models living at the art colony. Indeed, a parallel is made between Estella's encounter with the handyman and her encounter with the models. Estella's interest in Devlin is initially piqued when she clandestinely sees him nude (as do we) while masturbating on a rock near a pond. Devlin's strikingly large penis becomes a central part of his mystique when Estella later spies on him as he poses nude for Lindsay (figure 34). The film cuts from the image of Devlin posing to a shot of

Figure 34. *Sirens*

Figure 35. *Sirens*

Estella at the window, emphasizing her direct look at his penis (figure 35). From a similar position near the pond, Tony later secretly observes Estella and two of the female models as they all sensuously caress a third female model, who luxuriates in the experience. Estella is initially uncomfortable with the sexually assertive and uninhibited models, but she comes to enjoy their company, whereas her future encounters with Devlin are increasingly stressful. Indeed, she even fantasizes the female models erotically caressing her as she floats in the pond, whereas she literally runs away from Devlin when he tries to subtly caress her thigh under the table while sitting next to her at dinner.

As they prepare to leave the colony, Estella starts to confess her affair with the handyman to Tony, but he stops her, saying that some things are better left unsaid, thinking that she's going to tell him about her sexual activity with the models. The last scene of the film suggests that Estella has been sexually liberated by her experiences at the colony. While on a train, Estella and Tony sit across from each other in a small compartment surrounded by other passengers who are asleep. Estella removes her shoe and begins to stimulate Tony's penis through his pants with her foot. He's embarrassed at first but then relents, as all the other passengers—the surrogate gazers for the film audience—slowly awaken to covertly delight in the exhibition. As Estella stimulates Tony's penis, she closes her eyes and pictures herself standing nude with the other models on a mountain top—an allusion to the film's title. The film closes with that image of the women. Estella's sexual awakening and assertiveness can be attributed to her experiences with both Devlin and the women, but the final shot of the film suggests that the women had a greater impact on her. The body guy's exemplary lovemaking prowess linked to his large penis is displaced by the sensuality of her experience with the women.

Estella's sexual assertiveness results from a willingness to be open to experience with both sexes. A similar notion is suggested in *Shortbus* when a female character who has never had an orgasm finally achieves one after mutually kissing and caressing both members of a heterosexual couple in a ménage à trois, apparently without penetration sex occurring at all. On the other hand, she has been unable to have an orgasm with her husband, who vigorously performed hyperathletic penetration sex on her in various positions with his large penis. In 2004, *Sirens* director John Duigan further explored bisexuality in his film *Head in the Clouds* and directly connected the notion to political activism. The sexual ménage à trois involves Charlize Theron, Penelope Cruz, and Stuart Townsend. The Cruz and Townsend characters eventually go off to fight for the resistance in the Spanish Civil War, a cause about which they are passionate. Theron, an apolitical hedonist, stays behind in Paris but eventually risks her life to work with an underground movement fighting the Nazis. In *Sirens*, Duigan links bisexuality with sexual assertiveness; in *Head in the Clouds* it is connected to political awareness and activity, highlighting bisexuality's potential for political empowerment by undermining the conventional heterosexual male-female polarity.

Although bisexuality transgresses the cultural norm of heterosexuality and can definitely be considered alternative, its depiction in the body-guy narratives is conventional in that the sensual or sexual moments nearly always occur between female characters, invoking the male fantasy of lesbian lovemaking common to soft-core porn. Think about the casting of the conventionally beautiful

Theron and Cruz in *Head in the Clouds*, and the models Elle MacPherson and Portia de Rossi in *Sirens*. In addition, as we have seen in *Sirens*, the ideal of the body guy's large penis and pound-cubed sexual performance is maintained. However, the presence of so much conventional bisexuality in the body-guy films suggests there may be trouble in body-guy paradise. Even as the films celebrate his potent penis and gifted pound-cubed sexual performance, the women are drawn, if even only briefly, away from him to each other, an implicit recognition that for all that he has, it is not enough.

Buried within these soft-core heterosexual male fantasies of bisexuality there are indeed moments that provide a vision of what a true, radical bisexuality might be—one that erodes the masculine-feminine polarity rather than swings between it. In *Lake Consequence*, as the body guy watches the woman to whom he's been making love move into erotic embraces with another woman, his male fascination with the erotic spectacle gives way to a troubled look, suggesting that these women may somehow be complete without him. Their attraction to each other may be far from a fleeting erotic supplement to what the body guy "has." And this is precisely the image that disturbs Tony in *Sirens*. He sees the women caressing each other without men, and they are happy, blissful, and complete. He is so upset by the image that he cannot speak or hear of it, and even though he was mistaken as to the nature of Estella's confession, he was right. It's the image of the nude women alone together on the mountaintop that fuels Estella's fantasy at the end of the film, enabling her sexual assertiveness with her husband.

The old saying "opposites attract" acquires a whole new meaning. If by "opposites" one simply means males and females—and we would suggest that they are not opposites—our notion of radical bisexuality includes that but only when physical difference is separated from cultural, gendered positions. In other words, there is no reason why a man and a woman who are attracted to each other should not discover how to make love without privileging sexual difference around the penis that lies at the center of normal heterosexuality and that finds its ultimate celebration in the body-guy genre and its ultimate hero figure in the mythic body guy. In a sense, the glimpses of bisexuality in the body-guy genre that men sometimes witness hint at another narrative that would be the ruin of the body guy hero and the very genre itself. The heroes of this brave new world would not remotely resemble the body guy, and their penises would not conform to the norms of spectacular display or the performance standard so intricately woven with the notion of masculinity.

For many it is hard to even imagine what bisexual female pleasure "entirely detached" from the penis might be. And it is important to posit the same notion for men for whom it is almost unimaginable to have a sexual relationship with a woman that is not centered on their penis and penetration. We are suggesting something much more complex than these simple, predetermined, even alluring positions that can be summed up by the male fantasy of the man stepping aside to watch a woman to whom he has just been making love have torrid sex with another woman, a virtual soft-core porn fantasy masquerading as bisexuality. On the contrary we envision intelligent, creative work on the part of people committed to finding a way to give each other pleasure removed from the penis and penetration, pleasures grounded in unique and individual circumstances that require discovery—nothing that works for any two people can simply be repeated by another couple with predetermined maneuvers such as the "missionary position," the woman "riding" the man, or the man doing "pound cubed." Everything is unique and particular to the complex desires and preferences of the individuals. We are extending the notion of bisexuality to include relations between men and women that are not really heterosexual since heterosexuality always privileges the penis and penetration, nor are they homosexual since the partners are male and female, but not in the gendered masculine and feminine sense of the word. There is no place for "consummation" in such a relationship. There is never a moment that the man does something to the woman to make her complete. Indeed, it is possible to look at the woman as complete without any need of or even any place for the man to "enter" her—a penetrating penis would break something rather than complete something.

POLYMORPHOUS PERVERSITY AS LIBERATION

It is useful here to briefly return to the historical context of the late 1960s and 1970s. In her book *Screening Sex*, Linda Williams discusses *Coming Home*, which we analyzed above in the context of films with alternative sexual scenarios precipitated by catastrophic injuries and wounds to the male body causing impotence. Williams adds a different dimension, however, by placing the film within the context of Jane Fonda's career and films of the late 1960s and 1970s. Fonda was the first star to bring the issue of representing female sexual pleasure and orgasm to the foreground in Hollywood in such films as *Klute* (1971) and *Coming Home*. In a well-known scene in *Klute* she looks at her watch while having intercourse and going through the outward motions of orgasm. This "faking" orgasm is contrasted with a later "authentic" lovemaking scene in the film. Like us, Williams finds significance in the fact that the Fonda character in *Coming Home* achieves orgasm for the first time with a paraplegic man without penetration even though we have earlier seen her engaged in conventional intercourse with her husband, a hypermasculine military officer. Williams also documents the tension between Fonda and director Hal Ashby about this aspect of the film and Fonda's insistence on representing female pleasure as independent from the penetrating, erect penis.

Williams additionally considers Fonda's public persona, which during the late 1960s included the antiwar movement and in the 1970s her prominence in the personal fitness movement. She links Fonda's antiwar activism to her demand to represent orgasmic sexual pleasure as separate from the erect penis and penetration. "Make love, not war," was a popular slogan at the time, but Williams insightfully points to an oft-overlooked or forgotten aspect of the era: a strong interest in sexual activity that challenged the dominant definitions of normalcy with the focus on penetration and intercourse. A strand of counterculture celebrated "perverse" sexuality removed from a genital focus, which was viewed as a fixation tied to the dominant culture and its phallic militarism and hypermasculinity. That movement found its spokespersons in Herbert Marcuse and Norman O. Brown, who advocated a "regression," which, in Williams's words, "involved . . . a reactivation of pregenital polymorphous sexuality and a decline of genital sexuality" (157). Marcuse's influential book *Eros and Civilization* was originally published in 1955 but reprinted in 1966. In that same year Masters and Johnson published their highly influential *Human Sexual Response*, in which they documented that men and women derived the most intense orgasmic responses via masturbation by hand or mechanical devices, followed by having their partners bring them to orgasm by manipulating their genitals, with sexual intercourse being a "poor third" (162). In short, pound cubed was way overrated.

After this insightful chapter on Jane Fonda and the relation of sex to politics in the late 1960s and 1970s within the context of feminism, the counterculture, and the antiwar movement, Williams, however, returns to a notion of "hard core" that fully embraces the dominant model as if nothing of lasting value survived that time period. Thus, in her chapter on "Hard-Core Art Film since the 1990s" she does not even note, let alone comment on, the centrality of the big penis in her discussion of *9 Songs* and *Shortbus*. She implicitly assumes that whatever relevance and appeal Marcuse, Brown, and Fonda may have had, their notions of orgasm and pleasure were tied exclusively to the historical circumstances of the late 1960s and 1970s. She limits herself here, as she did in her book *Hard Core*, when she embraced the "frenzy of the visible" as defining pornography: big penises define hard-core art just like they define hard-core porn. Or more accurately, the same penile- and penetration-frenzied spectacle that defines "real sex" in hard-core porn continues to define it in "hard-core art."

We reject a definition of "real sex" or "hard-core sex" that privileges penile penetration within a sexual hierarchy. We are calling for a radical redefinition

Figure 36. *Angels and Insects*

of these terms—a definition that grants an equal place to alternative scenarios embracing polymorphous perversity and radical bisexuality. None of these forms of sexuality are more "real" or "hard" than the other. Polymorphous perversity rejects the traditional erotogenic zones associated with the genitals and embraces all the other areas of the body as sites of potential erotic and sexual pleasure. As such this idea is often referred to as pregenital sexual pleasure in that it more closely resembles an infant's delight in the entire body before learning to restrict the pleasures of the body to the culturally sanctioned zones. Such forms of nongenital sex include the feather, flowers, and hands that caress the surfaces of women's bodies in the films we discussed above: *40 Days and 40 Nights*, *1–900*, and *Sirens* respectively. Why should a caress be subordinate to penetration in defining real sex?

In addition to the tactile pleasures described above, our proposed redefinition of lovemaking includes visual pleasures that lie outside the predetermined cultural lexicon of what looks sexy, such as "tits and ass" or black lacy undergarments. In the film *Angels and Insects* (discussed in chapter 4) the main character, William, discovers, much to his surprise, that the sight of his colleague Matty's exposed wrist as she draws scientific illustrations for their work arouses him (figure 36). It's not just the sight of her wrist that captivates him but the precise manner in which she flicks her hand as she draws. He is so taken by the image that he envisions it as he makes love to his much more conventionally beautiful wife. Previous to this moment, William's relationship to his comparatively plain colleague, Matty, had been unromantic, although they shared a passion for the work they did together.

Visual pleasure can easily be extended into the realm of performance, as we discussed in *The Governess*, when Rosina insists that Charles photograph her as she enacts the story of Salome. In a variant of this scenario, Rosina later photographs the sleeping Charles after disrobing him and arranging his body in a way that pleases her. The same is true of alternative scenarios such as telephone sex. We are so used to thinking of sex as involving direct bodily contact that many of us can do little more than be disgusted by or laugh at disembodied sex involving technology and distance. In her *New York Times* review "A Love Life Less Ordinary," Lori Gottlieb quotes a psychoanalyst as observing, "Perversion can be defined as the sex that you like and I don't." Such is the nature and power of "normal" lovemaking and thus the need for learning to unmake love.

It may seem odd that William in *Angels and Insects* finds a particular movement of Matty's wrist erotic, but it is taken no further than that in the film. Although we never see their sexual relationship develop, presumably it will proceed along normal romantic lines. In our vision of remaking love, an alternative scenario like the flicking wrist could develop as follows. After discovering his unique erotic sensibility, William could share it with Matty, who would have to demonstrate open-mindedness rather than succumb to the usual cultural response of laughter or derision. William then could ask her to enact a scenario incorporating her wrist, and she could respond creatively and imaginatively. To complete the scenario, Matty could identify and articulate one of her desires that William could similarly fulfill. Or Matty could feel complete by simply providing William with the performative gift, wanting nothing in return, feeling satisfied with a kind of equivalent mental or emotional pleasure.

The Governess also provides an opportunity to imagine an alternative erotic scenario and, in fact, includes one within the film. Rosina thinks Charles will be pleased with the nude photograph she took of him, but instead he becomes deeply distressed and breaks off the relationship. In our alternative scenario, she might explain to him the pleasure she took from disrobing and posing him and ask him to incorporate it into a scenario for her. Charles would have to understand and empathize with Rosina's wishes and relinquish his usually controlling position to let her do with him what she will. Perhaps the pleasures from posing and photographing his body within the context of their erotic play arouses and fulfills her in a manner that is complete by itself and does not lead to orgasm—even orgasm is not essential in alternative scenarios. They might even incorporate the camera. We are not suggesting that certain scenarios are male and some female but rather that both partners must be completely open and responsive to participating in them. Whereas conventional penetration sex presumes a woman is incomplete until the erect penis penetrates her and completes the sex act, the alternative scenarios we are proposing are premised on the assumption that women are already complete. Insofar as the notion of completion makes any sense in such scenarios, it is in relation to the manner in which both the man and the woman participate in completing each other's scenario.

CELEBRATING POLYMORPHOUS PERVERSITY

Men in the current body culture are encouraged to define themselves and their masculinity around their penis and how well they perform sex in all the measurable ways we have documented throughout the book. If they have a big penis and can perform for extended periods, they should feel good about themselves. Ironically, however, these messages overvaluing the penis may be in direct response to a sexual reality that has, in fact, displaced the penis. In his book *Castration*, Gary Taylor tellingly entitles a chapter "What Does Manhood Mean?" Taylor suggests that manhood is no longer defined by the centrality of the penis because of widely used alternative practices such as mutual masturbation, fellatio, and cunnilingus. He observes, "The centuries-slow ebb of the reproductive imperative has licensed a panoply of heteromarital 'perversions' once condemned by church and state" (7). Furthermore, those alternative practices "are not anatomically restricted to couples composed of one he and one she; they can be performed just as easily and just as pleasingly, by he-pairs or she-pairs. A lot of the sexual activities being enacted, on any given night, by couples we call 'heterosexual' are also being performed that night by couples we call 'homosexual.' (They might be better described, using a less loaded term common in scientific descriptions of other species, as 'isosexual')" (7). Taylor links such isosexual practices, which do not distinguish between penetrator and penetratee, to what, from the reproductive point of view, has traditionally been called "unsexed" sex. This leads to his stunning insight: "By the late twentieth century, such castrated sensualities, had come to seem, to some, not deviant, but foundational" (8). Revealingly, the body-guy genre and the model of masculinity it promotes emerge just when the penile-centered form of sex it celebrates is no longer "foundational." Taylor offers the term "castrated sensualities" as the opposite extreme of what we have described as the body guy's phallic sexuality.

Furthermore, he links the new castrated sensualities to theorists who connected it with both polymorphously perverse sexuality and bisexuality; but regardless of what one terms it, all these views have profound similarities. The important point historically in Taylor's words is that "like Foucault's own *History of Sexuality*, these theories, all published in the last fifteen years of the millennium, challenge the 'natural' primacy of male-female intercourse: heterosexuality becomes just one late and suspect item on the bedroom menu" (8–9).

The "last fifteen years of the millennium" constitute precisely the heyday of the body-guy genre and the films we have analyzed in this book. Much like we have shown that the phallic sexuality of the body guy is a fearful reaction to the very real progress and power of women in the workplace during the 1980s and 1990s, it similarly betrays a fearful response to the manner in which peoples' actual sexual practices during that time period have moved away from the centrality of penile-centered intercourse. The seemingly powerful spectacle of the big penis and pound-cubed sex is in fact a fearful overreaction to the recognition of its loss of power on both fronts. In the crudest everyday slang, there are a lot of people who currently do not highly value fucking or being fucked.

What we are calling radical bisexuality fits in with alternative sexual scenarios, polymorphously perverse sexuality, and isosexuality. These are all different terms and ways of thinking about the same thing: a radical displacement of the penis and penetration sex, even in relations between men and women. Given that contemporary culture defines itself as heterosexual, it is not surprising that the dominant discourses of the body culture are heterosexual and that the body-guy genre that emerged within and gives support to that culture is predominantly heterosexual. But the bisexuality, limited as it may be within the genre, points to another important issue. The issues that we are writing about in this book are not linked to sexual orientation or sexual practice: the overvaluation of the penis and penetration is just as relevant to practicing bisexuals and homosexuals as to heterosexuals, and the hard work of intelligently imagining creative erotic alternatives applies to all.

It is within this context that we conclude this chapter with a discussion of *Man of Flowers*, Paul Cox's extraordinary 1983 Australian film about a seemingly "heterosexual" man who refuses to enter the world of "normal" adult sexuality, preferring instead a highly particular, personal alternative scenario. *Man of Flowers* emotionally involves the spectator in the rich if bizarre world of Charles Bremer (Norman Kaye). Charles is introduced to us in an unusual scene at the beginning of the film. We see a beautiful woman dance as we hear an opera. The dance turns into a striptease intercut with shots of Charles sitting and intensely watching (figure 37). Just as the woman is about to finish her performance the silent, mysterious man jumps up and rushes outside to a nearby church; cut to a shot of his hands playing intense but discordant music on the church organ. Cox plunges us into this mysterious world of aesthetics, eroticism, and alternative sexual behavior before we are even introduced to the characters and narrative in the conventional way. We soon learn that Charles is a rich, eccentric bachelor who has hired a "model," Lisa, to perform a striptease to the same piece of music every week for twenty minutes. Within our terms, this is his alternative scenario. It always follows the exact same script, including his fleeing the

Figure 37. *Man of Flowers*

room just as the woman strips naked. He does not touch her or speak to her, integrating his sexual arousal with the aesthetic world of music, which is a component of his scenario—he doesn't just observe as a voyeur; he also listens to the same operatic aria and plays music himself immediately following.

Later in the film, Lisa asks Charles why he wants her to perform this weekly ritual, and he replies that it gives him pleasure. She then asks how much pleasure and he calmly answers "enough." When she asks why it gives him pleasure, he simply answers that he does not know. The fact that he does not know does not in any way bother him; he simply accepts it. Such acceptance is precisely what we validate in this chapter: individuals can learn to pursue personal erotic scenarios that mysteriously reverberate within their own personal histories, and society can learn to be nonjudgmental rather than condemnatory about such erotic behavior.

Cox also asks us to accept and even identify with his eccentric protagonist, and he does so in part by graying the lines between the normal/abnormal opposition, specifically in regard to masculinity and alternative sex, issues delineated in a subplot. Lisa lives with her boyfriend, David, who fancies himself an avant-garde artist but is nothing but the most traditional of men sexually. He "fucks like a man," and he fucks casually. In one scene Charles visits David's studio and discovers him having sex with someone other than Lisa. Without stopping, David tells Charles to look at some paintings as he resumes his sexual activity. In another hilarious scene, David lies next to Lisa in bed after failing to get an erection. She tells him it could be a "symptom" of something, but he goes off on an incredulous rant about Charles's unusual relationship with Lisa. He can't understand how any man could pay a hundred dollars to simply watch a woman undress, then leave the room rather than fuck her. The irony of the situation is totally lost on him. He doesn't understand how Charles gets pleasure from his alternative scenario, even though he is still visibly frustrated from having failed just moments earlier to get any pleasure himself from normative penetration intercourse!

Cox also never presents Charles as a pathetic figure, one who can't make friends or get girlfriends. On the contrary, people like and befriend him. In fact, Lisa even wants to enter into a romantic relationship with him—and this after she's experienced the alleged sexual pleasure of the body guy and his pound-cubed performance. Charles shows no interest in personal relationships, however, but instead derives his pleasure from a heightened sense of aesthetics. He takes art classes, plays the organ, and lives in a beautifully decorated and well-maintained home. His is the world of the mind, and Cox manages to represent this world as rich and vital, even alluring. Charles prefers the world of aesthetic beauty to people and normative sexuality.

In common language, Charles is a "pervert" and socially maladjusted, but Cox depicts the world of so-called normal people as callous and banal. Furthermore, Lisa's boyfriend, David—the conventional male who knows how to fuck—turns out to be vapid and abusive. Charles's rigorously maintained aesthetic world is unique and individualized—delectable, compared to the violent conformity of the world David represents. Charles's individuality includes his intense sexual scenario, which gives him as much sexual pleasure as any "normal" man could get from pound cubed, but one that has nothing to do with building monogamous relationships, about which he cares nothing.

Figure 38. *Man of Flowers*

His choice to remain outside the normative monogamous relationship with Lisa leads directly to the final shot of the film. In a park by the sea, Charles stops walking to look at the setting before him. Slowly, three other men join him and stand with their backs to the camera, looking out over the water, contemplating the beautiful view, as an increasing number of birds fill the sky around them (figure 38). These men are not a social group in the normal sense of the word; they do not even acknowledge each other. The shot shows that Charles is not alone at the same time that it shows the isolated nature of the men who form this odd social collective—they stand perfectly still in visual contemplation of the world in front of them, mysteriously removed from its mainstream. Whatever Charles is contemplating, clearly it is beautiful, and clearly it is alternative.

CHAPTER 7

"Why Do You Say That as if It Were a Weakness? It's Not."

The opening scene of *Forgetting Sarah Marshall* (2008) got a lot of press from film critics, primarily because of the frontal male nudity. Indeed, the film may be a first. When penises appear in movies, most reviewers don't even mention them, let alone grant them detailed attention. Significantly, with this film the reception context began preopening, when the film's star and screenwriter, Jason Segel, talked in great detail to the press about his nude scene:

> And then I had this thought about the difference in nature between male nudity and female nudity. That, for men, they like all sorts of different types of women. They like fat women, skinny women, women with big breasts and small breasts, and blonde hair and brown hair. There aren't that many women out there who, like, love a small penis. [LAUGHTER] And so the judgment is very particular when you're doing male nudity. You're just gonna be having your junk examined. So, I was then terrified. And I was acutely aware of the ratings issue. So that I knew that I had to be flaccid, obviously. But you don't wanna be totally flaccid. ("Jason Segel Interview")

Referring to several of his recent films, producer Judd Apatow happily contributed by claiming that all his films would henceforth include a penis shot since "America fears the penis and that's something I'm going to help them get over" ("Apatow Makes Penis Promise").

Most viewers were thus primed for the now-infamous opening sequence where Sarah Marshall (Kristen Bell) walks in on her naked boyfriend, Peter, to announce that she is leaving him, something Segel told interviewers was based on an actual experience in his life. How humiliating to be caught with your pants down, so to speak, at such a moment. Indeed, Peter refuses to cover himself while he hysterically grieves for the remainder of the scene, linking the display of the penis to vulnerability and humiliation. The critics got it wrong, however, incorrectly describing the scene. Peter is *not* caught with his pants

Figure 39. *Forgetting Sarah Marshall*

down. Sarah actually walks in on him as he comes from the shower with a towel securely wrapped around his waist. When he sees her, he happily pulls the towel open and lets it drop as he swivels his hips so strongly that we hear the slapping sound of his penis hitting his thighs before we finally see the first notorious penis shot (figure 39).

What's the big difference whether she walked in on him when he was completely naked or if he dropped his towel upon seeing her? We have argued throughout this book that the common display of the body guy's penis is part of a widespread pattern of increased emphasis on the penis over the last three decades. We've also argued that the repetition and seeming embrace of the body guy is a backlash against women who have empowered themselves in the workplace in jobs previously reserved for men, affirming the spectacle of the penis as a privileged sign of what they have and women can never have. Women can have high-paying careers and rise to the highest levels of leadership, but they can never have a penis. They must come to men to get that prize if they want it. And it is precisely this that Peter thinks the professional woman Sarah has come for. He drops his towel to proudly display his penis and further emphasizes its presumed impressiveness by setting it in motion, creating a suitable slapping sound to accompany the swinging spectacle. Far from being caught naked, he creates the nude spectacle on the mistaken assumption that when Sarah sees what he's got, he'll get what he wants. But she is unfazed, as if there was nothing there—nothing to see. The ultimate dread—it goes unnoticed, has no impact, and might as well be *invisible*.

In this chapter, we look at *Forgetting Sarah Marshall*, *2 Days in Paris* (2007), and *Lady Chatterley* (2006), three films that opened during 2006 to 2008, to see what is currently happening in the body-guy genre and to identify significant trends within it. We also return to the "real-sex" films *9 Songs* and *Lie with Me*, from the same time period, from a different perspective than that in the previous chapter. All of these films are distinct in various ways: the dominant genre classification for *Forgetting Sarah Marshall* belongs to its producer Judd Apatow, who has created virtually his own brand of raunchy comedies mixed with slapstick and sentimentality aimed at young audiences; *2 Days in Paris*, a sophisticated romantic comedy, was made in France by Julie Delpy, an internationally renowned French actress, but features Adam Goldberg, an American actor; and *Lady Chatterley* is a literary adaptation of a British novel in the style of the European art cinema.

Strange bedfellows, yet these films are profoundly united. They incorporate, reflect, and comment on central features of the body-guy genre including the mind-guy / body-guy opposition, the centrality of the big penis, and penetration sex as a way of defining masculinity. They implicitly and sometimes explicitly refer to the ways in which the above crucial matters in film and even literature have been represented for decades, and they acknowledge national issues by crossing borders between the United States and France and England and France in complex ways. The tagline for *2 Days in Paris* was "He knew Paris was for lovers. He just didn't think they were all hers."

Forgetting Sarah Marshall is a comedy—and a very knowing one, at that. In his review of *The Pineapple Express* (2008), Owen Gleiberman insightfully notes of Judd Apatow, the film's producer, "In addition to being obscene as hell, his films are thrillingly and madly literate." Critics and the public alike quickly perceived how *Walk Hard: The Dewey Cox Story* (2007), which Apatow produced immediately prior to *Forgetting Sarah Marshall*, parodied the musical biopic, drawing heavily on such recent hits in that genre as *Ray* (2004), the Ray Charles story, and *Walk the Line* (2005), the Johnny Cash story.

We somewhat similarly argue that *Forgetting Sarah Marshall* can be best understood as a comic version of the body-guy genre, and the emphasis on the penis in the opening scene becomes significant within that context. Laura Hodes and Lisa Schwarzbaum have linked the comic use of the penis in this film to the sight of the penis in films in general, observing that penises are used for comic effect rather than the erotic objectification that occurs with female nudity in films. Even if there are many such comic instances, we caution against such generalizations since we have shown that images of penises that are meant to be anything but funny are not uncommon in movies. Furthermore, there are many different comic structures that function in quite different ways to quite different effect. The most common kind of penis humor in movies is penis-size jokes, where small penises, which are not seen, are the butt of the joke

(Lehman, *Running Scared*). And there are the unexpected images of penises in some comedies meant to be "gross" or shocking (*Walk Hard: The Dewey Cox Story* and *The Hangover* [2009]). The opening scene of *Forgetting Sarah Marshall* fits neither of these categories. The actor is not small, and there is no penis-size joke anywhere in the scene, and this is crucial. Peter easily embodies the ideal norm so central to the penis imagery we analyze throughout this book. He is in no way "lacking" or "deficient." Nor is the display of his penis gross or shocking. Why, then, is it funny for those who think it is? Because it is willfully displayed for an intended purpose for which it totally fails, and comedies can enable such moments in a manner dramas cannot.

Forgetting Sarah Marshall employs another clever comic conceit: the penis we see belongs to the mind guy, not the body guy. In many ways the film closely follows the dominant mind-guy / body-guy paradigm in which a beautiful woman must choose between the two after having her sexuality awakened by the body guy, in this case, Aldous (Russell Brand), the rock star for whom Sarah leaves Peter. A contrast of two montage sequences summarizes a central trope of the genre: we see a montage of Peter engaged in a series of slow, passionless missionary position thrusts atop unresponsive women, one of whom says she is coming in the same boring monotone with which she says everything else. She might as well be saying she is falling asleep, which it appears she is. Then we see a montage of Sarah and Aldous engaged in a variety of outrageously exaggerated athletic sexual positions, and Sarah appears ecstatic. Both men are musicians. Aldous clearly fits in with the recognizable type of the artist as body guy, which we have discussed. These figures are rebellious, dangerous, and outside the norms of society. Far from being settled down, they are typically on the move or well removed from domesticity, pursuing their vision. Aldous is Apatow's "madly literate" comic, spitting image of that character, every cliché in place. Peter, however, is a couch potato who simply supplies banal chords to orchestrate a *CSI*-style television show of which Sarah is the star. Although he is technically a musician like Aldous, the two are worlds apart; Peter represents the boring, successful, stable lover and future husband who lacks Aldous's "gift." *Forgetting Sarah Marshall* is the only film in which the mind guy and the body guy represent two poles of the same thing, a very clever conceit in making clear what is at stake.

The premise of the film is simple enough. Peter decides to go to Hawaii on a vacation to recover from his breakup with Sarah and checks into a resort where, of course, Sarah and Aldous are staying. A subplot continues the parallels with the body-guy genre. A young inexperienced honeymoon couple is staying in the resort. Aldous learns that the groom is a total failure at lovemaking. We see a scene where he tries but fails to enter his bride during lovemaking and one where he claims he is in, but she says she can't feel anything while he says it hurts. Aldous comes to the rescue as we see him teach the young man thrusting techniques, after which we see the newlyweds in marital bliss as they successfully engage in a variety of sexual positions. This scene clearly satirizes the body guy's sexual gift, which we have identified as a defining characteristic of his character's appeal in the genre. Another scene drives home this satiric quality. Aldous leaves Sarah after gleaning that she still loves Peter, who has actually become involved with another woman, Rachel. Aldous advises Peter that he should keep both women, to which Peter replies that he lacks the "sexual competence" for that. Aldous then off-handedly remarks that he had forgotten about his own gift, which sets him apart from ordinary men like Peter. In short, Aldous is an extreme comic version of what the body-guy films ask us to take very seriously: the body guy has a unique sexual gift that enables him to make love to a woman in a manner so special that her lover, indeed all her previous lovers and all her lovers to follow, will be comparatively inadequate. And there will be others because she invariably loses the body guy, sometimes returning to her boring lover or husband.

The scene in which Aldous discovers Sarah's love for Peter rhymes with the montage sequences described above in which Peter's lovemaking style is contrasted with Aldous's. Peter makes love to Rachel in his hotel room, which adjoins Sarah's and Aldous's room. The noise they make irritates the jealous Sarah, who awakens Aldous and mounts him. She then makes the motions of riding him while uttering loud sounds of sexual pleasure. Aldous, barely awake, lies passive, unaroused while Sarah mimics the motions and sounds of stereotypical lovemaking. When Peter and Rachel hear the presumed spectacle in the next room, they too exaggerate the pleasure they're actually experiencing, screaming louder and banging the bed against the wall in order to top the coinciding performance. The scene demonstrably lays bare the *performative* nature of the preferred lovemaking style and its representation in movies. It looks and sounds like it should, but it is all a hoax, one that the half-asleep Aldous barely grasps. In effect, it reduces Hollywood's lovemaking to nothing more than going through the motions, sound and fury signifying nothing.

In the classical Hollywood style, the film ends with yet another visual rhyme when Peter's new girlfriend, Rachel, walks in on him while he is naked. This time he really is naked and we briefly glimpse his penis as he quickly covers up. She has an amused, loving look on her face and even begins to laugh as he covers himself. He has seemingly learned his lesson. Rather than flaunt what he assumes to be the impressive display of his penis, he is wiser to cover it up. In an almost paradoxical sense, then, *Forgetting Sarah Marshall* is about both displaying the penis and covering it up. This process reveals something of the current crisis surrounding the representation of the penis in cinema: it reveals how ludicrous it is to take the body guy, his penis, and his stellar sexual performance seriously as we are asked to do in most other films of the genre. In the classic body-guy paradigm, we would see Aldous's penis, not Peter's, and instead of laughing at Aldous's sexual gift, we would be asked to be in awe of it and the penis he uses to give women his magic. Like so many comedies that venture into the sexual arena, *Forgetting Sarah Marshall* simultaneously mocks much of what we are normally asked to take seriously, while at the same time reinforcing it. It is okay to laugh at the penis if it belongs to the mind guy who then learns to cover it up, restoring its awe, mystique, and rock-star power.

2 Days in Paris, written and directed by Julie Delpy, is another romantic comedy that sheds light on many of the issues we've examined throughout this book, something which becomes all the more apparent when it is considered in relation to *Forgetting Sarah Marshall*. *2 Days in Paris* tells the story of Jack (Adam Goldberg) and Marion (Julie Delpy), two lovers vacationing in Europe. After a visit to Venice, disrupted by Jack's nonstop diarrhea attack, they decide to visit Marion's parents in Paris for two days on their way back to the United States. Marion's quirky family and her many former lovers all cause Jack great distress. In short, he is out of control throughout the entire film, a long-standing comedic tradition centered on men and failed masculinity.

Like *Forgetting Sarah Marshall*, *2 Days in Paris* contains an important image of the central male character's penis near the beginning and again near the end. Just when Jack seems to have survived the ordeal of a rabbit lunch with Marion's family and the worst seems to be over, the family get out a photograph of Jack that Marion had given them. This is a rather ordinary occurrence at a family get together, but the photograph, which we see in a brief insert, is a full frontal nude shot of Jack with three helium balloons tied around the shaft of his penis; the balloons floating upward around his torso and head. Jack looks on, mortified, while they all stare at the picture, and to his further embarrassment, the mother remarks that he has a "nice weenie." Near the end of the film, we see Jack's penis again when he drops his pants to stand fully nude in front of Marion. There are several other penis images and references throughout the film. Near the beginning of the film, as Jack and Marion prepare to make love, Jack has trouble putting on a condom. He complains that French condoms are too small for him, even tighter than Italian condoms. Thus, the mother's remark about his "nice weenie" confirms his impressive size. Marion's father runs an art gallery, and when they visit the opening of a new show, we see that the sexually explicit artworks include penises. Later, at a party, Jack has a conversation with one of Marion's former lovers. Using English awkwardly, he talks about the experience of when his penis "backs away." Wondering whether he has expressed himself correctly to Jack, he explains that he is referring to what happens when he gets cold or scared, in other words, when his penis retracts.

Both the penis imagery and all the penis chatter seem like the same old same old of the American cinema but the differences are significant, maybe even profound. There is a matter-of-fact quality to sex and the penis in 2 Days in Paris that contrasts with the almost hysterical quality in the American cinema. As noted, in the case of Forgetting Sarah Marshall the hysteria about the penis began with the publicity campaign before the film opened. Writer and star Jason Segel and producer Judd Apatow beat drums and shined the spotlight on the penis before people even saw it! 2 Days in Paris had been out for a year before either of us saw it, and even though we had read reviews of it, we did not know that it contained frontal male nudity.

Part of Jack's disorientation about Paris is precisely that sex seems to be no big deal. Everyone talks about it, looks at it, sees it, and responds to it in ways he cannot understand. Marion's mother walks in on Jack and Marion as they prepare to make love, looks at them in bed, then talks about doing the laundry and nonchalantly walks out. Marion is blasé about the large number of lovers she has had. Indeed, when Marion meets a former lover on the street, she casually tells Jack about the "blowjob" she gave him. Jack then gets upset, but even more upset about Marion's nonchalance—the blowjob is no big deal. After Marion's remarks that in relation to serious world problems it *is* of no importance, Jack replies that a blowjob put democracy in peril, referring to President Clinton and Monica Lewinski. When Marion's above-mentioned ex-lover talks graphically about his penis retracting, Jack is in a state of disbelief, as if the man is a psychotic. Who are these people who look at sex and penises this way and talk about it as if it and they were, well, nothing special? No big deal. Even when penises are big, they're "nice," maybe, but no big deal: "nice weenie." And sometimes they retract and shrivel up. No big deal. Which brings us back to the balloons.

In Forgetting Sarah Marshall, the initial image we see of Peter's penis occurs when he drops his towel and swivels his hips to impress Sarah and motivate her to run into his arms for sex. The first time we see Jack's penis, he stands befuddled with balloons tied around it. The balloons suggest playfulness on Marion's part. This is not about her being impressed with the spectacle of the big penis or of trying to impress others with it. It's about her having fun with it, playing with it, in a nice way, not making fun *of* it as in penis-size jokes, but not taking it all that seriously as a big important thing—the phallus—which it isn't to her or to the movie. We have noted throughout this book that the body guy has a playful, at times childlike quality about him that he brings to the woman. Here, it is reversed: she brings it to him, and she dares to do so with the privileged

cultural signifier of masculinity, virility, and sexuality—the penis. She ties balloons around it, takes pictures of it, and shows those pictures to her family.

Whereas in *Forgetting Sarah Marshall* Peter learns to cover up his penis, in
2 Days in Paris Jack learns to display it. Marion, her family, and her friends
implicitly give Jack the message that he should lighten up about his penis. His
response is to drop his pants and stand naked before her in all seriousness at the
height of a crisis in their relationship, suggesting it's the start of their salvation.
Is he learning that in order to be part of Marion's world he must stop taking his
penis so seriously? Whereas Americans are prone to such sentiments as, "Ah,
the French," here the more appropriate response is, "Ah, the Americans."

A minor miracle in this day and age stands at the center of *2 Days in Paris*:
the film does not invest for a moment in any sexual fantasy of the body culture,
including the body guy, with his magical penis and pound-cubed sexual performance. The world of sex depicted in the film is anchored in something
palpably real as opposed to fantasy. There is no hope that a Brad Pitt will mate-
rialize and make love to a woman in such a way that her life will be altered forever, that something will be awakened that she did not know about, that she
will think back on her previous lovers and realize how naive she was in being
satisfied with them. It is no coincidence that this film has no mind-guy / body-
guy opposition, as does *Forgetting Sarah Marshall*. It has many lovers current
and past, none of whom are thrown into competition with each other or played
off each other. Marion does not have a "rock star" body-guy former lover that
Jack has to win her away from, nor is he, with his big American penis, that lover
who has shown her the inferiority of her previous lovers. That model of sex,
and of the role of penises in such sex, has no place in this movie. This is not
a world of slow-motion montages of perfect bodies intertwined in perfectly
timed bliss, with intercourse going on and on and then continuing through the
night. The hysteria in this film is not centered on the penis and its powerful sexual performance but rather on an American man who can't understand why
there isn't more hysteria about it, like that of the Italian waiter in Venice who
almost stabbed Jack for putting parmesan cheese on his seafood pasta. Surely
penises warrant that level of hysteria. But not in this film.

2 Days in Paris raises the following opposition for us: adult attitudes and
behaviors versus childishness or immaturity. Although Marion's family and
some of her former lovers could be considered quirky, they represent an attitude toward sex and the penis that seems very mature. We have demonstrated
in our analyses of a wide variety of films that body guys are linked with play,
specifically the kind of play associated with childhood: food fights, jumping
from high places, and racing around. The validation of childhood in the body-
guy films implies that something is lost after we enter the adult world, and it

must be recaptured. Although it may be appealing to view the world with child-like wonder, curiosity, and enthusiasm, the nexus of connections between play and the body guys in movies has serious, disturbing ramifications for a concept of adulthood or maturity. The logic of body-guy representations may go as follows: body guys are linked to "proper" masculinity, proper sexuality, and play. They are opposed to mind guys; therefore, intellectuals are not properly masculine, not sexy, and at odds with playfulness. Play is linked to childhood; therefore, mind guys and intelligence are linked to adulthood. Adulthood is therefore unplayful, unmasculine, and unsexy—an unattractive, boring place. Within the logic of the body-guy genre, conforming to conventional masculinity takes precedence over this unattractive vision of intelligence and adulthood. Therein lies the danger of this body-guy / masculinity nexus: men and women who invest heavily in the notions of "manliness" and a fixed, secure masculinity with its attendant masculine privilege centered on the penis are lured away from both intelligence and maturity. The body-guy films validate the childish playfulness associated with the body while discouraging an examination of the play of the mind and true adult pleasures. It's ironic that pornography is called "adult entertainment" in that the simplistic or unexamined worship of big things such as titties and dicks, and of the long, loud, fast, and showy sexual performances central to porn is anything but adult.

Alongside such films as *Forgetting Sarah Marshall* and *2 Days in Paris* another recent challenge to the classical body-guy genre has arisen in the form of a subgenre that features sexually assertive women who appear to take their sexual pleasure into their own hands. On the surface, this strategy empowers the women, seemingly displacing the body guy's power to awaken and fulfill their sexuality. This genre transformation can be found in several of the real-sex films that we discussed in chapter 5 such as *9 Songs*, *Lie with Me*, and *Shortbus*. These films point to a dilemma for the body guy in that this subgenre hinges entirely on a category of women who conform, in part, to the definition of third-wave feminists. These are women who know about sex, care about it, expect it, and control it. In the movies, these female characters have turned the tables on the body guy: they don't wait demurely with a boring mind guy until the body guy comes along to fully awaken and fulfill their sexuality. They know what they want, and they go after it without a second thought. Zalman King, the titular pioneer of the genre, has told us that he recognizes this sea change in American culture and that he thinks the types of films he used to make no longer resonate within the contemporary milieu. Indeed he is now working in formats that feature these new sexually assertive women. He no longer includes the classic tropes of the body-guy genre: the opposition between mind guy and body guy and the awakening of a naive, deprived woman's sexuality.

The film *Lie with Me* (2005) provides a good example of this "new woman." The Internet Movie Database's "Official Synopsis" of *Lie with Me* is very helpful in articulating these shifting roles:

> Leila (Lauren Lee Smith) is a sexually voracious young woman who connects with men through brief physical encounters. One night at a crowded house party, Leila meets David (Eric Balfour) and it's lust at first sight. Later, as she has casual sex with a stranger just behind the house, David and his girlfriend mirror her actions in their car. Leila and David's eyes lock as they watch each other having sex with others, a courtship ritual that initiates their own sexual affair. Seduction is easy and very satisfying. Leila and David get to know each other—which means being intimate—in bed, at the park, on the roof, everywhere. For them, and for other members of their generation, sex is a form of communication.

The synopsis accurately identifies Leila as "voracious," but the description of the "casual sex with a stranger" scene omits something very important—she picks up the young man, sets up and controls the penetration sex, ordering him all the while not to "come." Leila describes herself in a voice-over narration at the beginning of the film as being on the "prowl" for men and sex, and she expects a man she has just met to perform perfectly to her desire the very first and only time they have sex, even though it is in a public place, with others watching and in an awkward physical position (he's up against a chain-link fence), and she expects him not to come too soon but to wait until the exact moment that she is ready for him.

Not surprisingly the synopsis notes that "seduction is easy," and while true, one might question the use of the word *seduction*: this is not a process in which an ostensibly resistant woman holds out while the alluring persistent male wears down her defenses (the usual connotation). This is a woman who lets men know she wants to fuck, tells them how she wants to do it, and then typically moves on afterward. "David and Leila get to know each other." Again, *know* may be the wrong word; they never speak or even know their names during these bed-park-roof do-it-everywhere encounters. The synopsis quite correctly interprets this kind of sex as generational, and this is key to these films: they represent a new world of sexuality that characterizes an actual segment of teen and young adult life in America. Referring to its cover story "Lust in the City," the front page of the 4 July 2008 issue of the *L.A. Weekly* declares "Women on the Prowl." A big kicker running across the center of the first page of the article inside asks, "Wondering why guys don't make the first move anymore, and other notes on lust in L.A." (Katz 29). The kicker on the following page quotes a man declaring, "There is identity chaos going on. The guys have become the sappy romantics, and the *women have become the shameless hussies*" (Katz 32).

The new assumptions about sex and gender totally destroy the narrative arc on which the body-guy genre is premised: women who are on the prowl are not *waiting* for the body guy to do *anything*, so in a sense there is nothing for him to do. His body, his good-sized penis, and his sexual performance style are all still intact and enshrined, but the narrative has to change—and change drastically. In the classic body-guy genre, as we have seen, the woman in-between frequently loses the body guy for one reason or another: he dies, society prevents their relationship, or he simply moves on. She is left longing for him and remembering him as an extraordinary lover in every sense of the word. In the new narratives, the sexually experienced women are the ones that call the shots, use the men as little more than sexual partners for short-term relationships, if anything, and frequently move on with little or no sentiment.

9 Songs illustrates this aspect of the new genre perfectly. Matt and Lisa have an agreement for a "summer of love," and then each will go their own way. Both are fully aware of the arrangement from the beginning; no one has been seduced or tricked into believing there would be more. Yet as the summer draws to a close and Lisa casually goes her own way as planned, Matt feels a desperate desire to keep her and then a devastating loss when she leaves. He has not been betrayed; he has simply fallen in love in a conventional manner and finds his life meaningless and barren without Lisa. The pattern is highlighted further in this film since it is the man, not the woman, who desires and needs the conventional relationship, the something-more-than-casual-sex. Lisa seems perfectly content in saying good-bye to her body guy, very big penis and all (see figure 29).

Zalman King makes the usual pattern perfectly clear in *Lake Consequence* when the film ends with the body guy returning the woman against her wishes to her life with her husband and family, prepping and coaching her for her reentry into her previous boring, mainstream life. Even in films where the body guy dies, like *Titanic*, he leaves his imprint forever upon the reminiscing woman he leaves behind. None of the classic body-guy films end with the body guy in a state of loss for the woman, loss is always on her side, even in *The Horse Whisperer* as the woman speeds away in her SUV from the lone rider in the western landscape. Strictly speaking, he has lost her as much as she has lost him, but the imagery of the film makes clear that the heavy loss is with her, returning to her mind guy husband and professional life in the East in comparison to the outsider lone cowboy figure, somehow romantically complete in himself in his relationship to his horse and the land.

9 Songs makes startlingly clear that one of the realities of this brave new world is that the body guy is at least as much at risk as the woman—his big penis, his pound-cubed sexual performance, and everything else notwithstanding, he has lost his mythic status. Within the almost clinical context of the real-sex films, it comes down to this: there are many other men out there with just as many inches, who can do it for just as many minutes, in just as many positions.

The real-sex films may ostensibly empower the female characters by giving them sexual agency, but they end up supporting conventional masculinity in that all the desired men have penises that meet or exceed the norm in size while flaccid and erect. These films all represent actual rather than simulated sex acts between the principal actors, a fact that seems to validate the notion that good sex requires a good-sized penis and a stellar athletic performance. The films implicitly say, "See, in these real-sex films, the body guys and their big penises really do exist, and they *can* do it in the manner suggested by the simulated sex of the conventional body-guy genre." These films address the female spectator as if to say, "If you don't have this kind of man and this kind of sex, it is not because he is only a product of the Hollywood dream machine—he really does exist." When it comes to sex, these films take on a pseudodocumentary quality: the sex is "real"—big penises, pound-cubed, and all. Far from truly threatening or dethroning the body guy, the "women on the prowl" subgenre is actually a dream for those who make and promote films of the genre. Under the guise of change and progress, these films present a "new" woman who wants big dicks and pound cubed from the get-go, and her ceaseless search for satisfying sex is the next logical step within the genre. In effect, we've gone from hard bodies in the 1970s and 1980s to the body guy with his big, hard penis in the late 1980s and 1990s to the hard women on the prowl in search of that penis and sexual performance in the first decade of the twenty-first century. These women know what they want and, as luck would have it, it is exactly what they have been getting and what men have wanted to give them for decades. The more things change, they more they stay the same.

If the phenomenon of prowling women looking for a good-sized penis is in actuality a false empowerment ultimately designed to restore shock and awe to the almighty penis, where are the representations of women who represent a more substantive power, and what does such power look like? In chapter 4 we discussed a pattern in which the female character's active investigative gaze both empowers her and potentially offers an erotic charge that often accompanies transgressive behavior. As we have seen, the female character in *Sirens* is linked to both a transgressive inquiring gaze and bisexuality—a notion that presents the possibility of decentering the penis. *Sirens* reveals but then contains the potential power of the inquiring or investigative gaze in culture by the fact that it must be associated with the body guy's penis in the film. Estella's enticement to act on her sexual desire is twice tied to an illicit sighting of the

body-guy Devlin's penis. At first she accidentally comes upon Devlin masturbating, but hides behind a tree in order to take a prolonged look. The second
time, she intentionally sets out to spy on Devlin and sees him posing nude for
Lindsay in his studio, which we see in long shot. We then learn it is a point-of-
view shot when the film cuts to her at the window with a look of fascination,
her eyes clearly fixed on his groin and strikingly large penis, which we have just
seen (see figures 34 and 35). With her curiosity about Devlin twice connected to
his penis, clearly she's got *it* on her mind when she later goes to him for sex. By
the film's conclusion, however, in her erotic imagination the image of the models caressing each other replaces the body guy with his strikingly large penis and
her memory of her sexual encounter with him.

Somewhat similarly in *The Governess* Rosina investigates Charles's laboratory and begins a series of interactions with him that culminate with the image
of his nude body and good-sized penis on display as she photographs him.
Unlike Estella, who is excited by the vision of the body guy's large penis and
seeks sex with him, Rosina doesn't even wake Charles up to have wild pounding sex with him. By the film's conclusion, she, too, rejects the spectacle of the
penis, in this case absconding with the photographic lens, a symbol of the substantive power that interests her rather than the promise of the penis. In effect,
by the end of both of these films, after encountering the spectacle of the
impressive penises at the heart of their investigative journeys, the central
female characters declare, "That's not it!"

To best understand what a significant alternative to the body guy, his gifted
penis, and stellar pound-cubed sexual performance might look like, it is appropriate that we return to the narrative that essentially began our investigation,
Lady Chatterley's Lover. In 2006, French director Pascale Ferran made *Lady
Chatterley* adapted from D. H. Lawrence's *John Thomas and Lady Jane*, the
second draft of what would become *Lady Chatterley's Lover*. This unorthodox
decision enables Ferran to come up with a fresh approach to a by now well
known story. To be sure, Lawrence's second draft fully participates in phallic
worship: "And then something awoke in her. Strange, thrilling sensation, that
she had *never known before* woke up *where he was within her*, in wild thrills, like
wild, wild bells. It was wonderful, wonderful, and she clung to him uttering in
complete unconsciousness strange, inarticulate little cries, that he heard within
himself with curious satisfaction. But it was over too soon, too soon!" (133,
emphasis added).

But, as if this were not enough, it is not over. In a paragraph after the above
lament Lawrence writes, "*Till he came into her again*, and the thrills woke up
once more, wilder and wilder. . . . When she awoke to herself she knew *life had
changed for her*" (133, emphasis added). Indeed, Lady Chatterley expresses how

"grateful" she is to Parkin, and Lawrence returns to the above theme: "She was aware of a strange woman awakened up inside herself" (134), and she comes to recognize, "He was but a temple servant, the guardian and keeper of the bright phallus, which was hers, her own" (136). Excessive as these passages are, in hindsight, the second draft actually downplays the penis as a phallic wonder capable of producing thrilling and uncontrollable orgasms in comparison to what would follow in the final version and it is this difference that opens the door for Ferran. She goes much further than Lawrence in toning down the phallic worship, and it is precisely the excess of the above language that Ferran implicitly critiques in her filmic version of the tale, along with the central notion of the glorious phallus that Lawrence increasingly embraced, and that his followers would reembrace in the late twentieth century. The brilliance of her film is closely tied to her groundbreaking decision to go back to an earlier draft of Lawrence's influential work since by virtue of its comparative obscurity it was also less calcified than the classic. When he wrote *John Thomas and Lady Jane*, even Lawrence had not yet discovered or fully articulated the extreme end point of the phallic worship that would emerge in the third version and in his essay about it entitled, "A Propos of *Lady Chatterley's Lover*." Ferran uses Lawrence's middle version to reimagine how his now archetypal story could have been told differently, with a much different legacy—one suitable to her vision of mature lovemaking in the early twenty-first century.

Ferran dephallicizes the penis, lovemaking, and masculinity in a profundity of ways. First, the casting of Parkin is quite unconventional in that the actor Jean-Louis Coullo'ch, although strong in appearance, is not buff or cut in the manner of other body guys. In fact, he may be described as stocky, his hair thinning and his face somewhat coarse rather than handsome in a chiseled way. He's no Brad Pitt or even a Sean Bean (voted Britain's second-sexiest man alive), the latest actor before Coullo'ch to play Mellors/Parkin onscreen in Ken Russell's made-for-TV British production of the tale from 1993. More important, the lovemaking itself deviates wildly from the usual body-guy pattern. Parkin and Connie have intercourse a total of six times in the film, with penetration ranging from thirty-seven to sixty-four seconds in "real time" from when Parkin enters her to his climax. This within a culture in which the media recently widely circulated a study documenting that the "satisfactory" range for actual penetration during intercourse was between three and thirteen minutes with "7–13 minutes" being "desirable" and "1–2 minutes" being "too short" ("Good Sexual Intercourse")! An Associated Press story even cited the editor of the *Journal of Sexual Medicine*, who reported that a previous study of fifteen hundred couples found the median time for sexual intercourse to be 7.3 minutes as documented by the women using stopwatches ("Sex Therapists Say").

Ferran does not use devices such as the montage typical of films like *Legends of the Fall* suggesting that the lovers went at it for a prolonged time, although they do have sex twice over the course of one evening. Only one of the six scenes fades out while they are still having intercourse, the others concluding within a minute of penetration. For the first two times they have intercourse, Connie (Marina Hands) does not even appear to have an orgasm. When she eventually does, it's depicted in an understated way, nothing equivalent to the above florid language from the novel. The two of them briefly moan, and then Parkin calmly comments that they both "came" together that time, to which Connie matter-of-factly replies "yes." Their sexual encounters are not depicted as boring or unsatisfying, however. Indeed, the two always appear exhausted after their lovemaking, but not from vigorous pounding sex in which they work up a pro-fusion of sweat. Their thrusting motions appear regulated for their mutual pleasure rather than to create a display of masculine bravura. Their sense of being spent is the result of the intense passion they feel for each other, a passion that Ferran does not link to wild athletic sexual performance.

Notably, within this context, the reception of *Lady Chatterley* in the United States marked the first time that mainstream critics in highly respectable news-papers and magazines reviewed the lovemaking scenes in detail, remarking on their departure from the clichés we've discussed throughout this book. Predictably at times, the critics lapse into an uncritical realism, but the main point is still significant: they recognize something different and something they can relate to that is within their lived experience, as opposed to the standard pound-cubed spectacle. They recognize mature lovemaking. Ferran herself contributed to this in interviews by talking about the importance of the love-making scenes and the time she devoted to rehearsing alone with just the two actors, isolated from the rest of the production. This exceptional departure from how lovemaking and especially intercourse is represented onscreen resulted, not surprisingly, from much work and careful attention to detail. Ferran has also given the same care and attention to the details of the all-important male body in her retelling of this archetypal tale of sexuality.

Connie's discovery of Parkin's body is about the discovery of her own body rather than about life-altering orgasms produced by a throbbing phallus. As in both novels, Connie is overcome with emotion at the first clandestine sighting of Parkin's shirtless torso as he bathes himself. Later that evening, Connie stands nude in front of a mirror and surveys herself, suggesting that the sight of Parkin's body triggers an investigation of her own body. (An almost identical pattern occurs in Clint Eastwood's *Bridges of Madison County* (1995). Meryl Streep's character sees Eastwood freshening his torso with water from a well and, later that night, looks at her nude body in a mirror.) Connie's investigation

Figure 40. *Lady Chatterley*

of her own body extends to Parkin as well, which brings us to another way in which Ferran maturely deviates from both Lawrence and the later conventional representation of the body guy. When Connie explores Parkin's body as he had explored hers, she is excited and full of wonder at the stocky hairiness of his legs, even though his body does not conform to the body-guy norm. Connie's exploration leads us to perhaps Ferran's most subversive representation of Parkin's body. At one point before they make love, Connie tells Parkin to remove his shirt with long tails, the only remaining article of clothing he has on. She then orders him to turn around before extinguishing the candle. He does so, revealing a nearly erect penis that appears to be at the small end of the normative range—not a porn penis by any means. Connie smiles in delight, quelling his slight discomfort. The next morning, Connie sees Parkin nude again and comments, "How curious. It's tiny now. Like a bud." We too see Parkin's penis, which is now flaccid and not only significantly smaller than his semierect state but also smaller than the expected norm (figure 40). Parkin chuckles at Connie's remark, not self-conscious at all, and she is shown smiling in delight, not in derision or disappointment.

Once again, it is instructive to carefully compare the visual construction of this sequence with Lawrence's account of it in *John Thomas and Lady Jane.* As in the movie she orders him to turn around as he undresses so that she can see: "He turned slowly, in the unwillingness of his roused, exposed nakedness. He saw her looking at his phallus . . . the erect phallus seemed sure, cocksure, a strange, wildly alert *proud* presence between the two beings" (236, emphasis added). Later, after their lovemaking, Connie thinks of "the erect, sightless overweening phallus," which she envisions as a "godhead." The penis, the phallus, and fucking are all explicitly conflated: "Because his phallus rose in its own weird godhead, with its own swarthy pride and surety, and 'fucking' went to the phallic roots of his soul" (238). This is not *just* fucking (what Lawrence associates with the modern jazz era); this is *fucking*: "The only thing which had taken her quite away from fear, if only for a night, was the strange gallant phallus looking round in its odd bright godhead" (239).

Nothing in the shot of Parkin's nearly erect penis in the film or of the images of their lovemaking or their postcoital conversations ever suggests anything equivalent to this kind of phallic worship. The image of his nearly erect penis is refreshing, attractive aesthetically without for a moment seeming impressive or "cocksure." Never does it look like a source of "pride" for Parkin or Connie, nor does it ever look like a "godhead." Indeed, it does not even have the fully erect quality that Lawrence emphasizes. Although Parkin is clearly aroused and very close to full size, his penis is still pointing downward. There is no trace of phallic worship here, either of the Lawrence variety, the hard-core porn variety, or even the tasteful art cinema variety of *9 Songs* or *Shortbus*.

Afterward, as in the film, the following scene takes place between Connie and Parkin: "And he turned to her, not ashamed now in his nakedness, the phallus little and sticky. . . . How strange it is!' she said with *a certain awe*, 'So little now, like a bud, and innocent. Little and innocent!'" (Lawrence, *John Thomas* 242, emphasis added). Interestingly, with the choice of the word *tiny* Ferran's adaptation uses a key word from the equivalent scene not in *John Thomas and Lady Jane* but, rather, *Lady Chatterley's Lover*: "'And now he's *tiny*, and soft like a little bud of life!' she said" (231). A following line makes explicit how the penis imagery, including that of the small penis, functions throughout both versions of this tale. Connie goes on to exclaim, "And he comes so far into me!" (Lawrence, *Lady Chatterley* 231).

For Lawrence's Connie Chatterley the tiny or small penis exists only in relation to the proud, erect phallus. What she finds attractive about it is directly related to its contrast with what she has just experienced. She likes it because of what it can become. As such, the small penis is always associated with vulnerability and femininity. Connie likes it not because it is an *alternative* to phallic male sexuality but because of its place *within* phallic sexuality. Lawrence makes this clear early in *John Thomas and Lady Jane* when he describes the "wilting of a poor little penis" (172) as follows: "And then, the strange *shrinking* of the penis was something so tender, so beautiful, the sensitive *frailty* of what was so *fierce a force*, she could feel her heart cry out" (173, emphasis added). The small flaccid penis can only be seen as poor, wilted, and shrunken; its meaning, value, and beauty is not within itself but only in contrast to the fierce force of the powerful, large erection.

But Ferran never grants the penis those qualities in her film. The penis never becomes the phallus, as Lawrence would have it. By choosing the word *tiny* from *Lady Chatterley's Lover*, Ferran emphasizes the small size of Parkin's flaccid penis. While seeming to closely follow Lawrence in her adaptation, Ferran has in fact pulled the small-penis imagery and language entirely outside of Lawrence's system of meaning. At this point in the early twenty-first century, Ferran understands that such phallic worship is not just ludicrous but also that it must be confronted within representation and cast aide if we are to move beyond it.

As Ferran recasts the body guy's appearance, penis, and sex style, she also exposes how these factors have been linked to the larger concept of masculinity—and she critiques this as well. Clifford Chatterley is linked to conventional masculinity through his control of Connie and his belief that he's entitled to dominate the people who work for him. He is distanced literally from his body through his paralysis but also speaks of bodies as if one is interchangeable with another, an attitude he held before his crippling wound. He tells Connie, "Oh, there's not much to know [about men]. One body's as good as the next. It's mere animal instinct." Clifford's certitude in his masculine mastery is contrasted with Parkin's insecurity—his wavering identity as it relates to masculinity. Connie becomes pregnant by Parkin and leaves on a holiday with her family to deceive Clifford as to the identity of the real father. She returns to Wragby soon after learning that Parkin has been beaten up by the town "brutes" and has resigned his post as gamekeeper to work in a factory. She pleads with him not to go and offers to buy a farm for him to tend. He replies that it's not right for a man to live off a woman. It's at this point he confesses that his move to the factory is an attempt to fit in with other people—other men in particular. He describes his perceived difference from "other folk" in gender terms: "When I was a kid, my mother kept calling me a girl. She said there was something in my character that was more like a woman than a man. Well, maybe she was right." Connie replies, "Why do you say that as if it were a weakness? It's not. You are more sensitive than idiots like Dan Coutts [the man who beat him up]. You should be proud of being sensitive." Note that Ferran's use of the word *proud* in the film refers only to Parkin's conventionally feminine trait of sensitivity, not to the cocksure godhead phallus of Lawrence's novels. Connie goes on to say that he has a gift, "the gift of life." Ferran raises the notion of the body guy's gift, but in this case it is not linked to his penis or his lovemaking abilities, as it is in other body-guy films, but to the larger package, so to speak, of what Parkin represents. His gift, in part, is that he is singularly unique, not the interchangeable body that Clifford supposes. He does not readily conform to cultural notions of masculinity either in the narrative or in Ferran's visual presentation of the character and his body.

Once again, Ferran's adaptation carefully follows *John Thomas and Lady Jane*. Parkin declares, " 'My mother allers said as I was on'y ha'ef a man' " (332). " 'I've got too much of a woman in me' " (332). And Connie assures him by saying such things as, " 'But why *should* you be like other men? . . . They're only stupid' " (332) and " 'You ought to be proud. . . . It's very good for a man to have a touch of a woman's sensitiveness' " (333). She also tells him, " 'You have got a gift—a gift of life. . . . Don't have silly ideas about being manly' " (333). Much of the dialogue in the film scene including the precise use of the words *proud* and *gift* that are so significant to our reading of it come directly from Lawrence.

Clearly, Ferran has a very delicate, sophisticated adaptation strategy. She has remade Lawrence's telling of this now mythic twentieth-century tale by seemingly remaining faithful to it, but the trick, so to speak, is in what she leaves out, what she does not attempt to represent in any way by action, visual imagery, dialogue, or narration. All of Lawrence's mythologizing about the penis/phallus, the importance of real "phallic" fucking as opposed to "just" fucking is gone. There is no trace of it anywhere—on the male body, on the penis, in the lovemaking scenes, or in the lovers' conversation. Nor do we hear about it in the film's limited use of voice-over narration. All of Lawrence's rhapsodizing about how the woman is changed in an instant and knows she is changed forever by having the body guy *in* her is gone, as is all the repeated emphasis on the woman feeling that the only time she is safe is when the body guy's phallus is *in* her. All these images of power—the phallic godhead, safety, real fucking—are gone, but we do hear and see, sometimes in combination, everything that ties masculinity, the male body, and the penis to women and the feminine. Ferran is shockingly faithful as it were to tracing that connection while totally silencing the other.

We have shown how excluding the small penis from representation is part of an effort to represent the penis as a visually impressive spectacle that clearly and dramatically marks the significant distinction between men and women. Lawrence, however, grants the small penis a place within representation and one that the woman finds attractive but only insofar as it is a shrunken, wilted trace of the fierce phallic power she has already known and values. Ferran's film, which was released as we were finishing this book, corroborates our main argument that the time is past to grant the penis/phallus any such privilege. In *John Thomas and Lady Jane* the aspect of Parkin that is like a woman is tied first and foremost to his character, what Connie calls his "sensitivity." His sensitivity is tied to his body, however, in that he is not fit to work the mines, but Lawrence grants his penis and fucking style the full force of phallic masculinity. Being like a woman does not refer to the penis and fucking, except in the moments where the shrunken penis is wilted and frail. To Ferran, a man not conforming to the norm of dominant masculinity is positive, and as we have shown in the last couple of chapters, we think this is also relevant to the penis. The penis, when "tiny" or "little," does not signify frailty; the truth of the small penis is that it makes clear how ludicrous it is to pin anything significant about the difference between men and women and between desirable masculinity and inadequate masculinity on one or two inches. And only about two inches separate small penises from the treasured norm. It is just as ludicrous to pin any significance on four inches! The truth of the small penis, in other words, makes clear how ridiculous it is to invest so much significance in any penis, regardless of its size. Men who embody or even exceed the norm tell us absolutely nothing about their masculinity, sexuality, or empowerment. Any sense of priv- ilege that these men (and the women who desire them) or dominant culture may attribute to their large penises can be eliminated in a moment by a word. The power of language far outweighs the power of the penis; a few words can cut any penis however large "down to size." Penises are not just inches away from being nothing; they are also moments away.

In Ferran's *Lady Chatterley*, when Connie asks Parkin why he wants to be like other men, she declares, "They're only stupid." In our terms, to make the penis conform to ideal norms in representation is also stupid, which includes representing it as an impressive visual display that promises desirable mas- culinity. Lawrence writes of Parkin in *John Thomas and Lady Jane*, "The idea that he was too womanly was terribly humiliating to him; and manliness meant stupid, unimaginative insentience to him" (332–33). It is time that we, like Ferran in *Lady Chatterley*, apply this equally to Lawrence's highly treasured phallus and to culture's continuing worshipful overvaluation of the penis. There is nothing humiliating about small penises. The so-called manliness that culture associates with normative and large ones is not only stupid but also unimaginative. If we want to free our imaginations, we have to break this con- nection between manliness and the penis.

In her highly influential 1970 book *Sexual Politics*, Kate Millett rightly notes of *Lady Chatterley's Lover* that "the celebration of sexual passion for which the book is so renowned is largely a celebration of the penis of Oliver Mellors, the gamekeeper and social prophet" (238). We have argued essentially the same thing about the body-guy genre that arose in the 1980s, traced back to Lawrence's novel. From this point of view the timing of Pascale Ferran's *Lady Chatterley* could not have been more fortuitous. Although we have shown that differing periods and nationalities all inflect these narratives differently, they continue to share a celebration of the body guy's penis that lies at their center. So important is this cultural imperative to call attention to the penis that the usual taboo on representing it in cinema has been abandoned. Yet Ferran does so with a fresh, reevaluative eye, in a sense grabbing the gamekeeper and his penis away from both Lawrence's ideological project and from that of the hordes of followers in the 1980s and 1990s who put their version of that legendary body guy and his magical penis to work in the service of their visions of masculinity and sexuality.

In 1971, the year following Millett's *Sexual Politics*, Hilary Simpson published *D. H. Lawrence and Feminism*. Simpson argues that Lawrence held a "growing belief that a masculine renaissance was required in order to correct the subjugation and apathy into which men had fallen" (128). Mellors is the new hero emerging from that renaissance. It is an understatement to say that Ferran has something different in mind. But many of the other body-guy films and the "new" masculinity that has arisen out of the current body culture has disturbing parallels with Lawrence's project. When Millett and Simpson wrote in 1971, the second wave of feminism posed a new threat to the dominant masculine world order. By the time Ferran revisited Lady Chatterley in 2006, that threat had been delivered upon. Indeed, the 1980s, 1990s, and first decade of the twenty-first century saw women move into positions in the workplace that were previously the primary domain of men, and they moved up into positions of power and leadership from which they had previously been excluded. Similarly, women were sexually active in a new, more extensive manner.

We have written this book in the hopes of making clear that many simple, fixed polarities are false and limiting to all involved, even those who seem like the winners or the lucky ones. Contrary to the way we were acculturated, much eroticism and sexual pleasure has nothing to do with norms about the penis, sexual positions, or how long penetration lasts (or even if it takes place at all). The norms and expectations of male sexual performance deemed "good sex" in the body-guy genre often derail rather than enhance sexual pleasure for both women and men. The effort to live up to those expectations blocks individuals from discovering their unique erotic and intellectual sensibilities, locking them into repeating the same old standardized scenarios.

But learning to unmake love is much more complex than just throwing away the ruler and the stopwatch and the formula of progressing from foreplay to the predetermined sexual positions. It requires an ability to see the male body, the penis, the mind, and masculinity in a fresh, new light. Penises do not indicate varying degrees of power and masculinity, nor need they be perceived and labeled impressive or unimpressive. The polar extremes here always go together. We can't have one or get rid of one without the other. If we want to

live in a world where we do not exalt the phallic power of the big penis, we have
to live in one where we do not deride the small one. Even if we are well inten-
tioned and wish to embrace the so-called feminine qualities of the small penis
as a way of celebrating tenderness and frailty as opposed to the power of the
large penis, in so doing we ensure the very continuation of both within a gendered system. Again we stress both language and visual perception. We have to
learn to *see* penises in a different light, and we can only do that if artists, including "amateurs" in this Internet era of user-generated content Web sites, represent them in manners that enable us to do so. We not only need variety, but we
need narrative contexts that shatter all the narrowly fixed images we've analyzed throughout this book. It will not take long before the "impressive" norm
loses its impressiveness and small, above-the-scrotum penises will simply
appear as a variation in shape and size.

Representational practice has to change. In *Lady Chatterley*, Pascale Ferran
has noticed and foregrounded these normally unspoken issues of the body and
lovemaking styles and made us rethink how we unquestioningly consume the
same thing over and over, as if it were fixed in some simple natural order. It
isn't. And Ferran shows us a possible alternative world in a carefully thought
out and rehearsed manner. Coullo'ch's Parkin and Sarsgaard's Martin of
Kinsey (see figure 28) offer a profound glimpse of a world with a much more
diverse representation of the male body and the penis, and perhaps it is no
coincidence that in both films these actors play characters who stand with full
self-confidence as they reveal themselves to their lovers. The characters in no
way seem brave, nor do they feel in any way humiliated by their comparatively
small penises, even when, as in *Lady Chatterley*, the lover comments on it.
These characters grant size no significance beyond that of a simple physical
attribute, one which may be observed and even enjoyed. Perhaps it is also no
coincidence that both characters are associated with a new or different masculinity, one so different that it's considered deviant from the perspective of
dominant masculinity. Martin in *Kinsey* is bisexual, and Parkin talks about
how he has always been "like a woman." Yet both these films present these
characters as profoundly appealing and sexually empowered.

The confident manner in which Parkin and Martin stand fully nude before
their lovers also points to the role that men with small penises can play themselves in determining how others perceive their size. The confidence and personality with which a man presents himself mediate the perception of his body.
If a man with a small penis sees himself as deficient and lacking, this negative
perception may have a similar impact on others. On the other hand, if a small
man displays a confident demeanor, he appears attractive, and he may even
invite a positive perception like that which we described in chapter 5, where the

small penis is valued as part of a package that enables a prominent display of the scrotum and an aesthetics of proportionality and harmony. Those who make images of bodies and those who respond to them do not have complete control.

Expectations people bring to the act of lovemaking are also relevant here. Men who feel good about themselves because they have a presumed impressive penis and can perform pound-cubed sex well, and women who feel good about their lovers for those same two reasons, fall prey to a notion of a fixed, plentiful, all-powerful masculinity that doesn't exist. In so doing they reassure themselves that they are normal but also ironically suppress their individuality. In other words, for many couples it is reassuring to know that the man's penis is of average size; they are having sex within the normative range of frequency, and intercourse lasts for an acceptable amount of time. We need to learn, however, to acknowledge difference and variety outside of narrow, limiting, judgmental values that blind us to range and opportunity. There is room for big penises, and there is room for pound cubed, but not as exalted privileged figures that come at the expense of small penises and alternative sexual scenarios. And penis size by itself, of course, does not determine whether a man will primarily favor penetration sex or alternatives to it. Nor does size determine how well he will perform any of those sexual practices. Furthermore, those who embody and embrace the norms for their pleasure do so differently if they understand and respect this range and diversity of bodies and sexualities rather than unreflectively conform to cultural pressure.

The veneration of the body guy, his penis, and pound-cubed sex in society and in the movies is a symptom of a larger anti-intellectualism in the culture. It is imperative that we reconsider the relationship between the mind and body in the formation of identity and self-worth. Creative lovers using the mind and the imagination rely less on the penis and more fully on the intellect. To illustrate this, let us imagine an alternative scenario involving Clifford Chatterley in *Lady Chatterley's Lover*. At this point, however, we want to move beyond the predictable ways in which a paraplegic man could engage in sex not tied to the penis, such as oral sex, and imagine representing him as a potent appealing mind guy. In Lawrence's novel and even in Ferran's adaptation, Clifford is a highly cerebral intellectual with a passion for reading and learning, and he shares this with his wife, Connie, in a regular ritual of reading aloud and engaging in meaningful conversation with her. Yet this is seen as limiting, tedious, and sometimes even grating, as if it is symptomatic of his disconnection from the pulse of real life, as indeed his symbolic paralysis suggests. Why not show Connie becoming intimately aroused in an exchange of passion with Clifford as he reads? For our project, it is not simply enough to displace the body guy and his gifted penis. We have to also resuscitate and learn to fully appreciate the living, vital, exciting world of the mind—a world that, far from being at odds with sex and eroticism, offers entrée into a sexuality of its own. We want to imagine movies in which mind guys who read and converse are sexy and erotic and where the qualities tied to them are part of their ability to be successful lovers.

We began this book by surveying how the openness and experimentation of the counterculture, the work of researchers on multiple intelligences, the second wave of feminism, and the development of academic gender studies all offered profound opportunities to redefine masculinity, sexuality, and notions of the mind and body. Those opportunities were lost on Hollywood and the movies as they went about business as usual—a cycle that continues. We can reject the easy anti-intellectual mythology of the body guy, the big penis, and pound-cubed sex by creatively integrating intelligence and the mind with eroticism and the body, or we can once again let the moment pass us by and succumb to more of the same old, same old. We cannot directly or immediately change Hollywood or the movies but we can change how we react to them and think about them. And we now live in a world where we can increasingly create and distribute alternative images and stories ourselves. We can learn to laugh instead of desire or emulate, and we can learn to imagine and explore instead of copy and strive. We can recognize and embrace multiple masculinities and sexualities and eroticisms just like multiple intelligences; we can dethrone the body guy with his preferred penis and sex style to identify and develop our own unique preferences instead. As we hope to have shown, movies can be most useful when we are critically aware of the limited options they often offer us and seize on those moments and those rare films that dare to break with the usual and the expected.

Notes

CHAPTER 1 — "EVERYTHING YOU ARE IS BETWEEN YOUR LEGS"

1. Even though many of these films were not box-office hits, box office is no longer the most accurate indicator of film audiences or revenues, especially for certain genre films or films made for niche markets. Many films find their primary audience on DVD, the Internet, pay-per-view TV, premium movie channels, and basic cable and network broadcasts. Some of these films are aimed at the women's market, which has long been undervalued and underestimated. They find their audiences, even if at the time critics dismiss them and the public doesn't rush out to the theater when they are released.

2. It is important to recall that it was not until 1959 that *Lady Chatterley's Lover* could even be legally published and sent through the mail in the United States, as Fred Kaplan documented in the *New York Times* on the fiftieth anniversary of the court ruling. Lawrence's work could not have been written and published as proper Victorian literature, and the films we examine here could not have been made in classic Hollywood. Pornography in both eras described and represented the penis and explicit sexuality, but we are dealing here with mainstream cinema and are far from classical Hollywood's fade to black and that era's body guys such as Clark Gable, John Wayne, and Marlon Brando.

3. With the exception of *Box of Moonlight*, all of the films we discuss here were directed by non-U.S. filmmakers, which suggests that showing the penis is particularly difficult for Americans and less charged for filmmakers in some other countries. Ironically, the body-guy genre touches a great American paradox: a puritanical tradition distrustful of the body and sexuality, and an anti-intellectual tradition distrustful of the mind. Perhaps the extremes that we find in the late twentieth-century body culture can only have arisen from such an impossible context. The stakes are currently very high for Americans, and specifically certain classes of Americans in a film genre that locates a man's sense of self-worth and well being in his sexual performance and his penis while denigrating the world of the mind and the sexual performance and adequacy of the men who live in that world.

4. Indeed, by 2008 the body guy and his penis had become so well known that his persona and sexual prowess could be easily represented even in PG-13 rated films that have no male frontal nudity or graphic sex. In *Australia* (2008), Hugh Jackman, *People Magazine*'s Sexiest Man Alive in 2008, plays the body guy. He is known only as the Drover in the film, a name that oozes body-guy connotations: cowboys, animals, rural life, ruggedness, sweat. In perhaps a not-so-subtle reference to Lady Chatterley, the beautiful woman is Lady Sarah Ashley (Nicole Kidman), who, though estranged from her aristocratic husband, travels from England to Australia to manage their ranch after he's murdered. Immediately upon Lady Sarah's arrival in the outback, her sexual and sensual lack—and a solution for

it—is established when a metaphoric penis is literally shoved in her face. An Aboriginal climbs atop a truck in which she's riding, and as he passes her open window, a large phallic item dangling from his crotch nearly slaps her in the face. She screams in shock while Drover looks on amused. In an even more direct reference to *Lady Chatterley's Lover*, Lady Sarah's interest in Drover is piqued for the first time when she sees him bathing, his shirtless torso all hairless and buff. We see Jackman from various angles and distances that emphasize his chiseled physique; Lady Sarah's dramatic transfixed gaze at the spectacle of the male body asks the audience to be spellbound as well. In an ensuing conversation, Drover discusses his sexual abilities, and all he has to do is put his hand down by his crotch highlighted by his partially undone pants for us to know that he is well endowed and knows what to do with it. We don't have to see his penis.

The term *well-endowed*, which we use here and elsewhere in the book in its commonly accepted meaning, descriptively connotes a desirable abundance of riches. We reject such connotations and even the assumption that the penis should be privileged as defining a man's "endowment."

5. See Anthony Easthope's *What a Man's Gotta Do: The Masculine Myth in Popular Culture* (1990); Kaja Silverman's *Male Subjectivity at the Margins* (1992); Peter Lehman's *Running Scared: Masculinity and the Representation of the Male Body* (1993); Steven Cohan's and Ina Rae Hark's anthology *Screening the Male: Exploring Masculinities in Hollywood Cinema* (1993); Dennis Bingham's *Acting Male: Masculinities in the Films of James Stewart, Jack Nicholson, and Clint Eastwood* (1994); Mark Simpson's *Male Impersonators: Men Performing Masculinity* (1994); Susan Jeffords's *Hard Bodies: Hollywood Masculinity in the Reagan Era* (1994); and the anthology *Constructing Masculinity* (1995), edited by Maurice Berger, Brian Wallis, and Simon Watson.

6. The novel raises the complex issue of nationhood and history in that Lady Chatterley's lovers in the movies are so often American men. The United States plays no role in Lawrence's novel; nevertheless, we have put the welcome mat out. Lawrence published *Lady Chatterley's Lover* in 1928, but we didn't put the welcome mat out then because of censorship issues. Several puzzles emerge when we consider the time frame of 1928 and 1988, when Zalman King made *Two Moon Junction*, jump-starting the body-guy genre in the United States. Most obviously, we have two drastically different time periods in regard to the history of sexuality. Lawrence wrote in the early modern era against a backdrop of presumed Victorian sexual repression, and, indeed, the Victorian novel (if we exclude the pornography of the "other Victorians") had no tradition of explicit sexual lovemaking. Good lovers had nothing to do with a preferred sexual style or penis. Furthermore, Lawrence wrote at a time when England had become a modern urban nation with thriving cities, a majority of the population far removed from the world of rural aristocracy, farms, and gamekeepers. Just like most urban Americans of the twentieth century never met real cowboys, undoubtedly most urban English people in 1928 had never met a gamekeeper. The western genre, with its cowboys and open plains, arose in America just as the "wild West" was, in fact, disappearing. This undoubtedly became a precondition for romanticizing the cowboy hero and the environment in which he lived. The same is true for the gamekeeper close to nature and animals in *Lady Chatterley's Lover*. He could be granted an extraordinary phallic sexuality precisely because Lawrence's readers were no longer part of that world.

By 1988 America had undergone what was popularly perceived as a "sexual revolution" twenty years earlier in 1968. Movie theaters all over cities like New York showed graphic triple-X-rated hard-core pornography. Indeed, by 1988 it had spread to people's homes via videotape and VCRs. Instead of being in the midst of what was popularly perceived as Victorian repression, we were in the midst of what was commonly perceived as an anything-goes sexual environment, in life, the arts, and the media. Sex and nudity were everywhere. And if Europe had just recently shifted from an agrarian to an urban society at the beginning of the twentieth century, by the late 1980s and 1990s in America that phenomenon was history, and the realities of the computer era were about to make it ancient history. Simply stated, the appeal of the working-class, man of the earth narrative had to be something much different and mean something much different to Lawrence's readers than its late twentieth and early twenty-first-century reincarnations do to contemporary readers and filmgoers.

CHAPTER 2 — REBELS, OUTSIDERS, ARTISTS, AND . . . BRUTES?

1. The following discussion does not depend on the circumstances of the film's production. We do not know, nor do we care, whether Dumont asked the actors to audition for the part nude. Either he cast Wissak in the lead role knowing that his penis is smaller than the norms of the average size in representation, or he cast him without knowing. If it is the former, the narrative trajectory and visual patterns we analyze were in some sense determined at the outset. Even if Dumont and no one associated with the production saw Wissak nude before they filmed the nude scenes, this in no way hurts our analysis since what matters is how they incorporated his body into the film as it was being made. They chose various techniques, such as camera angles, cutting patterns, actions, and dialogue, that emphasize his penis size in a certain manner. Katia, for example, puts her hand over David's penis as he lies down, removes it, and then sits up next to him while looking at him. All of the actions in this sequence—covering his genitals, removing her hand, and then sitting up and looking—bring the viewers' attention to David's penis in a manner that could easily have been avoided. Whether in advance or while making the film, Dumont made choices to foreground David's comparatively small penis in relation to the norms of representation in a manner that embedded it within the film's ideological project, which in this case unites his size with a terrible insecurity that finds an outlet in overcompensation that progresses from aggression, to violence, to homicidal rage.

CHAPTER 3 — "FUCK ME LIKE A COP, NOT A LAWYER"

1. The same stereotype of the well-hung black man applies, of course, to African Americans, who are noticeably absent as body guys across the genre. As is so often the case, the exception proves the rule. Films like *How Stella Got Her Groove Back* and *Heading South* invoke the conventions of the romance genre, where things heat up in exotic locales. But in this case something additional is going on. The black men in these roles inadvertently highlight their bizarre absence elsewhere. It is one thing to have them present in Jamaica and Haiti but another to erase them from Detroit and Atlanta. Why? In *Hung: A Meditation on the Measure of Black Men in America*, Scott Poulson-Bryant points out that despite the common sexual stereotypes, successful black actors almost never play highly sexual characters in Hollywood films. Furthermore, even the notorious long-circulated list of well-hung celebrities in Hollywood does not include black men. A culture that characterizes all black men as well-hung and hypersexual denies them such cinematic representation and denies the actors who portray them such qualities even as it breathlessly gossips about supposedly well-endowed white actors.

The body-guy genre intensifies this form of racism and poses another related dilemma. Insofar as the genre addresses professional working women who are most often implicitly white, it cannot risk the racial implications of embodying its hero in African American men (or in the case of European films, European black men). Furthermore, the genre demands a "special" quality to the hero's lovemaking abilities, and being well-hung and performing highly athletic sex are cornerstones of that gift. But the racial stereotype, of course, characterizes all African American men that way, meaning they are readily available. If, in fact, they are everywhere, that special once-in-a-lifetime quality disappears. But if American and European women (even black women, no less!) have to go to Jamaica and Haiti to find these men, both dilemmas are solved with one stroke: white American, European, and Australian body guys retain their special status, and women can dream on and keep searching for that one guy who can make all the other men they have known just that—ordinary, other men.

2. *Phenomenon* is unique in that the same character embodies both the mind guy and the body guy. The garage mechanic becomes a genius under mysterious circumstances. Revealingly, illness causes the genius; he has a brain tumor. This premise inadvertently raises two issues. Most obviously, it connects illness and abnormality to high levels of intelligence. Second, it points to the false distinction underlying the entire genre: body guys have a special sexual gift and sensitivity, while mind guys are sexually incompetent, clueless, and insensitive to women's "inner nature."

3. In a well-documented pattern, intelligent, educated, often-successful professional women are attracted to and prefer less-educated, working-class men of the earth. This is evident in books such as Pam Houston's *Cowboys Are My Weakness*, Sara Davidson's *Cowboy: A Love Story*, and Rosemary Daniell's *Sleeping with Soldiers: In Search of a Macho Man*, in which the body guy's sensitivity is emphasized, complementing his abilities as a lover. This phenomenon is worthy of further analysis.

CHAPTER 4 — "BRAIN WORK ISN'T MUCH OF A SPECTATOR SPORT"

1. Philip Roth's novels supply a complex exception. *The Professor of Desire* and *The Dying Animal* feature a highly sexual Jewish professor and the world of the mind, the intellect, and academia in general are represented as sexually charged. Roth does not oppose the penis to the brain. The film adaptation of *The Human Stain* functions quite differently within filmic traditions than it does within Roth's oeuvre. Both hinge on the secret that Coleman Silk, a highly sexual Jewish professor who is having an affair with a much younger woman, is really an African American pretending to be a Jew. In the movie this combines with the racial stereotypes to explain the quality and quantity of his lifelong sexual activity—Jewish men don't fuck like that, but black men do. In Roth's novels, however, Jewish men *do* fuck like that. Nevertheless, they are deeply dysfunctional in other ways.

Another interesting exception occurs in American film pornography, especially in the so-called golden era of theatrical hardcore, with a number of highly successful Jewish stars including Harry Reems, who starred in *Deep Throat* (1972), the film generally cited as kick-starting the genre, and the now legendary Ron Jeremy, subject of the successful documentary *Pornstar: The Legend of Ron Jeremy* (2001). We limit our analysis here to mainstream films and discourses that engage the mind-body issues we have identified. The Jewish porn stars did not play Jewish characters in their films, nor did they have well-established public Jewish personae known to the audiences of their films. In short, their status as Jewish actors was not widely known, they did not play Jewish characters, and their films thus did not deal in central ways with such issues as the depiction of intellectuals and successful professionals. Did Jewish porn stars challenge or alter the images of Jewish masculinity circulated widely in mainstream cinema? Did their success alter the public's perception of Jewish masculinity and sexuality? We do not think so, but even if that is the case, the question still remains, why were they so prominent in the genre?

2. Marty's movement toward "proper" rhythm starts with Bob Dylan, a musician whose music, performance style, and reputation are not generally associated with sexuality, and ends with Jimi Hendrix, a black musician legendary for his sexual endowment and prowess, as well as his driving, rhythmic music.

3. Both *Angels and Insects* and *The Governess* take place in Victorian England, a story-telling strategy that foregrounds the positioning of women within the culture of that time for the contemporary audience, in the process emphasizing both the extraordinary hurdles women had to overcome then in pursuit of their accomplishments while simultaneously drawing crucial parallels with women in the modern world.

4. *Erin Brockovich* intersects with the current spate of female investigators in television crime shows, particularly the Jerry Bruckheimer–produced *CSI* family of shows. The various female characters are often shown in the process of competently doing their work, whether in the field or in the lab—refreshing images. The shows are mainly about solving crimes with relatively little time devoted to personal subplots and backstories. The principal women, however, often wear tight, low-slung pants and tops that reveal ample cleavage. This is not our idea of how to make investigation sexy.

CHAPTER 5 — HUNG LIKE A HORSE . . . OR AN ACORN

1. It is important to emphasize another issue related to evolution: the value of the evolutionary distant past in explaining current human behavior. Explaining the present in such a manner has gained in popularity, owing to the appeal of its simplicity, and therefore it is particularly important to encourage caution. And in this era of reactionary attacks on evolution we want to be clear that it seems increasingly likely that female mate choice based on copulatory pleasure did, indeed, drive the evolution of the marked increase in penis size between male chimpanzees and prehominids and hominids. Like all scientists, evolutionary scientists continually gather new data and revise their hypotheses accordingly. As of this writing, it seems convincing that the small, inflexible penis of the chimpanzee who copulated for approximately eight seconds evolved because of female mate choice into a significantly larger, more flexible, hominid penis capable of copulating in many positions for longer periods.

As we have shown, there are some blind spots in the account that have yet to be addressed and refined, such as why the flaccid penis is not an accurate indicator of erect size. We are not attacking either evolutionary theory, with which we are in agreement, or the important recent work on how the penis evolved when it did. Such work is long overdue. We are, however, questioning the uncritical application of this work to explain contemporary human behavior. And this relates to the body-guy narratives and current representations of the penis.

2. Indeed, the majority of commentators on Celebrity Nudity Data Base emphatically remark about Sarsgaard's "small" or "tiny" penis.

Bibliography

Adkins, Trace. "(This Ain't) No Thinkin' Thing." *Trace Adkins Greatest Hits Collection.* Vol. 1. Capitol, 2003. CD.

Allen, James, Leon F. Litwack, and Hilton Als. *Without Sanctuary: Lynching Photography in America.* New York: Twin Palms, 2000. Print.

"Apatow Makes Penis Promise." 17 Dec. 2007. Web. 1 Dec. 2009. <www.contactmusic .com>.

Baker, Nicholas. *Vox: A Novel.* New York: Random House, 1992. Print.

Barber, Benjamin R. *Consumed: How Markets Corrupt Children, Infantilize Adults, and Swallow Citizens Whole.* New York: Norton, 2007. Print.

Berger, John. *Ways of Seeing.* London: Penguin, 1972. Print.

Berger, Maurice, Brian Wallis, and Simon Watson, eds. *Constructing Masculinity.* New York: Routledge, 1995. Print.

Bingham, Dennis. *Acting Male: Masculinities in the Films of James Stewart, Jack Nicholson, and Clint Eastwood.* New Brunswick, NJ: Rutgers UP, 1994. Print.

Biskind, Peter. "The Vietnam Oscars." *Vanity Fair* Mar. 2008: 266–80. Print.

Bordo, Susan. *The Male Body: A New Look at Men in Public and in Private.* New York: Farrar, Staus and Giroux, 1999. Print.

Bosworth, Patricia. *Diane Arbus: A Biography.* New York: Norton, 1995. Print.

Brings, Felicia, and Susan Winter. *Older Women, Younger Men: New Options for Love and Romance.* Far Hills: New Horizon Press, 2002. Print.

Brint, Steven, and Jerome Karabel. *The Diverted Dream: Community Colleges and the Promise of Educational Opportunity in America.* New York: Oxford UP, 1989. Print.

Brooks, David. "The Waning of I.Q." *New York Times* 14 Sept. 2007. Web. 15 Jan. 2010.

Celebrity Nudity Database. Web. 7 Jan. 2010. <www.cndb.com>.

Cohan, Steven, and Ina Rae Hark, eds. *Screening the Male: Exploring Masculinities in Hollywood Cinema.* London: Routledge, 1993. Print.

Collins, Wilkie. *The Evil Genius.* Orchard Park, NY: Broadview Press, 1886. Print.

Comfort, Alex. *The Joy of Sex: A Gourmet Guide to Making Love.* New York: Crown Publishing, 1972. Print.

Daniell, Rosemary. *Sleeping with Soldiers: In Search of the Macho Man.* New York: Holt, Rinehart, and Winston, 1984. Print.

Davidson, Sara. *Cowboy: A Love Story.* New York: HarperCollins, 1999. Print.

Dickinson, R. L. *Human Sex Anatomy*. 2nd ed. Baltimore: Williams and Wilkins, 1949. Print.

Durrell, Lawrence. Preface. *Lady Chatterley's Lover*. 1968. New York: Bantam, 2007. Print.

Dyer, Richard. "Don't Look Now: The Male Pin-Up." *Screen* 23.3–4 (1982): 61–73. Print.

———. *Only Entertainment*. New York: Routledge, 2002. Print.

———. *White*. New York: Routledge, 1997. Print.

Easthope, Anthony. *What a Man's Gotta Do: The Masculine Myth in Popular Culture*. New York: Routledge, 1990. Print.

Ehrenreich, Barbara. *Fear of Falling: The Inner Life of the Middle Class*. New York: HarperCollins, 1990. Print.

———. *The Worst Years of Our Lives: Irreverent Notes from a Decade of Greed*. New York: HarperCollins, 1991. Print.

Faludi, Susan. *Stiffed: The Betrayal of the American Man*. New York: Harper Perennial, 1999. Print.

Fixx, Jim. *The Complete Book of Running*. New York: Random House, 1977. Print.

Foucault, Michel. *The History of Sexuality*. Vol. 1, *An Introduction*. New York: Vintage Books, 1980. Print.

Gardner, Howard. *Frames of Mind: The Theory of Multiple Intelligences*. New York: Basic Books, 1983. Print.

———. *Intelligence Reframed: Multiple Intelligences for the 21st Century*. New York: Basic Books, 1999. Print.

Gleiberman, Owen. Rev. of *Pineapple Express*, dir. David Gordon Green. *EW.com*. Entertainment Weekly, 15 Aug. 2008. Web. 15 Jan. 2010. <www.ew.com/ew/article/0,,20217086,00.html>.

"Good Sexual Intercourse Lasts Minutes, Not Hours, Therapists Say." *ScienceDaily.com*. 2 Apr. 2008. Web. 15 Jan. 2010.

Gottlieb, Lori. "A Love Life Less Ordinary." *New York Times* 6 Feb. 2009. Web. 15 Jan. 2010.

Gould, Stephen Jay. *The Mismeasure of Man*. New York: Norton, 1981. Print.

Gowdy, Barbara. *We So Seldom Look on Love*. Hanover: Steerforth Press, 1998. Print.

Greene, Graham. *The End of the Affair*. New York: Penguin, 1951. Print.

Greenlee, Karen. "The Unrepentant Necrophile." Interview by Jim Morton. 1990. Web. 7 Jan. 2010. <www.nokilli.com/sacto/karen-greenlee.htm>.

Greider, William. *The Soul of Capitalism: Opening Paths to a Moral Economy*. New York: Simon and Schuster, 2003. Print.

———. *Who Will Tell the People: The Betrayal of American Democracy*. New York: Simon and Schuster, 1992. Print.

Hall, Stephen S. *Size Matters*. Boston: Houghton Mifflin, 2006. Print.

Haskell, Molly. *From Reverence to Rape: The Treatment of Women in the Movies*. Chicago: U of Chicago P, 1987. Print.

Heath, Stephen. "Difference." *Screen* 19.3 (autumn 1978): 51–112. Print.

Hodes, Laura. "Nude Men? You Must Be Joking." *Chicago Tribune* 11 May 2008. Web. 1 Dec. 2009. <http://archives.chicagotribune.com>.

Hofstadter, Richard. *Anti-Intellectualism in American Life*. New York: Vintage, 1963. Print.

Houston, Pam. *Cowboys Are My Weakness*. New York: Washington Square Press, 1992. Print.

Internet Movie Database. Web. <www.imdb.com>.

"Jason Segel Interview: *Forgetting Sarah Marshall*." *MoviesOnline.ca*. 2008. Web. 1 Dec. 2009. <www.moviesonline.ca/movienews_14484.html>.

Jeffords, Susan. *Hard Bodies: Hollywood Masculinity in the Reagan Era*. New Brunswick, NJ: Rutgers UP, 1994. Print.

Kaplan, Fred. "The Day Obscenity Became Art." *New York Times* 20 July 2009. Web. 1 Dec. 2009.

Katz, Dani. "Lust in the City: Hot, Sticky, and Bothered." *L.A. Weekly* 4–10 July 2008. 29–36. Print.

King, Zalman. Personal interview. 8 May 2008.

Kourlas, Gia. "The Bare Essentials of Dance." *New York Times* 12 Feb. 2006. Web. 1 Dec. 2009.

Lawrence, D. H. *John Thomas and Lady Jane*. New York: Penguin, 1927. Print.

———. *Lady Chatterley's Lover*. 1928. New York: Bantam, 2007. Print.

Lehman, Peter. *Running Scared: Masculinity and the Representation of the Male Body*. New ed. Detroit: Wayne State UP, 2007. Print.

Lehman, Peter, and Susan Hunt. "Severed Heads and Severed Genitals: Violence in *Dead Presidents*." *Framework* 43.1 (2002): 161–73. Print.

Lorenzi, Rosella. "Art News: Michelangelo's David Said Normally Built." *Discovery News* 24 Feb. 2005. Web. 15 Jan. 2010. <http://niwde.blogspot.com/2005/02/art-news -michelangelos-david-said.html>.

Marcuse, Herbert. *Eros and Civilization: A Philosophical Inquiry into Freud*. 1955. Boston: Beacon Press, 1974. Print.

Masters, William H., and Virginia E Johnson. *Human Sexual Response*. Boston: Little, Brown, 1966. Print.

Mayle, Peter. *"What's Happening to Me?" A Guide to Puberty*. 1975. New York: Lyle Stuart, 1989. Print.

McMillan, Terry. *How Stella Got Her Groove Back*. 1996. New York: NAL Trade, 2004. Print.

The Men of Oz: Nude Scenes from HBO's TV Series "OZ." Web. 7 Jan. 2010. <http:// acropolisvideo.com/menofoz>.

Miller, Geoffrey. *The Mating Mind: How Sexual Choice Shaped the Evolution of Human Nature*. New York: Anchor, 2000. Print.

Millett, Kate. *Sexual Politics*. 1970. Urbana: U of Illinois P, 2000. Print.

Morrison, Patt. "Giving Smart Its Due." *Los Angeles Times* 11 Oct. 2007: A21. Print.

Nin, Anaïs. *The Diary of Anaïs Nin*. Vol. 1, *1931–1934*. Ed. Gunther Stuhlmann. New York: Harvest Books, 1966. Print.

———. *Henry & June: From the Unexpurgated Diary of Anaïs Nin*. New York: Harvest Books, 1986. Print.

Pope, Harrison G., Jr., Katharine A. Phillips, and Roberto Olivardia. *The Adonis Complex: How to Identify, Treat, and Prevent Body Obsession in Men and Boys*. New York: Touchstone, 2000. Print.

Poulson-Bryant, Scott. *Hung: A Meditation on the Measure of Black Men in America*. New York: Doubleday, 2005. Print.

Reubens, David R. *Everything You Always Wanted to Know about Sex (But Were Afraid to Ask)*. New York: McKay, 1969. Print.

Rodgers, Joann Ellison. *Sex: A Natural History*. New York: Holt, 2001. Print.

Roth, Philip. *The Dying Animal*. New York: Vintage, 2001. Print.

———. *The Professor of Desire*. New York: Farrar, 1977. Print.

Schwarzbaum, Lisa. Rev. of *Forgetting Sarah Marshall*, dir. Nicholas Stoller. *EW.com*. Entertainment Weekly, 17 Apr. 2008. Web. 15 Jan. 2010. <www.ew.com/ew/article/0,,20192061,00.html>.

"Sex Therapists Say 3–13 Minutes Is Best." *Arizona Republic* 3 Apr. 2008, A13. Print.

Shamloul, R. "Treatment of Men Complaining of Short Penis." *Urology* 65.6 (2005): 1183–85. Print.

Sheets-Johnstone, Maxine. *The Roots of Thinking*. Philadelphia: Temple UP, 1990. Print.

Silverman, Kaja. *Male Subjectivity at the Margins*. New York: Routledge, 1992. Print.

Simpson, Hilary. *D. H. Lawrence and Feminism*. DeKalb: Northern Illinois UP, 1982. Print.

Simpson, Mark. *Male Impersonators: Men Performing Masculinity*. New York: Routledge, 1994. Print.

Slonim, Jeffrey, and Christina Tapper. "Kimora: Djimon Has a Huge . . . Billboard." *People Magazine* Apr. 2008. Print.

Stevenson, Robert Lewis. *Dr. Jekyll and Mr. Hyde*. New York: Scribner, 1886. Print.

Taylor, Gary. *Castration: An Abbreviated History of Western Manhood*. New York: Routledge, 2000. Print.

Williams, Linda. *Hard Core: Power, Pleasure, and "the Frenzy of the Visible."* Berkeley: U of California P, 1989. Print.

———. *Screening Sex*. Durham, NC: Duke UP, 2008. Print.

Wessells, H., T. F. Lue, and J. W. McAninch. "Penile Length in the Flaccid and Erect States: Guidelines for Penile Augmentation." *Journal of Urology* 156.3 (1996): 995–97.

Index

1–900, 141, 154
2 Days in Paris, 162–163, 166–167, 168
9 Songs, 131, 132, 135, 153, 163, 169, 171–172
40 Days and 40 Nights, 138–139, 154

Absent-Minded Professor, The, 80
Adkins, Trace, "(This Ain't) No Thinkin' Thing," 12
Adonis Complex, The (Pope, Phillips, and Olivardia), 19
Aerosmith, "Sweet Emotion," 140
Affleck, Ben, 80
Allen, Woody, 89
Altman, Robert, 140
American Gangster, 53
American Gigolo, 13
American Psycho, 42
Angels and Insects, 7, 98–100, 104, 154–155
Annaud, Jean-Jacques, 93
Ann-Margret, 76
anti-intellectualism: and ethnicity, 104; and the management of ambition, 83; and masculinity, 20, 169; and national identity, 12, 21, 38–39, 93, 98, 185n3 (chap. 1); and sexuality, 12, 21, 142, 183–184; and socioeconomic class, 3–4
Antonia's Line, 21, 97
Antonioni, Michelangelo, 43
Any Given Sunday, 73–76, 77
Apatow, Judd, 161, 163, 167
Apollo 13, 77
Arbus, Diane, 65, 67
Ashby, Hal, 144, 153
Ask the Dust, 33
Asylum, 63–65, 115
Atkins, Christopher, 16, 18

At Play in the Fields of the Lord, 7
Australia, 4, 185n4 (chap. 1)

Babenco, Hector, 7
Baker, Nicholas, *Vox*, 141
Bale, Christian, 42
Balfour, Eric, 132, 170
Bana, Eric, 42
Barber, Benjamin, *Consumed*, 40
Bassett, Angela, 58
Bataille, Georges, 92
Bates, Kathy, 3
Bay, Michael, 137
Bean, Sean, 174
Beautiful Mind, A, 77
Bell, Kristen, 161
Berenger, Tom, 7
Berg, Peter, 71
Berger, John, *Ways of Seeing*, 88
Bernabei, Pietro, 108
Bingham, Dennis, *Acting Male*, 186n5 (chap. 1)
Biskind, Peter, 144
Blue Lagoon, The, 16
Bobbitt, Lorena and John Wayne, 14
body culture, 10, 12, 13–15, 18–20, 23, 34, 57, 59, 74, 104, 105, 133, 156, 157
body guy: as artist, 33–38; as brute, 40–52; and capitalism, 28, 34, 39–40; and class (socioeconomic), 27–28, 46, 51–52; and closeness to the earth, 4–5, 8, 16, 27, 32–33, 34, 38, 44, 48; and family, 63–68; femininity of, 40–42, 68–70, 127–128, 178–179; gift, 9–11, 54–61, 178, 187n1 (chap. 3); and individualism, 31–33; as "Other," 10, 19; as outsider, 31–33; penis of, 6, 7, 23 (*see also* penis); penis of,

body guy (*continued*)
  emphasis on, 15–16, 29–30, 106; penis
  of, endowment/size, 110–112, 117–118;
  physique, 10, 14, 16, 19, 58, 186*n*4 (chap. 1);
  and playfulness, 38–40; as rebel, 38–40;
  sex style, 6, 8, 39, 42, 68, 95, 113, 116,
  137–138
body guy genre: character, 2–3, 5;
  definition, 1–4; and intellect, 53–54, 79,
  188*n*3 (chap. 3), 189*n*4 (chap. 4); and the
  mind guy, 1, 3, 8, 9, 11, 12, 53, 142, 164,
  169; and sexual incompetence, 20, 21;
  and socioeconomic class, 30–32, 52; and
  the woman in-between, 1–5 (*see also*
  women). *See also* body guy
Bonneville, Hugh, 63
Bordo, Susan, 113
Bordwell, David, 137
Born on the Fourth of July, 143, 145
Bosworth, Patricia, 66
Box of Moonlight, 7, 28, 31, 32, 37, 39, 40,
  68, 185*n*3 (chap. 1)
Brand, Russell, 164
Brando, Marlon, 185*n*2 (chap. 1)
Breathless, 14
Breillat, Catherine, 130
Bridges of Madison County, The, 175
Brint, Steven, 83
Brooks, David, 93
Brown, Norman O., 153
Bruckheimer, Jerry, 189*n*4 (chap. 4)

Cameron, James, 1
Campion, Jane, 54
Cape Fear (1991), 45
Carter, Helena Bonham, 41
Celebrity Nudity Database (cndb.com)
  (Web site), 50, 189*n*2 (chap. 5)
Cesar, Mènothy, 59
Church, Thomas Hayden, 94
Cohan, Steven, *Screening the Male*, 186*n*5
Collins, Wilkie, 44, 48; *The Evil Genius*, 44
Comfort, Alex, *The Joy of Sex*, 112, 129
Coming Home, 143, 152
community college/university opposition,
  81–84
Condon, Bill, 124
Constructing Masculinity (Berger, Wallis,
  and Watson), 186*n*5 (chap. 1)
Cougar Town (TV series), 61
Coullo'ch, Jean-Louis, 7, 174, 182
Cox, Courtney, 61
Cox, Paul, 157–160
Craig, Daniel, 61

Cruise, Tom, 145
Cruz, Penelope, 150
CSI (TV series), 189*n*4 (chap. 4)
Csokas, Marton, 63
Culkin, Rory, 85

Damon, Matt, 80
Daniell, Rosemary, *Sleeping with Soldiers*,
  188*n*3 (chap. 3)
David (Michelangelo), 107, 108, 115, 129
Davidson, Sara, *Cowboy: A Love Story*,
  188*n*3 (chap. 3)
Dead Presidents, 6, 86
Deep Throat, 188*n*1 (chap. 4)
Delpy, Julie, 163, 166
Demme, Jonathan, 102
De Niro, Robert, 45
De Palma, Brian, 102
Dern, Bruce, 144
De Rossi, Portia, 151
Diary of Anaïs Nin, The (Nin), 36–37
Diaz, Cameron, 73
DiCaprio, Leonardo, 1
Dickinson, R. L., *Human Sex
  Anatomy*, 109
DiCillo, Tom, 28
Diggs, Taye, 58
Dirty Dancing, 92
Dole, Bob, 14
Downey, Robert Jr., 66
Down in the Valley, 84–86
Driver, Minnie, 81, 100
Duchovny, David, 46
Duigan, John, 20, 150
Dumont, Bruno, 43, 187*n*1 (chap. 2)
Durrell, Lawrence, 24
Dyer, Richard, 19, 106
Dylan, Bob, "Subterranean Homesick
  Blues," 93, 188*n*2 (chap. 4)

Easthope, Anthony, *What a Man's Gotta
  Do*, 186*n*5 (chap. 1)
Eastwood, Clint, 175
Ehrenreich, Barbara, 28, 41; *Fear of
  Falling*, 28; *The Worst Years of Our
  Lives*, 28
Einstein, Albert, 38, 79
End of the Affair, The, 35–36, 38
Enemy at the Gates, 53, 93–94
Erin Brockovich, 103–104, 189*n*4 (chap. 4)
Europa, Europa, 90, 91

Faludi, Susan, 138
Fiennes, Joseph, 53

Fiennes, Ralph, 89
Fenn, Sherilyn, 9
Ferran, Pascale, 32, 173–182, 185
Fight Club, 40–42, 44, 47
Fincher, David, 40, 103
Fiorentino, Linda, 70
Fixx, Jim, *The Complete Book of Running*, 13
Flynt, Robert, 123–124
Fonda, Jane, 13, 143, 152–153
Forbes, Michelle, 46
Forgetting Sarah Marshall, 15, 161–166, 167–168
Foucault, Michel, 112; *The History of Sexuality*, 156
Foxx, Jamie, 74
Freud, Sigmund, 13, 107–108, 113, 117, 128, 129
Fur: An Imaginary Portrait of Diane Arbus, 63, 65–68, 120

Gable, Clark, 185n2 (chap. 1)
Garber, Victor, 3
Gardner, Howard, *Frames of Mind*, 21–23
Gerber, Mark, 7
Gere, Richard, 13
Giamatti, Paul, 94
Gift, The, 45
Girl 6, 140–141
Gleiberman, Owen, 163
Goldbacher, Sandra, 100
Goldberg, Adam, 163, 166
Goldberg, Whoopi, 58
Goldwyn, Tony, 92
Good Will Hunting, 80–84
Gorris, Marlene, 21
Gottlieb, Lori, 155
Gould, Stephen Jay, *The Mismeasure of Man*, 21–23
Governess, The, 7, 100–102, 104, 142, 155, 173, 189n3 (chap. 4)
Gowdy, Barbara, 146
Grant, Hugh, 148
Grant, Richard E., 34
Greene, Graham, 36
Greenlee, Karen, 147
Greider, William, *Who Will Tell the People*, 28, 31, 41
Gulisano, Massimo, 108

Haas, Belinda and Philip, 98
Hall, Stephen S., *Size Matters*, 19
Hands, Marina, 175
Hangover, The, 164

Hark, Ina Rae, *Screening the Male*, 186n5
Harvey, Paul, 126
Haskell, Molly, *From Reverence to Rape*, 79, 82, 101
Heading South, 59–60, 187n1 (chap. 3)
Head in the Clouds, 150
Hellman, Jerome, 144
Hendrix, Jimi, "Purple Haze," 93, 188n2 (chap. 4)
Henry & June, 34–36, 38, 65
Heston, Charlton, 75
Hitchcock, Alfred, 102
Hodes, Laura, 164
Hofstadter, Richard, *Anti-intellectualism in American Life*, 38, 39, 93, 98
Holland, Agnieszka, 90
Horse Whisperer, The, 48, 62, 171
Hounsou, Djimon, 14
Houston, Pam, *Cowboys Are My Weakness*, 188n3 (chap. 3)
Howard, Ron, 77
How Stella Got Her Groove Back, 58–59, 60, 65, 127, 187n1 (chap. 3). *See also* McMillan, Terry
Human Stain, The, 188n1 (chap. 4)
Hung (HBO series), 15
Hunter, Holly, 55

ideas/people opposition, 73–78, 80–84, 99
Inventing the Abbotts, 33
I.Q., 20, 38, 79

Jackman, Hugh, 185–186n4 (chap. 1)
Jacobson, David, 84
Jeffords, Susan, *Hard Bodies*, 18, 186n5 (chap. 1)
Jeremy, Ron, 188n1 (chap. 4)
Jewish male: and the cowboy mystique, 85, 92; and Holocaust imagery, 87–88, 89–91, 93–94; sexuality of, 86, 89, 91–92, 188n1 (chap. 4)
Johnson, Virginia E.: *The Kinsey Data*, 109; *Human Sexual Response*, 109, 153
Johansson, Scarlett, 62
Jordan, Neil, 34
Junior, 80

Kalifornia, 46–47
Kaplan, Fred, 185
Karabel, Jerome, 83
Kaufman, Philip, 34, 36, 37
Kaye, Norman, 157
Keaton, Michael, 77
Keitel, Harvey, 7, 55–56

Kensit, Patsy, 98
Kidman, Nicole, 66, 185n4 (chap. 1)
King, Zalman, 8, 30, 102, 119, 169, 171,
    186n6 (chap. 1)
Kinsey, 124, 182
Kinsey Report (research study), 13, 109
Kissed, 146–147
Klein, Calvin, 10, 14, 16, 58
Klute, 152
Koehler, Fred, 90
Kravas, Heather, 88

Lady Chatterley (film), 7, 32, 162–163, 173,
    175, 180, 182. *See also* Lawrence, D. H.
Lake Consequence, 102, 151, 171
LaLanne, Jack, 13
Lane, Diane, 92
Last Seduction, The, 70–73, 105
Law, Jude, 53
Lawn Dogs, 7, 29–30, 31, 38, 40
Lawrence, D. H., 4, 24, 44, 106, 116,
    129, 130, 132, 186n6 (chap. 1); *John
    Thomas and Lady Jane*, 173–180; *Lady
    Chatterley's Lover*, 4, 5, 7, 8, 24–26, 44,
    116, 129, 173, 185n2 (chap. 1), 186n4
    (chap. 1), 186n6 (chap. 1)
Lee, Spike, 140–141
Legends of the Fall, 5, 31, 38, 44, 53,
    129, 175
Lehman, Peter, *Running Scared*, 108, 186n5
    (chap. 1)
Leigh, Jennifer Jason, 140
Lewis, Juliette, 46
Lie with Me, 132, 133–135, 163, 169, 170–171
Loeb, Heinrich, 109
Lombardi, Vince, 74
Looking for Mr. Goodbar, 60

MacPherson, Elle, 151
Madonna, 61
Madsen, Virginia, 95
Man of Flowers, 157–160
Mapplethorpe, Robert, 14
Marcuse, Herbert, *Eros and
    Civilization*, 153
Martin, Dean, "When You're Smiling," 93
masculinity: multiple (masculinities), 19,
    184; "new" (Simpson), 181; and penis
    size, 49, 51, 52 (*see also* penis), and
    sexual performance, and violence,
    42–52
Masters, William H.: *The Kinsey Data*,
    109; Kinsey Report, 13; *Human Sexual
    Response*, 109, 153

Mayle, Peter, *What's Happening to
    Me?*, 127
McGregor, Ewan, 7
McMillan, Terry, *How Stella Got Her
    Groove Back*, 58, 60, 127
Meat Loaf (singer/actor), 40
Medeiros, Maria de, 34
*Men of OZ: Nude Scenes from HBO's TV
    Series "OZ"* (Web site), 90
Miller, Geoffrey, *The Mating Mind*, 110,
    112, 113–119, 129, 130
Millet, Kate, *Sexual Politics*, 180, 181
mind/body opposition, 8, 9, 21–22, 54, 80,
    168, 185n3 (chap. 1), 188n2 (chap. 3)
Moonlight and Valentino, 27
Moore, Demi, 61
Moore, Julianne, 34
Morrison, Patt, 79
Morse, David, 85
Mortensen, Viggo, 92
Mother, The, 60
Munich, 42–43, 90

Nash, John, 77–78
Neeson, Liam, 124
Neill, Sam, 148
Night in Heaven, A, 16–19, 61
Norton, Edward, 40, 85
Notebook, The, 65
Nunn, Bill, 71
Nutty Professor, The, 80

O'Brien, Kiernan, 131
Obsession, 102
Oh, Sandra, 95
Ormand, Julia, 53
OZ (HBO series), 90
Ozu, Yasujiro, 136

Pacino, Al, 73
Paper, The, 77
Paquin, Anna, 55
Paris, Texas, 43
Payne, Alexander, 94
penis: and Asian men, 105; big (big dick),
    9, 14, 31, 60–61, 71–72, 112, 117–119,
    127–129, 130–133; big, centrality of,
    137–139, 153, 163; big, in pornography,
    129, 153; big, in real sex films, 172,
    182–184; big, spectacle of, 167; and black
    men, 105, 187n1 (chap. 3); erect vs.
    flaccid, 111–112; and full-frontal nudity,
    in film, 7, 13, 15–16, 29–30, 50, 67, 90,
    106, 120, 187n1 (chap. 2); good-sized, 6,

7, 23, 31, 50, 68, 70, 79, 82, 105, 128, 172;
in human evolution, 110–112, 117–118,
189n1 (chap. 5); Jewish, 86, 88, 89–90;
and male/female differentiation, 23,
127–128, 182; medical measurement of,
108–109, 111–112; norms, 107–112, 126;
opposed to brain, 101, 105; as phallus, 19,
79, 167, 179; and race and ethnicity, 106,
187n1 (chap. 3); representation and
regulation in representation of, 79–82;
size and boy/man differentiation,
126–127; size jokes, 105, 122, 167; vs.
scrotum, 116–117; small (above the
scrotum), 15, 50–52, 67, 86, 105–106,
112, 115–118, 120, 122–123, 126–130, 187n1
(chap. 2), 189n2 (chap. 5)
people/ideas opposition. See ideas/people
opposition
Perfect Moment, The, 14
Perfect Murder, A, 33
Phenomenon, 65, 188n2 (chap. 3)
Piano, The, 7, 54–57, 65, 68, 69, 129
Pillow Book, The, 7
Pineapple Express, The, 163
Pitt, Brad, 3, 42, 44, 46, 53, 168, 174
Playgirl (magazine), 13
Pornstar: The Legend of Ron Jeremy, 188n1
(chap. 4)
Portal, Louise, 59
Poulson-Bryant, Scott, *Hung: A
Meditation on the Measure of Black
Men in America*, 187n1 (chap. 3)
Psycho, 51, 102
Pullman, Bill, 70

Raimi, Sam, 45
Rampling, Charlotte, 59
Ray, 163
Rea, Stephen, 34
real sex films, 130–135
Redford, Robert, 32, 48, 62
Red Shoe Diaries (Showtime series), 30
Reeves, Keanu, 45
Reagan, Ronald, 18
Reuben, David R., *Everything You Always
Wanted to Know About Sex*, 108, 109
Rhys Meyers, Jonathan, 7
Richardson, Natasha, 63
River Runs Through It, A, 32–33
Rockwell, Sam, 7
Rodgers, Joann Ellison, 116
Roth, Philip: *The Dying Animal*, 188n1
(chap. 4); *The Professor of Desire*, 188n1
(chap. 4)

Russell, Ken, 174
Rylance, Mark, 98

Sarsgaard, Peter, 124, 182, 189n2
(chap. 5)
Schipisi, Fred, 20
Schindler's List, 90
Schreiber, Liev, 92
Schwarzbaum, Lisa, 164
Schwarzenegger, Arnold, 13
Scott Thomas, Kristen, 62, 98
Seinfeld (TV series), 14
Segel, Jason, 15, 161, 167
sex: necrophilia, 145–148; non-penile-
centered (nonpenetration) 137, 144,
147–148, 150, 152–159; paraplegic,
143–145; penetration, 2, 6, 23, 36, 112,
118, and stasis vs. motion, 136, 138, 144,
152; styles, 6, 8, 39, 42, 47, 68, 98, 113,
116, 118–119, 137; telephone, 140–143;
vigorous (pound-cubed), 6, 7, 26, 133,
135, 138, 152, 153, 168, 172, 175
sexuality: bisexuality, 148–154, 156–157;
polymorphous perversity, 152–157
sexy mind, 79, 82, 94–99, 142; and
alternative sexual scenarios, importance
of, 138, 144–145, 173, 177, 182–184; and
investigation, 100–104; and language/
eroticism, 95–97, 102, 104; and play,
38–40; and rhythm, 92–93, 95, 188n2
(chap. 4)
Sheets-Johnstone, Maxine, *The Roots of
Thinking*, 110
Sheffer, Craig, 32
Shields, Brooke, 16
Shortbus, 131, 132, 148, 153, 169
Short Cuts, 140
Sideways, 94–98, 104, 115, 140
Silence of the Lambs, The, 102
Silverman, Kaja, *Male Subjectivity at the
Margins*, 186n5 (chap. 1)
Simpson, Hilary, *D. H. Lawrence and
Feminism*, 181
Simpson, Mark, *Male Impersonators*,
186n5 (chap. 1)
Sirens, 20, 148–151, 154, 172–173
Skarsgard, Stellan, 80
Sling Blade, 44, 45
Smith, Lauren Lee, 132, 170
Soderbergh, Steven, 103
Spielberg, Steven, 90
Squid and the Whale, The, 80
Stanford-Binet I.Q. test, 21
Stern, Howard, 13, 105, 129

Stevenson, Robert Lewis, 44, 48
Stewart, Martha, 41
Stilley, Margo, 131
Stone, Oliver, 73, 77, 145
Stopkewich, Lynne, 146–147
Streep, Meryl, 175
Sunset Boulevard, 57
Sunshine, 89–90, 91
Swayze, Patrick, 92
Sweet Home Alabama, 4
Szabo, Istvan, 89

Taylor, Gary, *Castration: An Abbreviated History of Western Manhood*, 116, 129, 156
Taxi Driver, 85
Thelma and Louise, 5
Theron, Charlize, 150
Thomas, Henry, 53
Titanic, 1–4, 38, 171
Tokyo Story, 136
Townsend, Stuart, 150
Turturro, John, 28
Twentynine Palms, 43, 44, 47–52, 115
Two and a Half Men (TV series), 15
Two Moon Junction, 8–12, 15, 54, 115, 148, 186n6 (chap. 1)
Tyson, Richard, 9

Van Gogh, Theo, 141
Vanishing, The, 80
Vanity Fair (magazine), 144
Van Sant, Gus, 80
Viagra, 14
Voight, Jon, 143

Wahlberg, Mark (Marky Mark), 14
Walk Hard, 163

Walk on the Moon, A, 92–93
Ward, Fred, 34
Warren, Leslie Anne, 16
Waterdance, The, 143
Wayne, John, 145, 185n2 (chap. 1)
Weisz, Rachel, 53
Wenders, Wim, 43
West, Mae, 136
Wexman, Virginia Wright, 137
Wilkinson, Tom, 100
Will, George, 12
Williams, Linda: *Hard Core*, 136, 137; *Screening Sex*, 152, 153
Williams, Robin, 80
Winter, Susan, *Older Women/Younger Men*, 61
Winslet, Kate, 1
Wissak, David, 50, 187n1 (chap. 2)
Without Sanctuary (ed. Allen), 87
women: and artistic expression, 65, 101–102; and careers, 54, 57–66, 73–77; as *femmes fatales*, 70–73; and intelligence, 53–54, 79; and investigation, 100–104; and motherhood, 62–66, 75–77; older women/younger men, 57–62; on the prowl (cougars), 61; in Victorian era, 189n3 (chap. 4). *See also* body guy genre: the woman in-between
Wood, Evan Rachel, 84
Woodstock Festival, 13, 16, 29, 93

Yoakam, Dwight, 45
Young, Karen, 59
Young Adam, 7, 33

Zabriskie Point, 43
Zane, Billy, 1
Zodiac, 103

About the Authors

Peter Lehman is the director of the Center for Film, Media and Popular Culture at Arizona State University. He is the author of numerous books, including *Running Scared: Masculinity and the Representation of the Male Body*, and *Roy Orbison: The Invention of an Alternative Rock Masculinity*. He is the editor of *Pornography: Film and Culture*.

Susan Hunt has taught community college for the past twenty years. She has coauthored numerous articles on film and sexuality for a variety of journals and anthologies and has been active in the media literacy movement. She currently lives in Los Angeles and teaches film studies at Santa Monica College and Pasadena City College.